VALUES
AND
PUBLIC
POLICY

VALUES

—— AND ——

PUBLIC
POLICY

Henry J. Aaron
Thomas E. Mann
Timothy Taylor

Editors

The Brookings Institution
Washington, D.C.

Copyright © 1994
THE BROOKINGS INSTITUTION
1775 Massachusetts Avenue, N.W., Washington, D.C. 20036

Library of Congress Cataloging-in-Publication data:

Values and public policy / [editors] Henry J. Aaron, Thomas E.
  Mann, Timothy Taylor.
      p.   cm.
  Includes bibliographical references and index.
  ISBN 0-8157-0056-3   ISBN 0-8157-0055-5 (pbk.)
  1. Social values—United States.   2. United States—Social
policy.   3. Social ethics—United States.   I. Aaron, Henry J.
II. Mann, Thomas E.   III. Taylor, Timothy.
HM216.V47   1994
303.3'72—dc20   93-38466
                                                                      CIP

9 8 7 6 5 4 3 2 1

The paper used in this publication meets the minimum requirements of the American National Standard for Information Sciences—Permanence of Paper for Printed Library Materials, ANSI
                    Z39.48-1984.

Foreword

Popular discussion of contemporary social and economic problems increasingly centers on the role played by individual values. Poor school performance, welfare dependency, youth unemployment, and criminal activity are often seen by ordinary citizens as resulting more from shortcomings in the personal makeup of individuals than from societal forces beyond their control. Impulsive, self-indulgent, indecent inclinations seem to underlie a range of behaviors that trouble many Americans and frustrate policymakers trying to design effective interventions.

This public debate about values and public policy, often conducted as ideological warfare among contending political forces, has left the scholarly community distinctly uncomfortable. One reason is that public policy scholars find many appeals to values simplistic and overly judgmental, reflecting a tendency to blame the victim and minimize the importance of circumstances and laws. Another, perhaps more telling, reason for this discomfort lies with the traditional approach to public policy analysis.

Analysts usually treat preferences—values, beliefs, and interests—as given, beyond the reach of public policy. Their task is to examine the incentives people face and to ask why rational, utility-maximizing individuals behave as they do. If behavior leads to undesirable outcomes, the challenge of public policy is to rearrange the incentives in a way that induces socially optimal behavior. However, a growing body of analysis suggests that this approach is inadequate. Individual values and social norms are shaped by experience, including lessons taught by family, friends, and community, and are subject to change; and responses to public policies depend on people's preferences.

This volume, which grew out of a series of seminars conducted at Brookings, is an initial effort to consider the analytic and substantive implications of a more values-centered approach to public policy research. It explores how values and norms are influenced directly or indirectly by public policies and how the resulting norms and values in turn condition the efficacy of public policies. Most important, it argues that the formation of preferences is as essential a subject of investigation for public policy analysts as incentives and behavioral responses.

Values and Public Policy was edited by Henry J. Aaron, director of the Brookings Economic Studies program, Thomas E. Mann, director of the Brookings Governmental Studies program, and Timothy Taylor, managing editor of the *Journal of Economic Perspectives*. The authors are George Akerlof and Janet L. Yellen of the University of California, Berkeley; Nathan Glazer, Harvard University; Jane Mansbridge, Northwestern University; David Popenoe, Rutgers University; James Q. Wilson, University of California, Los Angeles; and Daniel Yankelovich, the Yankelovich Group.

Commentators in the seminar series at which the essays in this volume were originally presented and discussed were Douglas Besharov, Gary Burtless, John J. DiIulio, Jr., Edwin Dorn, William Galston, Christopher Jencks, Frank Levy, Franklin Raines, Isabel Sawhill, Thomas Schelling, Charles L. Schultze, and Peter Skerry.

Susan Thompson provided administrative assistance. Judy Chaney, Lisa L. Guillory, Sara C. Hufham, Inge Lockwood, and Kathleen Elliott Yinug helped prepare the manuscript for publication. Theresa B. Walker edited the manuscript, David H. Bearce and Laura Kelly checked it for accuracy, and Susan Woollen prepared it for typesetting. Florence Robinson constructed the index.

The editors wish to gratefully acknowledge the generous support of the Brown Foundation, Inc., Houston, Texas, and Robert S. McNamara.

The views expressed here are the chapter authors' alone and should not be ascribed to those acknowledged above or to the trustees, officers, or other staff members of the Brookings Institution.

Bruce K. MacLaury
President

November 1993
Washington, D.C.

Contents

Table

Figures

Index   211

Introduction

Henry J. Aaron, Thomas E. Mann, and Timothy Taylor

A peculiar and distressing gulf separates scholarly and popular discussions of many social issues. Ask an economist or a sociologist why families go on welfare and stay there, and you are likely to get a learned disquisition on how declining wages have contributed to an increase in welfare, on how payment formulas drain the economic gain from employment and make staying on welfare easier than leaving it, and on how welfare rules undermine family stability. Ask an ordinary citizen the same question and you are likely to get an earful on sloth, shortsightedness, and lack of morality in welfare recipients and, perhaps, even a few racist comments about how "they" behave. Ask educators why test scores are falling, and you had better be ready for a discourse on why student performance is sensitive to curriculum, teacher skills, and school management and organization. Ask ordinary citizens and you may hear judgmental remarks, at least in comments on other people's children, about parents who care too little to make their children do homework, about the distractions of television, and about peer pressures.

In short, social scientists—especially economists—evaluate public policies and institutions by examining incentives and behavioral responses. These scholars usually take values, habits, and social norms as given—beyond analysis and the reach of public policy.

1

Popular discussion dwells precisely on alleged differences in values and norms that people believe lead to social and economic problems. Policy analysts usually take tastes and preferences as given. Ordinary citizens treat values as objects that must be changed if problems are to be solved.

The tendency of scholars, particularly economists, to take values—tastes or utility functions, in the terminology of economists—as given has several origins. First, economics emerged from utilitarian philosophy, which regards the maximization of given individual preferences as the objective of the good society. Personal utility, tastes, or values have traditionally occupied a position in policy analysis similar to postulates in Euclidian geometry—fundamental properties to be accepted as they are and not themselves subject to analysis.

Second, values or tastes are hard to quantify independently of the behaviors they engender. Imprecise concepts are impossible to embody in formal models that are the mode of discourse in economics and, increasingly, in other social sciences. Hypotheses about unquantifiable phenomena are difficult or impossible to test. Furthermore, supposedly analytical statements about values often are simply elaborate criticisms of the behaviors they purport to treat nonjudgmentally. Suppose, for example, that one constructs a model in which people save only when the return on saving exceeds their preference for present over future consumption. Suppose further that one observes that people save little. It adds nothing of significance to then comment censoriously that those who save little have scant regard for the future.

The third reason that scholars have not paid much attention to the source of tastes, intellectual *cachet*, is related to the second. Many of the best and brightest scholars in the disciplines generally most concerned with public policy—economics, political science, and sociology—have been engaged in the grand and productive intellectual venture of creating mathematical behavioral models constructed on the assumption that people maximize satisfaction based on *given* tastes. The intellectual resources devoted to exploring the *formation* of tastes in the policy-focused disciplines have been negligible. Instead, with a few notable exceptions (Thomas Schelling in economics; Aaron Wildavsky and James Q. Wilson in political science) the discussion of tastes has been the province largely of those not in the intellectual vanguard. Many appeals to values in public policy debates are facile, simplistic, judgmental, and ill considered. Emphasis on values is often used in what might charitably be called a protean way, its meaning shifting in every use. Value-based arguments are sometimes presented as if some great eclipse has cut the less favored off from the moral sunlight. All society can do is condemn the sinners and pray for them to come to their senses. In extreme cases, value-based arguments can be used to blame bad people for social problems and to minimize the role of circumstances, institutions, or laws.

Little wonder, then, that social scientists have tried to steer clear of such arguments. Academics like their terms well defined and their analytical methods rigorous; their world is peopled with rational humans who are neither good nor bad; and they see explanations for social phenomena in events, rules, and policy, not in value judgments.

A growing body of analysis suggests, however, that this approach is, if not wrong, at least oversimplified. After all, values are not entirely determined, like eye color, by genetic inheritance. They emerge from lessons taught by family, friends, and community. In the jargon of the social sciences, analysts have begun to recognize that values and norms are not "exogenous," or independent of public policy. And the idea that values can change, combined with the recognition that responses to policies depend on people's preferences—that is, their values—leads to thinking about how public policy might change values directly or indirectly and thereby change the responses to public policies themselves. Though value-based explanations of various kinds of behavior remain distressingly fuzzy, there are good analytical reasons for paying attention to them. Anyway, they are simply too prevalent for social scientists to ignore.

In a study of the British health care system, one of the editors of this volume encountered a graphic illustration of the way in which public policy shapes preferences. British and American physicians receive similar training. They study the same texts and journals. Many physicians from each country have spent periods in residence in the other. So one might expect British and American physicians to have similar standards for care. In fact, they do not. Because per capita health care spending in Britain is well below half of that in the United States, British physicians cannot do as much as their American counterparts. However, British physicians do not in general describe their situation as one in which resource limits prevent them from following best practice. Rather, resource-constrained British physicians have adapted standards for what is medically indicated to fit available resources. One British physician put the matter plainly:

> There are many situations where resources are sufficiently short so that there must be decisions made as to who is treated. Given that circumstance, the physician, in order to live with himself and to sleep well at night, has to look at arguments for *not* treating a patient. . . . He states the reason for not going forward in medical terms . . . but that formulation in many instances is in no small part conditioned by the fact that there really aren't enough resources to treat everybody, and there is a kind of rationalization which is, perhaps, influenced by resource constraints.[1]

As if to illustrate this process, a British general practitioner explained why he regarded as sound the British practice in the early 1980s, incomprehensible in the United States, of denying dialysis for virtually all patients over age 50 who suffer chronic kidney failure, an invariably fatal condition. His explanation, stated quite seriously and without irony, was "Well, you know, everybody over age 50 is a bit crumbly." Resource constraints in Britain have contributed to attitudes toward medical care much different from those in the United States. Such attitudes would not change quickly if resource constraints were suddenly relaxed, and they might not change significantly.

A conviction that people's values and social norms are shaped by experience and that the resulting values and norms condition the efficacy of public policy led Brookings to organize a series of seminars on values and public policy. The chapters in this book grew out of that seminar series, spanning the year September 1991 to September 1992. The papers originally presented at those seminars have been revised substantially to take into account comments presented at the time and since.

The Affluence Effect

Daniel Yankelovich describes the evolution of values in the United States in "How Changes in the American Economy Are Reshaping American Values." During the period just after World War II, U. S. economic growth was rapid, but people carried a fear born in the Great Depression that the good times would not last. Sometime in the 1960s querulousness gave way to optimism that growth would continue endlessly. A renewed and disorienting fear that affluence is in jeopardy emerged during the 1980s and manifested itself powerfully in the 1992 presidential campaign.

Particular changes in views on central questions of personal and public behavior marked each of these periods. Yankelovich finds a long-term decline in the importance attached to obligations to others. The importance of conventions of class or the larger society has lessened. Acceptance of different ethnic groups and of diverse lifestyles has increased. The positive good of pleasure, including bodily pleasures, has increased. Censoriousness toward "incorrect" sexual behavior has diminished. The importance of self-fulfillment and the expression of one's individualism has increased, especially among women. The value of sacrifice as a moral good has diminished. The ethic of work as intrinsically valuable and meritorious has lost ground to a view that work is good only if it provides personal satisfaction. Concern about the environment has increased. Reverence for the family has remained high, but the definition of family has broadened, and the norms for sharing responsibilities among partners have become more egalitarian. One of the more chilling shifts Yankelovich finds is the sharply higher proportion of the young than of the old who are willing to do anything as long as it is not illegal.

Yankelovich argues that the key factors shaping these changes in values are whether the society is actually becoming more affluent and whether society believes that trend will continue. He argues that in the 1960s and 1970s Americans believed that affluence had arrived and would stay—and in such a climate people press against the bonds of constraint and "revel in expanding their life choices." Yankelovich thinks that Japan, in particular, is just entering that stage. However, he argues that because Americans now feel that one can no longer take affluence for granted, "Americans in all walks of life are adjusting their expectations downward and adapting to

what they see as a more difficult, less open, less fair, more demanding, and more stressful economic environment."

Culture, Incentives, and the Underclass

In "Culture, Incentives, and the Underclass" James Q. Wilson
examines the perennial tension between explanations of social problems based on incentives and those based on personal characteristics
of the badly behaved and, in particular, of criminals. Changes in
incentives, he argues, cannot explain much of the increase in many
social problems. Reductions in the likelihood of arrest and duration
of punishment cannot explain more than a small minority of the
increase in crime rates. Changes in welfare benefits, earnings, and
other objective conditions cannot explain much of the increase in
the numbers of unwed mothers and welfare recipients. Labor market developments can explain only part of the reduction of employment among young men. In each case, objective developments have
exacerbated problems but cannot come close to explaining what has
gone wrong.

Something else is clearly at work. Wilson focuses on destructive
values held by a minority of Americans. He argues that certain
patterns of dysfunctional behavior seem to run in families, including
crime, drug use, and violence. He believes that these patterns are
set early in life, that these patterns are heavily influenced by family
and community environment, and that policy tools to correct the
problem must be focused on improving the habituation of children.*

Wilson then moves into a discussion of such interventions, including Head Start, boarding homes, the school system, and military
service. Although these policies offer a few potentially promising
insights—for example, the thought that making home visits to
young parents to teach them about parenting may be useful—the
overall record is not encouraging. Wilson ends up arguing that creating well-functioning two-parent families is the key to better ha-

---

*Wilson uses the term *habituation* "to refer to the process whereby
people acquire a constant, often unconscious, way of doing something, a
regular inclination to behave in ways that are either impulsive or reflective,
self-indulgent or other-regarding, decent or indecent."

bituation of the underclass. But how to make families function better than they do remains elusive. Moreover, the focus on today's children offers little guidance on what to do about teenagers and adults who have already been habituated in what Wilson would describe as a destructive fashion.

Families, Values, and Family Values

In his chapter, "The Family Condition of America: Cultural Change and Public Policy," David Popenoe argues that "by most quantitative measures, American families are functioning less well today than ever before, and less well than in any other advanced, industrialized nation." Popenoe sees each society as seeking a balance between "personal autonomy and self-fulfillment on one hand, and social order and cultural harmony on the other." He refers to the proper balance as "communitarian individualism" and argues that such a balance is crucial to the personal and economic welfare of the nation.

In several ways, Popenoe's thesis echoes arguments in some of the earlier essays. Popenoe, like Yankelovich, emphasizes a balance between individual and community. He develops one of Wilson's key themes in his emphasis on the importance of early socialization for children. But in the end, Popenoe's argument is distinctly his own. Unlike Yankelovich, who sees a conflict among legitimate values, Popenoe unabashedly judges that America has moved too far from social order and cultural harmony. Unlike Wilson, who focuses on children in a minority of the population, Popenoe challenges majority values.

A democracy may well have difficulty dealing with the problems that Popenoe describes; after all, if a majority embraces one set of values, will that same majority support public policies to alter those values? Although he mentions various government policies that might provide greater support for families, Popenoe seems to pin most of his hopes on social cycles and trends that might make family values more attractive. For example, children of the "divorce revolution" of the 1960s and 1970s, having seen the problems that divorce can cause, might be more determined to make divorce only a last resort.

Multiculturalism

Because the stakes in childhood development are large, multi-cultural instruction in schools has become a bloody battlefield in the debate about educational reform. Is multicultural instruction a boon or a bane, or neither? Nathan Glazer reports from the front lines of this war over educational curriculum in "Multiculturalism and Public Policy." As a critic of some aspects of the content of multicultural curricula who nevertheless sees virtue in many of the objectives of those curricula, he has been pilloried by both sides. Some supporters of multiculturalism argue that biases and exclusions in current curricula are disproportionately felt by those who are left out. Opponents argue that the "oppression studies" curriculum proposed by multiculturalists is at best divisive and self-serving and at worst an outright falsification of history.

Curriculum choices would be simple if the line between historical accuracy and ethnic or nationalistic cheerleading were clear and bright, but Glazer shows that curriculum decisions have been and remain controversial. Arguments that today would be designated "multicultural" have raged since the nineteenth century and continue in recent attempts to alter the curricula in New York and California.

Glazer asks the advocates of multicultural curricula to attend to scholarly accuracy and reminds the opponents of multicultural instruction that what is chosen from the infinity of possible subjects of instruction is inevitably subjective. Ethnic cheerleading, far from being the discovery of contemporary multiculturalists, has long been a major ingredient of American schooling. Glazer acknowledges the difficulty of defining a fair and balanced curriculum and expresses a willingness to alter the curriculum with time, while still arguing that truth and historical accuracy (as best understood at any time) should remain a paramount value. His position calls for a compromise between legitimate competing values in a battle where neither side is taking any prisoners. "We are serving three masters in social studies,"—he writes, "truth, national unity, and civil harmony. The first two seem somewhat short-changed by our concern for civil harmony."

Public Spirit and Private Interest

In her contribution, "Public Spirit in Political Systems," Jane Mansbridge emphasizes that people must be motivated by something greater than personal self-interest if democratic society is to work. For example, going to the time and trouble of voting is irrational from the standpoint of a self-regarding individual, because no single person's vote is likely to decide an election. An even more pointed example is that of the couple who drove overnight so that he could vote for one of two candidates and she for the other. Going to considerable effort for no tangible result is hard to rationalize; but if everyone behaved self-interestedly and without public spirit, no one would vote and democracy would collapse.

The corollary is that behavior that is not self-interested in the short run can be genuinely and deeply self-interested in the long run. Mansbridge's emphasis on public spirit clearly is at odds with a narrow emphasis on self-interest. If it is true that rational self-interest leads to a lack of public spirit, nonparticipation, and (eventually) social collapse, this would imply that one's self-interest is self-destructive—a contradiction in terms suggesting that self-interest was not properly understood by the model of rational selfishness in the first place.

How can society build a sense of public spirit? Mansbridge points out that the process of deliberation can shape public-spirited values: because people may be directly persuaded, because the process of deliberation itself helps to build a public spirit, and because involvement in deliberation helps produce commitment to the ultimate decisions. The other authors in this volume focus either on changing the values of children growing up, or helping adults to manage their conflicts of values. Mansbridge, however, takes seriously the proposition that the values of adults might be changed after they are already adults, and that this process of change might be salutary both for individuals and for society.

Crime and the Community

Nowhere is the disjunction between scholarly analyses by economists and popular commentary larger than in the discussion of crime. Economists have traditionally focused on rewards from crime versus the severity and likelihood of punishment. Popular writing focuses on the collapse of security in particular neighborhoods, the pervasive cloud of fear under which many people live, and the fact that much crime involves the delivery of goods and services people want or are induced by their friends and neighbors to want. While most previous models of crime have concentrated on the interaction between law enforcement agencies and criminals, to examine the costs and benefits of criminal behavior, George Akerlof and Janet Yellen build on and enrich the traditional analyses of the costs and benefits of crime to criminals by placing such behavior in a social context.

Their analysis, "Gang Behavior, Law Enforcement, and Community Values," emphasizes that the rewards of criminal activity and the likelihood of punishment cannot be understood apart from the community, its sense of justice, and its interaction with potential criminals. The community constrains both criminals and the police. If criminal behavior becomes too invasive, criminal threats and retaliation will not stop at least some of the community from cooperating with the police. On the other side, if overaggressive law enforcement alienates the community, then the job of law enforcement becomes harder, not easier.

Akerlof and Yellen thus view the task of law enforcement as hinging sensitively on the development of a community consensus against crime. In contrast to earlier analyses in which crime rates varied smoothly and continuously with rewards and with the severity and likelihood of punishment, Akerlof and Yellen explore the consequences of including the role of the community as a determinant of the level of crime. In an appendix, for the more formally inclined, they demonstrate that these ideas can be expressed and manipulated in a mathematical model.

Values and Preferences, Norms, and Habituation

Traditional analyses of public policies take human motivations as given. These motivations govern how people respond to incentives. The analysis of public policy is the attempt to determine how personal behaviors can be modified by changing the incentives people confront.

The incompleteness of this framework, as commonly practiced if not in principle, is a principal focus of this book. Children do not enter the world bearing fully developed preferences and habits. People acquire values and preferences through infancy, childhood, and adolescence under the influence of parents, schools, neighbors, and the media, all subject to genetic inheritances and predispositions. These values and norms continue to evolve gradually during a lifetime of adult experiences. People live within a social context, subject to the influence of community norms. Throughout this process, habituation shapes how people will later respond to the incentives they face.

The authors of the chapters in this book explicitly perform two tasks: they express judgments on the state of values and behavior norms in the United States, and they examine what public interventions might constructively alter those values and norms. By implication, they also provide a critique of the traditional framework used for analyzing public policy.

Defining the Problem and Fixing It

The authors implicitly make three different judgments on why the values Americans hold are problematic. One perspective views most value problems as conflicts between justifiable and worthwhile, but irreconcilable, impulses. From this point of view, the problem of values is the travail of the majority trying to work its way toward a common view. The title of a book by Daniel Yankelovich, *Coming to Public Judgment*, encapsulates this stance. Mansbridge and Glazer take a similar approach.

The second perspective on values emphasizes the fear that a broad public consensus on values is crumbling. From this perspective, the issue is not a conflict between worthwhile values, but rather the subtle contagion of "bad" values infecting our culture. That is Popenoe's focus.

The final perspective focuses on the values of a minority—those who commit crimes, have children out of wedlock, remain too long on the public dole. The problem is viewed neither as a conflict among worthwhile values nor as a societywide malaise, but rather as a failure of the mainstream to pass on healthy values to a particular subgroup. Wilson takes this perspective as, in a different way, do Akerlof and Yellen.

On how policy might change values, the authors divide up differently. At least five approaches, intertwined in various ways, are in evidence in their chapters.

One source of change in values might be the very incentives on which economists focus. Such incentives may emerge from economic trends or public policy. The effects of economic trends on values are well illustrated by the increase in oil prices that began in the mid-1970s. People and businesses initially griped about prices but did little to conserve fuel. As capital equipment was replaced, additional conservation measures were undertaken. Then, attitudes favoring conservation in general intensified. Perhaps an even more dramatic example was the change in personal norms regarding sexual behavior that followed discovery of effective methods of birth control.

The role of public policy in influencing values may be more controversial. Prohibitions of certain forms of racial discrimination that forced changes in public behavior may also have led to a decline of prejudicial attitudes and changes in personal behavior and social norms. Regulations banning or limiting smoking have not only restricted the places where smokers can light up, but have helped to convert smoking from a fashionable behavior flaunted on stage and screen into something unchic. President Clinton's recent abortive effort to permit gays and lesbians to serve openly in the military can be thought of as another attempt to build on (what he perceived as) an expanding tolerance for homosexuality and push it still further.

In each of these cases, people rationalize behaviors forced on them by changes in incentives in ways that extend and intensify the originally intended effects. Furthermore, changes in behaviors of neighbors and friends transform community norms that may exercise a distinguishable influence on behavior. Yankelovich and Popenoe stress that many changes in values evolve from broad social or economic trends—rising incomes, the civil rights movement, or increased education. By arguing that communities cooperate with police who behave fairly and punish appropriately, Akerlof and Yellen make this argument in perhaps the strongest way. Several of the possible solutions offered by Popenoe and Wilson to the breakdown of the family also rely on the notion that changes in incentives, over time, may cause values to shift.

Improved child rearing, either at home or at school, is a second way to change values. Wilson and Popenoe argue persuasively that strong families produce well-adjusted children; they argue less persuasively for particular methods of creating strong families. Glazer not only stresses the role of school in imparting facts, concepts, and skills but also highlights the need for schools to motivate children to participate with some degree of commitment in the educational process. Glazer's recognition of the importance of nurturing this commitment is exactly what underlies his sympathetic consideration of some forms of multicultural education.

Since "ought" statements frequently rest on perceived facts, a third way to change values expressed as declared preferences is to correct misperceptions of fact. Many health experts believe people would be less willing to endorse such statements as "everyone is entitled to health care as good as that available to the president" and might be more willing to support curbs on health spending if people were informed, perhaps on their pay stubs, just how much of their total compensation goes for health insurance.

A fourth approach to altering values goes beyond the presentation of information to persuasion by public figures. Yankelovich writes of the need for experts to improve their ability to communicate with the public. Popenoe argues that the attitudes of public figures might help to arrest the decay of families. And Mansbridge, perhaps more than any other author here, presents a case for the importance of public deliberation. None of the authors, however, describes how a nation like the United States, which is both diverse and committed to the right of individuals and groups to communicate their views freely, can organize to use authority figures to set good examples—or even what that means.

Insofar as individual values emerge from the norms of neighbors and frequent associates, the evolution of local institutions and developments also shapes the formation of individual values. The growth or decay of neighborhood voluntary organizations—the YMCA and YWCA, neighborhood clubs, the Boy Scouts, the Elks, churches—and policies or economic events that affect them become important forces in the formation of personal values and social norms. Wilson concludes his paper by explicitly pleading the importance of nurturing such organizations, although he acknowledges that no one knows how to do it. Such organizations are part of Popenoe's civil society. The very affluence effect to which Yankelovich attaches so pivotal a role has increasingly enabled people to provide for themselves many of the services through which such organizations once bound people together. Greater income has brought greater freedom from community pressure—and community nurturance.

Final Thoughts

The chapters in this volume run against a deep taboo among many social scientists and particularly among economists. Such analysts are concerned with behaviors, tangible actions, not attitudes. What people say or think or feel has importance in many contexts, it is acknowledged, but not in analyzing how public policy can change behavior. One should focus, it is argued, on how measurable behavior is related to the various kinds of incentives that people face. All else is speculation.

And so it is. But this stance raises a difficult puzzle that can be expressed best in terms commonly used in policy analysis.

To carry out such analysis, two kinds of models are used. One category relates certain events to certain influences, usually expressed in mathematical form, but the model is not supposed to express the actual structure of behavioral influences. For example, the price of a particular commodity may follow an annual cycle, so that the price can be related to the calendar date. No one thinks that the passage of the days intrinsically determines commodity prices, but a model that relates price to calendar date may perform serviceably as a forecasting device. Such constructs are called "reduced form" models.

Other models purport to represent the underlying structure of the process at work. A commodity price might be related both to factors governing supply, such as weather, and factors governing demand, such as personal income, unemployment, and exchange rates. Such a model goes beyond calendar regularities to represent the underlying forces that determine commodity prices. Such constructs are called "structural models."

The research issue embedded in the topics examined in this book is whether models that purport to reveal the structure of relationships between incentives and behaviors really go deep enough. This book raises the question of whether research methods used in designing and evaluating public policy, which take motivations and values as given and which downplay how individual behaviors cumulate to form the community norms that eventually influence the individual behaviors from which those norms emerge, are adequate to the task.

In this sense, Akerlof and Yellen point out one way to advance research. Using traditional analytic methods, they extend the range of relevant behaviors to include community norms and show how such norms feed back to transform the behaviors that produced them. Although personal characteristics at some level remain outside their framework, the preferences that determine willingness to cooperate with the police are explained within their model. As an alternative, researchers might adopt a two-stage approach. Initially they would follow current practice, assuming stable preferences and inquiring how changes in incentives affect behavior. At some point they would step back to inquire whether changes in policies and induced changes in behavior will lead to changes in preferences.

Not every analyst must build a model that integrates behavior and preferences as Akerlof and Yellen have done. But it is time to stop the pretense that stable values can be postulated and then set aside, as a matter of no real interest to the serious researcher.

Note

1.   Henry J. Aaron and William B. Schwartz, *The Painful Prescription: Rationing Hospital Care* (Brookings, 1984), p. 102.

How Changes in the Economy Are Reshaping American Values

Daniel Yankelovich

In the past few years, scholars studying values in advanced industrial democracies, such as Germany, France, Britain, Italy, Japan, Belgium, Holland, and Switzerland, have noted a striking similarity in their own countries to the value changes taking place in the United States, with a five- to ten-year time lag separating these countries from the United States. These researchers see an extensive transformation of values in Western Europe and Japan as well in the United States.

Rapid advances in technology, the end of the great struggle between Soviet-style command economies and democratic capitalism, the troubled outcomes of various national experiments with the role of government in the welfare state, and many other changes contribute to the transformation. But one cause, especially important to the interplay of values and economic thinking, stands out above all others. It is the reaction of people in the industrial democracies to the experience of affluence during the half century since the end of World War II.

After the war, each nation gradually recovered from the Great Depression of the 1930s. For several decades all enjoyed unprecedented economic growth and mounting affluence, which in more recent years has begun to slacken off, imperceptibly in some nations and more obviously in others.

The impact of affluence on peoples' values has proved powerful but curiously indirect. Economic changes do not by themselves transform values; what does is people's perceptions of their own, and their nation's, affluence (referred to throughout this paper as "the affluence effect"). There is, of course, a link between perceptions and reality. But the link is distorted. People often feel poor when they are objectively well-off, and well-off when they are actually growing poorer. In some nations, people who are relatively well-off feel poorer than their neighbors in other nations, and vice versa. Except at the extremes of the economic spectrum among the very rich and the very poor, value changes are mediated by people's interpretations of their own economic condition and its future prospects, interpretations that lag behind objective economic reality as an economist might describe it.

To explore the impact on values of the affluence effect, this paper is organized into three parts. The "Overview" develops the hypothesis that the affluence effect is a powerful driver of changing cultural values, especially when seen in the context of America's most stable and enduring values. "Truth and Relevance" discusses how the hypothesis of the affluence effect bears on the purpose of this book, namely, to consider whether formal economic analysis ought to expand its scope to take values into account in its search for solutions to America's social and economic problems. "Major Changes in Values" draws on the large body of survey research findings to identify six areas of value changes influenced by the affluence effect: greater tolerance and acceptance of pluralism; sweeping changes in family-related values; the changing meaning of success; a new relationship between work and leisure; changes in social morality; and new values in relation to health and physical well-being.

Overview

The affluence effect is the meaning that people give to their affluence or lack of it. For most people feeling affluent means freedom and empowerment. They believe that affluence brings the power to do whatever one wants to do. This meaning of affluence has had a dramatic effect on cultural values that the slower growth of recent years has blurred but not changed in its essentials. Because of it, many traditional values, rooted in generations of want and scarcity, have been swept aside and tens of millions of people find themselves experimenting with new forms of self-expression and individuality that were unthinkable or impractical in earlier periods.

Since the end of World War II, the affluence effect has evolved in three stages, with some industrial democracies now in the third stage and others still in the first two stages. The first stage occurs when affluence is new, and people suspect that their economic well-being may not be real. Incomes may be rising, but people fear it will not last. Confidence is low. Values remain conservative and traditional. The focus is on social bonds, sacrifice, hard work, and saving for the future; and personal choice is limited.

Except for its college youth, the United States persisted in this first "it-can't-last" stage until the late 1960s. The depression may have ended with World War II, but it was not until the late 1960s that Americans who had lived through the depression were able to put their depression psychology, and the fear, insecurity, and outlook it engendered, behind them. In West Germany and Japan, the combined effects of depression, defeat in war, inflation, and poverty were so traumatic that the outlook they engendered persisted throughout many years of growing affluence as economists would define it. Only in the early 1980s did these two economic giants move into the second stage.

Psychologically, a startling discontinuity takes place between the first and second stages of the affluence effect. From an objective economic point of view, incomes may be rising slowly and steadily. But subjectively, the transition is abrupt. Remarkably, people swing from undue skepticism about their economic prospects to undue optimism. They leap from doubting the reality of their affluence to assuming that it is a permanent condition and that they and their nation can now spend freely without worrying about tomorrow. They believe they can indulge themselves and make up for lost time, and their nation can address long-neglected problems and fix them. Almost overnight the feeling changes from "it won't last" to "it will go on forever, and now we can afford to do anything we want."

In stage two people revel in expanding their life choices. Indeed, greatly enhanced personal choice is the hallmark of this second stage, and people relish their new freedom to choose careers and life-styles in accord with their individual bent, not in conformity to the expectations of others or as a concession to economic constraints.

In this stage of the affluence effect, the quest for self-expression and self-fulfillment grows less inhibited. People assume that only when they feel (and are) well-off economically can they start to live for today and for their own self-satisfaction, on the assumption that tomorrow things will take care of themselves.

Stage two came to Japan later than to the other industrialized democracies and so can be seen most clearly there. By the late 1980s the Japanese began to show familiar signs of the second stage. Especially pronounced were the following:

—A rising level of individualism and less conformity (for example, a shift away from group travel to individual travel to enjoy life and "invest in myself");

—A tendency to take affluence for granted and to spend freely and carelessly;

—An increase in live-for-today, short-term satisfaction;

—A decline in the willingness of people to sacrifice for their children; and

—A willingness to be more venturesome and take more risks in their personal lives.[1]

The third stage, fear of the loss of affluence, a painful adaptation to the unexpected economic reality that one can no longer take affluence for granted, also arrives abruptly. People begin to feel cornered and disoriented. They realize they had better begin to think about tomorrow once again. They grow apprehensive that opportunities for jobs, income growth, home ownership, higher education for their children, and retirement are at risk. My firm's research shows that the United States moved squarely into this third stage in the two years preceding the 1992 presidential election. Indeed, the results of that election are best understood in the context of the economic anxieties generated by this third stage, anxieties far exceeding those associated with an ordinary economic recession.[2]

Americans in all walks of life are now adjusting their expectations downward and adapting to what they see as a more difficult, less open, less fair, more demanding, and more stressful economic environment.

How the Affluence Effect Changes Values

In his book, *Life Chances*, sociologist Ralf Dahrendorf presents a historical context for understanding how the affluence effect influences cultural values.³ Dahrendorf sees all historic shifts in Western culture as efforts to balance *choices* and *bonds*. Choices enhance individualism and personal freedom; bonds strengthen social cohesiveness and stability. In societies where the bonds that link people to one another and to institutions are rigid, the individual's freedom of choice is limited. As people struggle to enlarge their sphere of choice, the bonds that bind them together slacken.

The tension between bonds and choices characterizes the evolution of American cultural values in the post-World War II period. Driven by the affluence effect, the quest for greater individual choice clashed directly with the obligations and social norms that held families and communities together in earlier years. People came to feel that questions of how to live and with whom to live were a matter of individual choice not to be governed by restrictive norms. As a nation, we came to experience the bonds to marriage, family, children, job, community, and country as constraints that were no longer necessary. Commitments were loosened. We witnessed an explosion of divorces, single households, latchkey children, children born out of wedlock, job changes, second careers, dropping out of school, returning to school, and restless moving about from place to place.⁴

Gradually, as the affluence effect evolved, Americans began to shape a synthesis between expanded choice and the need for enduring commitments. The young affluent Americans on the leading edge of this trend learned that total freedom of choice undermines the bonds that give personal relationships, the family, the community, and the nation their meaning and stability.

People do learn from experience, and as they do, they modify their values. Americans have learned a great deal from their bruising encounter with new self-expressive values. They learned, for example, that their expanded life choices created time stress and mounting financial debt that suddenly grew frightening when they became concerned about their economic prospects.

Many have also learned that the world of work can be less satisfying and less secure than they assumed, and that giving too much to work and career can undermine family and quality of life, especially in an economic climate in which loyalty is a one-way affair (the employer expects it but does not give it in return).

The quest for greater self-expression, Americans have learned, can take a heavy toll on personal relationships. Children suffer.

Families are at risk. Relationships between men and women grow distressingly complex and often unstable. People's powerful needs for affiliation become frustrated, and some forms of pleasure seeking prove deeply unsatisfying.

This learning experience does not mean that Americans are returning to traditional marriages and families, to older definitions of status and success, to social conformity and togetherness. They are not. They are inventing distinctive blends of bonds and choices, shaping novel patterns of culture.

The affluence effect is like one of the consequences that eating the apple had for Adam and Eve. After the apple, Adam and Eve were never able to return to their previous state of innocence. The taste of freedom from traditional bonds apparently has a similar powerful effect. So strong is the appeal of greater freedom to express one's individuality that, once experienced, people find it very difficult to return to a more constricted world. Thus, even the combination of lowered economic expectations and the bitter learning experiences associated with the new values are not enough to cause people to go back to a traditional world of close but restrictive bonds. The struggle to retain as much self-expressive freedom as possible, whatever the economic circumstances, is a striking feature of the affluence effect.

Outside the United States in the other industrial democracies, similar cultural changes are occurring in less extreme form: a reaction against the constraints of traditional bonds followed by a striving for a synthesis that will retain some traditional bonds while leaving plenty of room for greater individual choice, whatever the ups and downs of the economy. In each culture, the pattern takes a distinctive form, reflecting the history, institutional structure, and material conditions peculiar to it. But in all advanced industrial democracies today, the tension generated by the affluence effect underlies the churning, groping, restless, nervous energy of modern industrial democracy.

Summary of Value Changes

The following list summarizes the American values that have changed in recent years:

—The concept of duty. Less value placed on what one owes to others as a matter of moral obligation.

—Social conformity. Less value placed on keeping up with the Joneses.

—Respectability. Less value placed on symbols of correct behavior for a person of a particular social class.

—Social morality. Less value placed on observing society's rules.

—Pluralism. Greater acceptance of differences in ethnicity and life-style.

—Sacrifice. Less value placed on sacrifice as a moral good, replaced by more pragmatic criteria of when sacrifice is or is not called for.

—Expressiveness. A higher value placed on forms of choice and individualism that express one's unique inner nature.

—The environment. Greater value placed on respecting and preserving nature and the natural.

—Technology. Greater value placed on technological solutions to a vast array of problems and challenges.

—Sexuality. Less moral value placed on "correct" sexual behavior; a loosening of some but not all norms of sexual morality.

—Pleasure. Less puritanism about pleasure, especially bodily pleasures; pleasure regarded as a good.

—Family. A high value placed on family life, but with a vastly expanded concept of family beyond the traditional nuclear form.

—Husband-wife relationships. A far-reaching shift from role-based obligations to shared responsibilities.

—Health. Greater value placed on one's own responsibility for maintaining and enhancing health.

—Work ethic. A shift from the Protestant ethic valuation of work as having intrinsic moral value to work as a source of personal satisfaction, and therefore less tolerance for work that does not provide personal satisfaction.

—Women's rights. A higher value placed on women achieving self-fulfillment by paths of their own choice rather than through roles dictated by society.

This enumeration is far from complete, but it does suggest the breadth of change. Some of these changes are so extensive that they virtually reverse previously held values. For example, social conformity and respectability were once the norm of the land, but individualism and choice of life-style are now the norm. The almost universal rule of marriage once revolved around sharply differentiated roles for men and women. Now roles have blurred, and a different conception of marriage has taken hold among most Americans.

America's Core Values

Before documenting specific areas of changed values, I want to emphasize that all American values have not changed. Despite the affluence effect and other agents of change, many of America's most important traditional values have remained firm and constant.

Since the focus of this paper is on changing values, I will keep my inventory of the values that have *not* changed brief. The list that follows is a familiar one, but mere familiarity should not blind us to the importance of the fact that while many traditional values are in upheaval, a small number continue to win the allegiance of most Americans.

The unchanged values are the following:

—Freedom. Valuing political liberty, free speech, freedom of movement, freedom of religious worship, and other freedoms from constraints to the pursuit of private happiness.

—Equality before the law. Placing a high value on having the same rules of justice apply to one and all, rich and poor, black and white.

—Equality of opportunity. The practical expression of freedom and individualism in the marketplace, which helps to resolve the tensions between the values of freedom and equality.

—Fairness. Placing a high value on people getting what they deserve as the consequence of their own individual actions and efforts.

—Achievement. A belief in the efficacy of individual effort: the view that education and hard work pay off.

—Patriotism. Loyalty to the United States and dedication to the way of life it represents.

—Democracy. A belief that the judgment of the majority should form the basis of governance.

—American exceptionalism. A belief in the special moral status and mission of America.

—Caring beyond the self. Placing a high value on a concern for others such as family or ethnic group; neighborliness; caring for the community.

—Religion. A reverence for some transcendental meaning extending beyond the realm of the secular and practical.

—Luck. A belief that one's fortunes and circumstances are not permanent and that good fortune can happen to anyone at any time.

Each one of these values has a rich and complex heritage that is not captured by its mere mention. Despite the transformations in America's life-styles, these core values have endured. Virtually all Americans share them; compositely, they make American culture distinctive. The United States is a nation of immense diversity—geographically, ethnically, economically, politically. And yet, this tiny cluster of values holds Americans together as a single people and nation. They are the *unum* in the national motto, *e pluribus unum*—the unity amid the variety of American life.

Truth and Relevance

The hypothesis of the affluence effect is intriguing because of its great breadth. Not confined to the United States, it appears to have equally large effects on Western Europe and Japan, shedding light on how the societies of the advanced industrial democracies are evolving. Its effects are also broad in that they cover a wide swathe of social values including family values, acceptance of pluralism, social morality, the relation between work and leisure, preferred life-styles, feelings of altruism, how people define success and quality of life, and many other important arenas of life.

To link the hypothesis of the affluence effect to the purpose of this book, two questions should be posed and answered. How is the affluence effect relevant to solving social and economic problems? And how do we know it is valid?

Relevance

The affluence effect is relevant to public policy in many ways. It has a direct and obvious influence on people's attitudes toward whether social problems are to be addressed, how they should be paid for, what the role of government should be, and how the problems are to be solved. From the late 1960s to the mid-1970s, when the second stage of the affluence effect was in full bloom, the typical American attitude could be paraphrased as, "I'm doing okay. Why shouldn't others get a break too?" Majority attitudes toward government and private sector programs to help minorities were positive. The war on poverty and entitlement programs for the needy enjoyed large-scale support. People were willing to help others and, if necessary, to pay extra taxes to do so.

One of the most typical attitudes of the period was a let's-fix-it mindset. The dominant sentiment of the day was, "If we can put a man on the moon, surely we can do something about poverty (or illiteracy or housing or insuring a comfortable retirement for older people or helping people in inner cities, and so on)."

Then, as the affluence effect evolved into its present less optimistic phase, people's outlooks became transformed. The attitude became, "It's rough out there, so we had better look out for ourselves." Instead of altruism supported by the conviction that there was enough for everyone, abruptly the struggle for existence came to be perceived as a zero-sum game, negatively affecting people's willingness to devote resources to solve other people's problems.

In the period of transition from the rising expectations associated with stage two to the diminishing expectations associated with stage three (the two years before the presidential election of 1992), Americans were in a state of semishock and anxiety. People were persuaded that the country had lost its way and that their own personal lives were spinning out of control. They grew fearful that the budget deficit was taking the nation's future as hostage, that the next generation would not live as well as the present generation, and that somehow government entitlements needed to be questioned.

Following the election, people began to adapt their outlook to the harsher economic environment and to seek, once again, to exercise control over their lives. A new attitude of pragmatism began to take hold, replacing the prolonged mental holiday that had characterized the 1980s. Americans began to reconsider, favorably, the role that government should play in their lives and to give top priority to fixing the long-term problems plaguing the economy, such as slow growth, lagging competitiveness, a ballooning federal budget deficit, and high unemployment.

A changing attitude toward entitlements is, perhaps, the best example of how value changes tied to the affluence effect bear on solving social problems. In stage two of the affluence effect in the 1970s, the public endorsed two different definitions of fairness relating to entitlements. One was the traditional concept of fairness based on deserving, for example, "I'm entitled to X because I worked for it and I deserve it." This is how people feel, for example, about seniority on the job and social security. The other was a newer conception of fairness based on need, for example, "I'm entitled to X—welfare, housing, a college education, health care—because I *need* it."

In the early years of the entitlement programs, Americans supported both definitions, fairness based on need and fairness based on getting what you deserve, because times were good and the second stage of the affluence effect dominated the national mood. The public did not realize the contradictions and conflicts between the two definitions.

Eventually, however, the conflicts began to hit home. People in interviews would say things such as, "I skimped and saved for my kid's college education, but who got the scholarship? Not my kid, but the kid next door whose parents spent every dime they ever made. It's just not fair."

The conflict between the two conceptions of fairness raises fundamental questions about the moral basis of public policy. Individuals have great latitude about how to allocate their resources. But when it comes to social policy, as represented by government-mandated benefits, the concept of need-based entitlements, where nothing is expected in return, leads the country into contradictions and conflicts. There are no limits to what people need and therefore no limits in theory to entitlements. (We see this issue played out in the controversy about rising health care costs.)

In the more practical mood of stage three of the affluence effect, the public has reached a new value consensus. The data suggest that the public is ready to shift the moral foundations of entitlements from a one-way street—if you need it, you are entitled to it—to a more balanced social contract. If the society gives you a benefit, you must, if you are able, pay it back in some appropriate form. Most Americans today embrace the concept of reciprocity. What the public is saying is that most government programs should require some form of reciprocity: people should no longer expect something for nothing. Above all, they should not expect something for nothing as a matter of right.

To the extent that the value orientation of the public now embraces the doctrine of reciprocity rather than need-based entitlements, few social policies will remain unaffected.[5]

It is difficult to imagine any realistic strategy for dealing with social problems that does not take this kind of shift in values into account.

Limited Documentation

While its relevance is easy to establish, the validity of the affluence effect is another matter. From a strict scientific standpoint, evidence to support it is spotty and incomplete. It comes from making inferences from a number of sources, none of which is as systematic and well documented as one might like. In the pages that follow I present evidence of value changes (largely from the survey research literature) supporting the affluence effect hypothesis, so that readers can reach their own judgment about its validity.

A major source of discomfort is the virtual absence of time-series data on cultural values. The available data are unsystematic. Generally speaking, it is not until changes in values are well advanced that they begin to be measured. By then, however, the opportunity to establish a baseline has been lost. Unlike economics, which is rich in time-series data conducted year after year, values research is often done in ad hoc studies conducted sporadically, some published, most unpublished, some in the public domain, much of it not.

A great deal of opinion poll data on attitudes and values has in recent years been gathered at the Roper Center in Storrs, Connecticut, an invaluable resource for scholars in the field. I have drawn heavily on this data base for this paper. My own research firm has made its proprietary data base available—the DYG SCAN[SM], a trend identification program. It is also a principal source of documentation for the value changes reported here.[6]

Another methodological problem is semantics. Values are notoriously difficult to define, let alone measure, and it can be confusing when measures of values are mixed interchangeably with measures of opinions, attitudes, beliefs, motivations, and other subjective states of mind and feelings. In the literature, values are usually defined as the most stable and enduring of these predispositions, opinions as the most superficial and volatile, with attitudes falling somewhere between the two.

In many contexts, these distinctions are useful. For purposes of public policy, however, they may be more confusing than helpful. For one thing, they do not always hold up under careful scrutiny. According to the convention, opinions are supposed to be easy to change, values very difficult to change. In practice, however, one will sometimes find rock solid opinions (on the death penalty, for example) that resist change, and fundamental values (on the sacredness of human life, for example) that yield to change.

Furthermore, for public policy purposes, understanding people's surface attitudes and opinions may be just as useful as knowing their deeply rooted values. For most public policy purposes, it is not too important whether cultural changes involve values in the narrow sense of the word, or attitudes, opinions, and beliefs, or a blend of all. What is important is that cultural change has taken place and thus affects public policy.

Finally, most value change is not linear but dialectic. The most typical pattern of change starts with a swing to the opposite extreme, which is then followed by a series of multidirectional movements as people struggle to adapt their new values to more traditional ones and to changing circumstances. Unless one understands the dynamics of the adaptive process, how people juggle the old and the new, the measures of value change recorded in the literature appear patternless or are interpreted as backlashes or cyclical swings of the pendulum.

The pendulum analogy is particularly popular and almost always wrong. A pendulum swing backward implies a return to an older pattern, and this movement almost never occurs. We never really return to the past. People's efforts to synthesize the old and the new always lead to new patterns. Sometimes radically new patterns may even parade superficially as a return to the past. For example, Americans in the 1990s yearn for the family values that dominated the country in the 1950s. But what Americans meant by family in the 1950s is not at all what they mean by family in the 1990s.

When people's values conflict, they manage the conflict in an immense variety of ways. The most frequent pattern is one in which people vacillate between old and new values, trying to hold onto both until the conflict grows so uncomfortable that they have to choose one or the other or evolve some sort of compromise. Unfortunately, these patterns cannot be measured along elegant, unidirectional trend lines.

For all of these reasons those unfamiliar with the field of values research will feel some discomfort in their first encounter with it. With these caveats in mind, I will now describe and document a half-dozen value changes driven by the affluence effect.

Major Changes in Values

Some of the clearest trend data on changing American attitudes and values depict a shift away from xenophobia and toward greater acceptance of diversity—a striking manifestation of the live-and-let-live philosophy associated with the affluence effect.

Greater Tolerance and Acceptance of Pluralism

The early days of public opinion polling, in the 1930s and 1940s, portrayed an America openly and vigorously anti-black, anti-Catholic, anti-Semitic, anti-foreigner, and opposed to equality for women.

The opinion polls of the 1930s focused on attitudes toward Jews, because of Hitler's persecution of the Jews. These polls showed that anti-Semitism was widespread throughout the country. In a 1939 Roper poll for *Fortune* magazine, Roper found that a majority of Americans (53 percent) felt that Jews are different from other Americans and should be restricted in various ways, including preventing Jews from "mingling socially where they are not wanted" and even deporting them to a "new homeland."

Almost forty years later, in January 1987, a Gallup poll asked Americans whom they would *not* like to have living next door to them as neighbors. Only 3 percent mentioned Jews.

One of the most compelling bits of evidence for declining xenophobia in America is a time-series question that Gallup and National Opinion Research Center (NORC) have been asking for many years: whether voters would or would not vote for a Jew for president, a black for president, or a woman for president (the presidency

being the most universal symbol of social acceptance). On willingness to vote for a Jewish presidential candidate, the nation moved
from an even split in 1937 (47 percent to 46 percent) to an 8:1
positive ratio fifty years later (82 percent to 10 percent).[7]

The question of attitudes toward African-Americans is more ambiguous. But even so, clear cut trends are discernible. When, in May
1944, an NORC survey asked a cross-section of Americans whether
they felt "Negroes in their town" had the same chance as whites to
get a good education, the overwhelming majority (84 percent) answered yes. When asked why they were not as well educated as
whites, the majority (54 percent) cited lower intelligence or lack of
ambition. When asked "Do you think Negroes are as intelligent as
white people—that is, can they learn just as well if they are given
the same education?" more whites answered no than yes (47 percent
to 44 percent). And when at the end of a long series of similar
questions, white Americans were asked whether "most Negroes in
the United States are being treated fairly or unfairly," only one out
of four answered "unfairly."

As recently as 1968, a majority of white Americans (55 percent)
endorsed the view that they had a right "to keep blacks out of their
neighborhood if they wanted to, and that blacks should respect that
right." NORC has asked this same question every year since 1968,
and the trend line is unambiguous: by 1990, the 55 percent majority
who felt they had a right to keep blacks out had dwindled to a 22
percent minority.

Even more dramatic is the trend line on whether Americans
would vote for a black for president, rising sharply from a 38 percent
minority as reported in a 1958 Gallup poll to a strong 84 percent
majority in a 1990 NORC study.

Changing attitudes toward women show a similar pattern. In an
April 1946 Roper survey for *Fortune* a cross-section of Americans
were asked about the comparative qualifications of men and women
for various jobs "when men and women are given an equal chance."
The results are wondrously one-sided. Men were selected as "making
the best welders in a factory" (80 percent to 5 percent), the "best
lawyers" (78 percent to 8 percent), the "best department store ex-
ecutives" (55 percent to 22 percent), the "best high school teachers
of history" (41 percent to 33 percent), and the "best baby doctors"

(46 percent to 31 percent). Women were selected overwhelmingly for only one type of job—as making the "best stenographers" (86 percent to 5 percent). The reason men were thought to enjoy such greater potential in the eyes of Americans was implicit in a Gallup poll conducted that same year: in answer to the question, "Generally speaking, which do you think are more intelligent, men or women?" men were chosen over women by two to one (40 percent to 20 percent).

The trend line on the acceptability of a woman for president could hardly be more dramatic: a 2:1 ratio of respondents saying they would *not* vote for a woman in a 1937 Gallup poll to a nearly 7:1 ratio (82 percent to 12 percent) in a 1987 Gallup poll saying they would.

What do these trends mean? Clearly, as the Los Angeles riots and similar events demonstrate, they do not mean enlightened race relations and easy acceptance of pluralism. There are many reasons for this unpleasant reality. Greater pluralism in society requires more skilled management; the institutions on which we depend for fair and effective management, especially the schools and the justice system, do not work well; and economic hard times exacerbate tensions. But knowing that the public has grown less xenophobic is important in considering policy solutions to the problem of rising racial tensions.

Consider the troubled question of affirmative action. In response to a Gallup/*Newsweek* question in April 1991 on whether affirmative action quotas are necessary to achieve fairness in education, hiring, and promotion, whites reject the use of quotas by two-to-one margins (59 percent to 29 percent), while the reverse pattern holds for blacks: by more than two to one (61 percent to 26 percent), blacks believe that quotas are necessary.

How should one interpret these findings in the light of the secular trend toward greater pluralism? Unlike the America of the 1930s, the American public today accepts a pluralistic society in which women and minorities have access to equal opportunities with white males. Various opinion polls show that some forms of affirmative action—those that include outreach, remedial training, scholarships, and good faith efforts to find qualified candidates for schools or jobs—are acceptable. But anything that smacks of preferential treatment, such as selecting candidates on the basis of race or gender (or giving these factors *any* weight), is so unacceptable to the public that it has grown into a divisive political issue.

A study conducted for the Democratic Leadership Council in May 1992 found that the main reason for the sharply divergent attitudes between blacks and whites on quotas reflects mistrust on both sides far more than it does racial prejudice. Whites fear that with quotas, less qualified minorities will get the good jobs; blacks fear that *without* quotas, less qualified whites will get the good jobs. Black Americans' fear reflects a deepening pessimism. Over the past several decades the optimism of black Americans about their progress has declined steadily and sharply. In 1970 almost two-thirds of blacks (64 percent) believed the situation of black people in this country was improving. A decade later in 1980, black optimism had slipped to 49 percent. By 1988 it had declined further to 33 percent, and by April 1991 had eroded still further to a mere 21 percent.[8] In sharp contrast, an October 1990 Gallup poll shows that 61 percent of the public overall believe the quality of life of blacks has improved over the past ten years.

In the debate over various forms of affirmative action, one of America's strongest core values is seen to be at risk. Traditionally, Americans balance the conflicting claims of freedom and equality through adherence to the concept of equality of opportunity. (See earlier inventory of core values.) The almost sacred principle of equality of opportunity depends utterly on rigid respect for people's qualifications. The idea that a less qualified person should get the job for whatever reason violates America's faith in individual effort and in merit. Forms of affirmative action that guarantee equality of opportunity receive strong majority support (at the two-thirds level). Forms that seem to violate this core value are rejected vehemently.

Without denying that racial prejudice still exists, the practical ramifications of these findings on values and attitudes for public policy are important. They suggest that policy initiatives that threaten our core values will inevitably invite backlash and undermine the policymaker's good intentions. If the heart of the problem is mistrust, then the policy emphasis shifts from legalistic solutions to enforce "numerical targets" (that is, quotas) to efforts to engage and reduce mistrust, especially justified black mistrust that existing job qualifications are biased to favor white candidates because they emphasize formal education over ability to do the job.

Successful policies should reinforce core values, not undermine them. A review of current policies designed to strengthen pluralism will, I believe, show that more often than not they ride roughshod over American core values, thereby insuring their defeat and giving rise to the mistaken impression that popular prejudice not the obtuseness of policymakers is to blame.

In the examples that follow, the pattern is dialectic rather than linear—a swing to the opposite extreme, followed by an effort at synthesis as people struggle to reconcile the old and the new.

Marriage and Family

The chief impact of the affluence effect in all of the advanced industrial democracies has probably been on family life and the role of women. The affluence effect causes a shift from traditional roles in marriage to personal relationships. In the past, roles in marriage were sharply differentiated: the men as breadwinners and providers and the women as caretakers and homemakers. Now these roles have grown blurred.

The shift is a difficult one for our societies. Historically, marriage has been so squarely based on sharply defined roles for husbands and wives that when these expectations blur people have to relearn how to behave. As a result, there is a great deal of confusion: marriage becomes a major source of tension.

The combined effect of greater individualism, greater independence and autonomy for women, more choice, less automatic sacrifice, and more questioning of traditional roles has been to place the family under great strain. Maintaining family life in the face of such strain has become the most important value of tens of millions of Western Europeans, Japanese, and American families.

Structural changes in American family composition have proved radical. The Bureau of the Census shows that in the 1950s, most households—approximately 70 percent—consisted of a male breadwinner, a female homemaker, and two or more children under the age of 18 living at home. When the word "family" is used, most Americans still conjure up this image. Today, however, a mere 8 percent of households fit this model. An additional 18 percent consist of dual-earner households with one or more children under 18 living at home. Thirty percent of families comprise married couples without children. Eight percent are single parents. Eleven percent are unmarried couples and others living together. And a whopping 25 percent (up from 17 percent in 1970) are people living alone—one out of every four households.

These transformations are not solely because of shifts in values, but value changes contribute significantly to them. For example, in 1943 Gallup asked a cross-section of 25–35-year-old women to choose among three alternatives: being unmarried with a successful career; being married with a successful career; and being married and running a home. Three out of four (73 percent) chose the third alternative, and among those who did want a career *and* marriage, four out of five said that if they had to choose, they would drop the career—a total of 87 percent choosing running a home over a career.

In 1938 Gallup showed that Americans disapproved of married women working outside the home by a ratio of almost 4:1 (78 percent to 22 percent). By February 1986, a study by NORC shows that the pattern had totally reversed: almost 4:1 approved (77 percent to 22 percent).

In the mid-1950s I conducted a study among married women to learn how much choice they felt they had about whether or not to have children. When I raised the question, the women stared at me uncomprehendingly. The gist of their response was, "If you are married, you have children. It is not even a question, let alone a matter of choice. Having children is what being a married woman means."

In a series of studies on what it means to be "a real man," our research findings were equally unequivocal: until the late 1960s, being a real man meant being a good provider for the family. No other conception of what it means to be a real man came even close. Concepts of sexual potency, or physical strength, or strength of character (manliness), or even being handy around the house were relegated to the bottom of the list of traits associated with masculinity. By the late 1970s, however, the definition of a real man as a good provider had slipped from its number one spot (86 percent in 1968) to the number three position, at 67 percent. It has continued to erode.[9]

Family values have become the main arena for the showdown between the new expressive values of seeking greater choice for the self and the more traditional claims of family bonds, commitments, and obligations. At one and the same time, the majority of Americans profess that family values are the most important values in their lives and that they are satisfied with their own family life, and yet as soon as one probes, one encounters a wave of fault-finding and pessimism about the future of the family.

If anything, the importance of the family as a value has increased in the past two decades. In 1976, 83 percent of the public declared family life a very important value; by 1991, the number of Americans holding this point of view had increased to 93 percent.[10] A series of NORC studies over the past twenty years shows that three-quarters of all Americans say they are satisfied with their family life.[11]

Yet the evidence is strong that Americans are worried about family and the prospects for the institution of marriage.

—By a ratio of more than 4:1 (62 percent to 14 percent), Americans believe family values have grown weaker in recent years, not stronger.[12]

—More than two out of five Americans (43 percent) feel that changes in the traditional family structure "severely threaten" the American Dream.[13]

—From the middle to the late 1980s, the number of Americans who believe that "the family is the place where most basic values are instilled" declined from 82 percent to 62 percent.[14]

—When asked in a July 1989 Roper poll for Virginia Slims whether or not marriages have improved since the 1970s, by a ratio of 45 percent to 35 percent, women say they have gotten worse (the ratio for men is similar—43 percent to 33 percent).

—Even more tellingly, when people were asked whether the "kinds of marriages" people have today require change in order to make women's lives better, 78 percent of women said that change was needed, and almost the same number of men (70 percent) agreed.[15]

—Asked in a November 1989 Gallup poll whether they feel the divorce rate will get better or worse in the next ten years, by more than two to one (46 percent to 22 percent), Americans think it will get worse.

—Asked about the future prospects for family life in America, only 5 percent felt they were excellent, in sharp contrast to a 59 percent majority who feel they are "only fair" (30 percent) or "poor" (29 percent).[16]

What underlies this pervasive feeling of pessimism? One factor that people cite in survey after survey is that parents have less time to spend with their children. This is the number one answer to the question, "Which is the most important cause of family values having grown weaker?" When people are asked to list the ways in which family values should be strengthened, the top rated-answer (55 percent) is that parents should spend more time with the family.

Also high on the list are greater efforts to teach family values in churches, synagogues, and schools, and better role models on television. At the bottom of the list are such policy issues as having business allow workers to do more work at home, providing day care for children of working parents, and allowing more flexible work schedules. This does not mean these issues are unimportant to people; it does mean that people feel these social policies are not as important as the less tangible factors cited above—partly because they do not make the connection between them and parents having more time with their children. (This is another example of the relevance of values to social policy.)

When we probe the question of what "family values" mean, we begin to see how Americans are attempting to meld the new expressive values with the traditional ones. When people are asked how they define family values, eleven meanings receive majority endorsement. Of these, six are clearly traditional:

Value	%
—Respecting one's parents.	70
—Being responsible for one's actions.	68
—Having faith in God.	59
—Respecting authority.	57
—Married to the same person for life.	54
—Leaving the world in better shape.	51

The other five are a blend of traditional and newer, more expressive values:

Value	%
—Giving emotional support to other members of the family.	69
—Respecting people for themselves.	68
—Developing greater skill in communicating one's feelings.	65
—Respecting one's children.	65
—Living up to one's full potential as an individual.	54

Significantly, some important traditional family values of the 1950s fail to be endorsed by most Americans. Fewer than 50 percent cite "being married" (47 percent) as part of their definition of family values, or "having children" (45 percent). Fewer than 4 out of 10 include "earning a good living" (39 percent) or "being financially secure" (37 percent). And a mere 20 percent include "having nice things" in their definition.[17]

Americans want very much to hold onto those intangible aspects of tradition that center on religion, respect, discipline, and responsibility. But they also want to graft onto these traditional values the newer emphases on freer communication of feelings and the opportunity to live up to one's full potential as an individual.

Despite their pessimism about marriage and family, most people (78 percent) feel they are better off today than their parents were at a comparable stage in life. By three to one (44 percent to 15 percent), they feel their family life has turned out better than they expected, and, as they look to the future, 81 percent expect eventually to lead a more satisfactory life than their parents did.

Comparing their lives with those of their parents, people acknowledge that some things will be more difficult and others easier. By 49 percent to 30 percent, they think they will have more difficulty than their parents did in finding the money to put kids through college and by 41 percent to 32 percent they think owning a home will be more difficult. Conversely, however, by 47 percent to 14 percent, they believe it will be easier for them to be in good physical health. Of equal importance, by 44 percent to 16 percent they think it will be easier to have an interesting job, and even easier (by 42 percent to 31 percent) to earn enough money for a good living.[18]

These findings show that Americans today realize that they are better off in many ways than their parents were. But at the same time, they are aware that many of the new values and life-styles threaten the family—an institution that has come to mean more to them now that it can no longer be taken for granted.

The Meaning of Success

One of the most sweeping changes in postwar American cultural values relates to the meaning of success. In the 1950s Americans shared a certain definition. Success meant getting married, raising children who would be better off than oneself, owning a home and an automobile, and working one's way up the ladder of social mobility. The trappings of success were largely external and material, a matter of keeping up with the Joneses.

When in November 1962 Gallup queried cross-sections of the public on the "formula for success in today's America," two answers dominated all others: get a good education (50 percent) and work hard (31 percent), followed by honesty and integrity (17 percent). Only 6 percent mentioned having a job that one enjoys doing, and a paltry 3 percent cited the importance of self-confidence and self-esteem.

Then came the 1960s campus rebellion and its iconoclastic attitudes toward the 1950s. For millions of college students the shared meaning of success shifted from owning a Cadillac to fulfilling one's unique inner potential.

In the 1970s the majority of Americans were intrigued but still unconvinced of the virtues of the new outlook. A January 1971 Harris poll asked people, "Do you think the desire on the part of many young people to . . . turn their backs on economic gain and success . . . is a healthy or unhealthy thing?" Only 13 percent thought it healthy. In mid-decade (April 1974) the leading responses to a Gallup question about "what really matters in your own life," were a decent and better standard of living (31 percent), good health (25 percent), adequate opportunities for one's children (23 percent), a happy marriage and family life (15 percent), and owning one's own home (12 percent)—all traditional, fifties-like conceptions.

By the 1980s, however, most Americans were attempting to graft the new values onto the old ones. In response to a May 1983 Gallup question about which factors are most important for "personal success in America today," the top ranking ones were good health (58 percent), a job one enjoys (49 percent), a happy family (45 percent), a good education (39 percent), peace of mind (35 percent), and good friends (25 percent). Note that the traditional emphasis on education and family remains an important part of the definition of success, but newer values such as having a job one enjoys, peace of mind, and good friends have now been elevated to a status equal to or higher than the traditional ones. It is characteristic of the 1980s that people wanted material well-being and the new forms of inner fulfillment extolled in the 1960s and 1970s.[19]

Now in the 1990s we are witnessing a further evolution of the shared meaning of success. Increasingly, Americans are coming to think of success as self-defined rather than conformity to the expectations of others. Over a five-year period, the DYG SCAN[SM] has measured a significant increase in the ratio of those embracing a conception of success as self-defined. By 1987 it had already reached a 5:1 ratio (63 percent to 12 percent), and by 1991 it had grown to more than a 7:1 ratio (68 percent to 9 percent).[20]

There are some modest demographic differences, mainly related to age and income. People between 40 and 60 with higher incomes (above $50,000 a year) lean slightly more often toward the self-defined measure of success, while people younger than 40 with lower incomes lean slightly more often toward conformity to group definitions of success. Some minor gender, education, geographic, and race differences also occur. What is significant is not the differences but that all groups in the population follow the dominant pattern of shifting away from older, more objective, conformist definitions of success to more subjective definitions.

If Americans define success in their own terms, what do they mean by it? Money and tangible possessions are still dominant. By a two-to-one margin (40 percent to 22 percent), Americans in 1991 gave priority to the material over the intangible. Here the pattern has been markedly dialectic—with a heavy emphasis on tangibles in the 1950s, a swing toward intangibles in the following few decades, and an edging back toward tangibles in the 1980s and 1990s. Demographic differences are pronounced and in the expected direction: the less educated and lower-income segments of the population emphasize tangibles because they do not have them. Those in the higher income brackets lean moderately toward intangibles because they have been better able to satisfy their material needs.[21]

What are the intangibles that Americans associate with success? The current emphasis is on quality of life. Glimpses of what Americans mean by quality of life can be seen in several studies:

—Having good family and personal relationships with loved ones.

—Getting one's time under control.

—Saving money and getting one's finances under control (for example, less debt, being a smarter consumer by outfoxing the seller).

—Reducing other forms of stress.

—Doing more to enhance health and personal appearance.

—Becoming more "green" conscious about the environment.[22]

In the 1990s, Americans know they can not have everything, and they are adapting their definition of success in life to this new reality. People's feelings about being squeezed in the 1990s go deeper than recession or slowdown in economic growth. The affluence effect elevated the importance of expanded life choices and self-expressive values. And people are struggling to hold onto those values in an affordable form even under difficult economic conditions.

Work and Leisure

The emphasis on expressive values associated with the affluence effect also carries over to the world of work and helps to shape a new work ethic. In the old work ethic, people were expected to postpone gratification: it was not assumed that they would find their work interesting or enjoyable. Quite the contrary. It was assumed that work would mean drudgery, fatigue, and sacrifice.

The new work ethic revolves around the idea that people have a right to derive personal satisfaction from their work, which should be enjoyable, challenging, and fulfilling. In both instances the word ethic is appropriate because work is being endowed with a moral value over and above its pure economic exchange value—in the old work ethic, the moral value of sacrifice for others; in the new work ethic, the moral value of finding personal satisfaction in doing something useful and productive.

Research evidence shows that the meaning of work is changing not only in the United States but in all of the advanced industrial democracies. An international survey documents the changing meaning of work in six countries —the United States, Japan, West Germany, the United Kingdom, Sweden, and Israel.[23] The study identifies three basic motivations for working—the ancient and traditional function of working for sustenance and survival, working to improve one's standard of living and material well-being, and working as an expression of self-actualization.

The research found varying patterns among the working population of each of the six countries. Israel was the only country of the six where a majority say they work mainly for survival and sustenance (54 percent), the United Kingdom had the largest number of people who worked primarily for material success (65 percent), and Sweden, the largest number whose principal motivation for working is to realize expressive values (23 percent).

The Swedish study is particularly suggestive. The results show that working for sustenance and survival is the dominant motive for those born in the early years of this century when Sweden was still an agrarian society. As Sweden evolved into an industrial society, working for material success became more important, and it is the dominant motivation of middle-aged and older Swedes. Expressive values are strongest among those born around 1955.[24]

This international study and others show sharp erosion of the old Protestant work ethic with its view that work derives moral worthiness from the sacrifice required to make a living at an arduous, wearying, and uninteresting job.

The evolution of the shared meaning of work in the United States follows a fascinating dialectic pattern with many twists and turns over the past four decades that can only be hinted at here.

In the 1960s the affluent young were contemptuous of their fathers' work-driven, nose-to-the-grindstone way of life and in reaction turned the relationship of work to leisure upside down. Instead of work as the center of life with a little time left over for leisure, the pursuit of leisure was exalted and work was relegated to the sidelines as the enemy of self-fulfillment. Self-fulfillment, it was assumed, would come through leisure time spent in cultivating friendships, communing with nature, finding suitable forms of artistic self-expression, and so on.

Then in the 1970s and 1980s, baby boomers made a great discovery that went largely unnoticed at the time. They learned that some types of work could serve self-fulfillment better than leisure. These were forms of work that offered challenge, autonomy, the development of new skills and ways of testing oneself, expressions of creativity, a satisfying social milieu, and a game to be won. Because it met both practical and expressive needs, work became a prime focus of baby boomer energy. In a mid-eighties study, a majority of 30- to 40-year-old men and women (54 percent) said they were deeply committed to their careers, and an even larger number (60 percent) said they placed much more emphasis on "pursuing satisfaction in a career" than their parents did (compared with 13 percent who gave their careers less emphasis).[25]

For the past decade, Americans have been attempting to find the proper balance between work and leisure, work and family, and inner satisfaction and economic productivity. The present state is one of ambivalence, confusion, and conflict. On the one hand, when people are asked whether they would welcome or reject "less emphasis on working hard," 70 percent say they would reject it. In response to this same question a decade earlier, only 45 percent rejected it. This is a very large swing.[26]

On the other hand, when those with some college education were asked whether they would put more or less time on their job if they had their lives organized the way they "really wanted," only 9 percent would give their job more time, with three times as many saying they would give the job less time.[27] When a series of *Los Angeles Times* polls in the 1980s asked, "Which is more important in life: working hard . . . or doing the things that give you personal satisfaction?" the working hard response declined from 59 percent in 1980 to 49 percent in 1989, while the "personal satisfaction" response increased from 34 percent to 44 percent in this same period.[28] In May 1990, Gallup asked a cross-section of Americans whether they would be willing to work between twelve and fourteen hours a day if such effort were guaranteed to make them rich. Only one out of four (25 percent) said they would, and almost half (47 percent) rejected the idea.

Sooner or later, Americans will clarify their ambivalent attitudes. What seems abundantly clear, however, even from this confusing pattern of survey findings, is that the shared meaning of work has shifted markedly in the post-World War II era. In the 1950s, people valued their jobs primarily as a source of income. Today, however, Americans expect more from their jobs than just income. By margins of more than 4:1 (59 percent to 13 percent), people look to their jobs not only for income but also for personal satisfaction.

What about the relationship of leisure to work? In the 1950s there was precious little leisure for most Americans, and what there was came as a well-earned reward for hard work. In this spirit, women might give themselves a brief coffee break from housework and men might relax on Sunday after a week of exhausting work. These moments of leisure were seen as an unproductive but morally justifiable pause in the routine of work.

Today, there is more opportunity for leisure, but its uses have changed. The dominant view is no longer that leisure is a time for relaxation from work, but that leisure time ought to be used in a productive manner. This view is held among Americans today by a ratio of almost two to one (43 percent to 24 percent), a pattern that has remained constant for the past five years.[29]

There are some striking age differences. The younger the person, the more committed he or she is to the leisure-as-a-time-for-productive-effort point of view. People who are 18 to 24 years old hold this view by a margin of 3:1, compared with those 60 and older, where the ratio is closer to 1:1.

Changing values in relation to work and leisure are good illustrations of the impact of the affluence effect. In the period of rising expectations, people came to feel that their work should serve their self-expressive needs as well as provide them with a living. As expectations now adapt themselves to slower growth, people refuse to abandon these new values, setting themselves up for a lot of tension.

Social Morality

The broad idea of social morality covers many domains of values. One of the most important is the conflict Americans feel between what might be called "market values" versus "communal values." Market values reflect the view that the price mechanism should dominate the distribution of goods and services. Communal values reflect what sociologists call "sacred values," in the secular sense that one can not and should not put a price on them. The simplest way of thinking about communal values are those that people regard as so important that they wish to exclude them wholly or partially from market forces.

Americans do not want market forces to prevail exclusively when it comes to such matters as health care, education, housing for the homeless, food for hungry children, and a helping hand for the blind, the mentally ill, and other Americans who cannot help themselves.

Survey data suggest the public is aware that the country's value orientation has become less generous in outlook. When people between the ages of 18 and 44 are asked whether being "a concerned citizen involved in helping others in the community" is more descriptive of their own or their parents' generation, a majority (53 percent) cite their parent's generation. When asked whether this change is for the better or worse, an impressive 77 percent feel it is a change for the worse.[30] When a cross-section of Americans are asked about the importance to themselves of helping their community, two out of three (65 percent) give this value top importance.[31]

Despite the harsher economic climate, Americans care deeply about reconciling communal with market values. Typically, Americans resolve the conflict by a compromise that makes room for both values. There are several forms such compromises can take. One of them, the food stamp model, subsidizes recipients in keeping with communal values but leaves market forces dominant for the providers of services. Medicare and medicaid are variants of this model, but less pure because, especially in medicaid, there is intervention in the price structure.

The form of compromise that most Americans favor is one in which market forces are given priority, but a safety net is provided to protect victims from excessive harm by the market. Public attitudes toward farm policy are a good example. An exclusive reliance on market values would lead to the elimination of farm subsidies and perhaps to the demise of most small farmers and the consolidation of farming in giant farm enterprises. The trend has moved in this direction for many years. But communal values resist this stark outcome.

Farmers in general, and small farmers in particular, elicit a strong response based on American communal values. A 1984 Roper poll shows that more than three out of four Americans (78 percent) believe that small farmers are so important to this country that special programs must be devised to insure their survival. In keeping with market values, Americans want to eliminate all subsidies to farmers. In keeping with communal values, however, they also want small family-owned farms to be protected and preserved.

A March 1985 Roper study shows how Americans would resolve these conflicting pulls. Fewer than half the public lines up on the extremes. Only 15 percent opt for the uncompromising market value that farmers should succeed or fail like any other business. At the other extreme, 28 percent believe the government should guarantee farmers a reasonable income. The compromise favored by most Americans tilts toward the market position: a free market for farm products but a safety net in case of disaster.

Role of Government

Attitudes toward the role of government lie at the center of the conflict between market and communal values, with government seen as the principal vehicle for implementing communal values.

The broadest set of communal values relates to concern with the poor and the victimized (people who are unemployed through no fault of their own, victims of storms, floods, earthquakes, and so on). But communal values also extend more broadly, for example, to the role of government in strengthening the economy, a central issue in today's politics.

The public's attitude here is strikingly pragmatic and nonideological. Do whatever works. If intervention in the economy works, then the government should intervene. If hands off works, then hands off it is. The public's values come into play in relation to partisan and sectarian interests. People's sense of social morality is violated when partisan bickering or business-government or business-labor adversarial interests stand in the way of the public interest. Overall, attitudes at present favor active government, on the grounds that only government can represent the national interest.

Over the past half century, attitudes toward government have followed a marked dialectic pattern. Strong progovernment attitudes prevailed in the fifties and sixties, and an antigovernment mood dominated the seventies, and particularly the eighties. In the 1990s, however, sentiment has swung away from a minimal role for government, and today an almost 2:1 ratio of Americans say that government should play a major role in the country's economic and social affairs, partly to strengthen the economy but partly to implement the compromises that people feel are needed to balance market and communal values in other arenas. There are marked differences in these views, with women, young people, low-income people, and the less well educated taking a stronger progovernment stance than men, the college educated, and the well-to-do. Those whom the market has rewarded most favor it; those who have received lesser rewards prefer more government intervention.

Beating the System

An important aspect of social morality is the extent to which people are willing to observe the rules over and above legal requirements, rather than finding ingenious ways to beat the system. Currently, only about four out of ten Americans (41 percent) hold strong moral convictions about respecting the system and following the rules even when the law does not force one to, with almost three out of ten adhering strongly to the opposite "beat the system" morality.

The most noteworthy aspect of this dimension of social morality is a remarkable set of age-related differences. Americans 60 years of age and older favor "respecting the system" by more than 2:1 margins (55 percent to 22 percent), while younger Americans (aged 18—24) favor trying to "beat the system" by almost 2:1 (39 percent to 24 percent).

This is one of the few instances of changing social values where subgroup variations are obscured by aggregate responses. On virtually all other value changes, subgroup differences reflect mere nuances, with all groups moving in the same overall direction. Here, however, the aggregate masks a sharp age-related split in our society.

No doubt the split is partly due to the traditional rebelliousness of youth. But, based on other data, I believe that something more complicated is at issue. As young people receive pervasive messages of unfairness, injustice, nonresponsiveness, greed, and institutional self-interest, they become cynical and more convinced that manipulation of the system is a more adaptive response to today's America than obeying the rules.

Sexual Morality

The most frequently measured aspects of sexual morality are moral approval (or disapproval) of premarital sexual relations, married people having sexual relations with someone other than the marriage partner, and people who are not married living together.

A fifty-year-old Roper survey in March 1943 asked, "Do you consider it all right, unfortunate or wicked when young men have sexual relations before marriage?" Only 14 percent felt it was "all right," 42 percent thought it "unfortunate," and 37 percent condemned it as "wicked." When the same question was asked about women, a mere 5 percent found it acceptable, 43 percent thought it was "unfortunate," and 46 percent "wicked." Almost twenty years later, in June 1962, the Gallup poll asked a cross-section of women whether in their opinion it was acceptable for a woman to have sexual relations before marriage with "a man she knows she is going to marry." An overwhelming 87 percent of women, married and unmarried, said it was emphatically *not* acceptable. As recently as July 1969, a 68 percent majority of the public continued to condemn sexual relations before marriage as morally wrong. But shortly thereafter, the pattern began to change year by year until by 1990 it had totally reversed, with only one out of three now condemning premarital sex as morally wrong (33 percent), and 60 percent saying it is not morally wrong.[32] (An exception is made for young teens (14 to 16 years old). The overwhelming majority of Americans condemn premarital sex for these youngsters as morally wrong.

In sharp contrast, moral condemnation of extramarital sex has not budged for many years. An 84 percent majority rejected it as "morally wrong" in the early 1970s; in 1990 an 84 percent majority continued to condemn it, an unchanging pattern of public response to extramarital sex over a nearly twenty-year period.[33]

On the question of people living together without benefit of marriage, Americans are divided and no clear-cut pattern emerges. In the 1970s a majority (52 percent) had come to feel that cohabitation was not a moral issue but merely a question of individual lifestyles.[34] A decade's experience, however, has revealed some hesitancy and reservations, with the majority (54 percent) now expressing doubts about its morality.[35]

Many other aspects of our changing social morality are worthy of discussion, for example, values regarding strict punishment for crime versus leniency and compassion, tolerance for diverse life-styles, orientation toward the present versus the future, absolutism in moral norms versus situational ethics, and so on. All are relevant to our concerns but cannot be covered in this chapter.

Health

The concern of Americans with their health and fitness has grown into one of the nation's top priorities. But health-related values have shifted a great deal in recent years.

A generation ago, people felt their health was the responsibility of the doctor rather than their own. Health was defined as the absence of disease, and disease was visualized as caused by germs, viruses, infections, and other invasive entities that physicians were trained to diagnose and banish. It was not unusual to hear people wax eloquent on the importance of good health while actively pursuing the couch potato way of life, demolishing fat-marbled steaks, and smoking several packs of cigarettes a day. As long as the definition of health as the absence of disease prevailed, people did not see how their behavior made much difference to their health one way or another.

Today, Americans endow health with a much more positive meaning, and they have come to accept much greater personal responsibility for their health, while appreciating how their behavior (and the behavior of others) affects their health. Americans are increasingly conscious of the importance of prevention, of acting prudently with respect to the environment, and of taking a long-run perspective in recognition of the new possibility of living a long, vital life. People have expanded their definition of health to include their emotional well-being, the importance of loving relationships, of enjoying a sense of achievement, and of reducing the stress in their life.

Today, the focus on fitness and a healthy, vibrant appearance is being reinforced in several ways: by its connotations of pleasure, because it is a morally justifiable way to be preoccupied with oneself, and because one does not need a lot of money to be physically fit.

Leaders concerned with health policy are constrained by health-related values that limit their flexibility. Health care is regarded as a maximum entitlement. An April 1987 Harris poll shows that a whopping 91 percent endorse the view that "everybody should have the right to the best possible health care—as good as the treatment a millionaire gets." More than seven out of ten Americans believe that "health insurance should pay for any treatment that will save lives, even if it costs one million dollars to save a life." Fewer than one out of four political leaders (23 percent) agree with this statement.

People have odd ideas about health insurance. If people are covered by insurance, they do not see health care as costing them money. The only costs people clearly associate with health care are the out-of-pocket costs they themselves incur. The old attitude, "When it comes to my health (or my spouse's or parents' or children's health), money is no object," remains as potent as ever.

There is a huge gap between the experts and the public on the burning issue of how to control health care costs. To explain rising health care costs, experts emphasize the increasing number of older people in the population (the average person over 65 costs our health care system more than three times the amount spent on a person between the ages of 19 and 64) and the explosive costs of technological innovations in medicine. When average Americans are confronted with this reasoning, they find these ideas new and shocking. In their view, technology should reduce costs, not raise them, and most people have never considered the idea that a price tag is associated with the graying of America.[36]

People have their own well-formed convictions about why health care costs are rising: experts see technology and the aging of America, but the public sees greed, high doctors' fees, corruption, drug company profiteering, unnecessary testing, malpractice, overbilling, duplication, and waste. The common view is that too many people are skimming vast amounts of money from the reservoir of dollars flowing through the health care system. Everyone has a horror story to tell, and all the horror stories are vivid, concrete, personal, and persuasive to those who experience them. The experts see skyrocketing health care costs as essentially a new problem caused by factors the system has not dealt with before. The public sees the problem as a very old one, the age-old human failing of greed and failure to resist temptation.[37]

The Sacredness of Human Life

Changes in attitudes toward the value of human life are directly relevant to public policy on health care. The DYG SCAN[SM] measures the prevalence of the belief that human life is so sacred that anything and everything should be done to keep individuals alive for as long as possible, regardless of circumstances, in contrast to the belief that circumstances must be taken into account and that heroic measures to keep people alive may not always be appropriate. Significantly, over a five-year period, those holding the latter point of view have increased from a 48 percent minority to a 60 percent majority, a large shift in a brief time. The shift is particularly marked among older Americans. People over 60 years of age have shifted from a 40 percent endorsement of the circumstantial view in 1988 to 64 percent currently.[38]

Conclusion

The economist's theory of human motivation is the weakest part of that profession's conceptual toolkit. The image of people as rational maximizers of their interests is an abstraction whose relationship to actual human behavior is quite simplistic. For many years sophisticated critics have wanted to replace this weak link with a more adequate conception. Doing so would immensely strengthen the economist's search for solutions to real social problems such as those relating to affirmative action, family policy, and rising health care costs.

An empirically based understanding of the nation's value system and how it is changing is not a complete answer, but it is not a bad start. As a practical matter, policy analysts interested in actually solving social problems will want to immerse themselves in the inventory of America's core values presented in the first part of this paper and add to or subtract from it. They will surely want to understand, in practical terms, which present and proposed policies reinforce these values and which ones ignore or violate them. They will be surprised, perhaps startled, at how this review changes their perspective on what constitutes sound policy.

Strategically, they can focus mainly on a subset of these core values, especially those relating to fairness, equality of opportunity, achievement, and caring beyond the self. These core values are at risk in today's America, and public policies designed to strengthen them are almost guaranteed to win public support.

A focus on core values is not enough, however. It must be supplemented by a working understanding of how changing cultural values interact with the core values. Again, it is unnecessary to be encyclopedic; concentration on a handful of changing values will do for most policies.

I recommend special attention to three values in this category, all related to the affluence effect. The first is choice. The ability to choose reinforces the powerful American drive to exercise some autonomy and control over one's destiny. The second is reciprocity. The shift from entitlement to reciprocity is one of the most powerful moral forces in America today. This shift has the potential to transform compassionate but unworkable social policies into effective ones. The third new cultural value is respect for the public's clamor to participate in shaping the decisions that affect people's lives. Americans are increasingly unwilling to accept the traditional constraints of representative democracy whereby their representatives make the key decisions, and then in theory the public holds them accountable through the electoral process. All too often, this remote form of accountability does not work. People crave a more direct say in truly important policies, especially if such policies demand sacrifice.

My own conclusion is that a working knowledge of values added to the powerful modes of formal economic analysis could significantly improve the effectiveness of public policy formation.

Notes

1. Memorandum from Professor Sumiko Iwao, Keio University, Japan, March 17, 1989.
2. DYG SCAN^SM—A Trend Identification Program, 1991. The DYG SCAN^SM is a product of DYG, Inc., of Elmsford, N.Y.

3.   Ralf Dahrendorf, *Life Chances: Approaches to Social and Political Theory* (London: Weidenfeld and Nicolson, 1979).

4.   For a detailed description of these changes see Daniel Yankelovich, *New Rules: Searching for Self-Fulfillment in a World Turned Upside Down* (Random House, 1981).

5.   Daniel Yankelovich, "American Values and Public Policy: How Reciprocity and Other Beliefs Are Reshaping American Politics" (Washington: Democratic Leadership Council, 1992).

6.   The surveys discussed in this chapter were obtained from the archives of the Roper Center for Public Opinion Research at the University of Connecticut at Storrs using the data base, POLL. POLL is a question level index of more than six decades of public opinion research.

7.   For more details see Daniel Yankelovich, "German Behavior, American Attitudes," *Dimensions*, vol. 4, no. 3 (1989), pp. 5–10.

8.   See Louis Harris and Associates, March 1970; Gallup for *Newsweek*, May 1980; Gallop for *Newsweek*, February 1988; and Gallup for *Newsweek*, April 1991.

9.   For elaboration see Yankelovich, *New Rules*, pp. 100–05.

10.   Gallup, February 1991, and Yankelovich, Skelly and White for General Mills, December 1976, families with children under thirteen years of age.

11.   National Opinion Research Center, 1973–90.

12.   Mellman and Lazarus polling firm for Massachusetts Mutual, June 1989.

13.   Roper for the *Wall Street Journal*, October 1986.

14.   Mellman and Lazarus for Massachusetts Mutual, June 1989, and Research and Forecasts for Ethan Allen, September–November 1985.

15.   Roper for Virginia Slims, July 1989.

16.   Mellman and Lazarus for Massachusetts Mutual, June 1989.

17.   Mellman and Lazarus for Masschusetts Mutual, June 1989.

18.   Gallup, February 1991.

19.   For further discussion see Yankelovich, *New Rules*.

20.   DYG SCAN^{SM}, 1991, pp. 3.112–13. Numbers do not add to 100 percent because they reflect the two ends of a spectrum of intensity. The reader can assume a third category of people who fall in-between and who are not reported here. This note applies to all subsequent citations of SCAN data.

21.   DYG SCAN^{SM}, 1991, pp. 3.84–85.

22.   Hilton Hotels Time Values Survey, Americans' Use of Time Project, University of Maryland, cited in Carol Hymowitz, "Beating the Clock: Trading Fat Paychecks for Free Time," *Wall Street Journal*, August 5, 1991, p. B1; and DYG SCAN^{SM}, 1991.

23.   Daniel Yankelovich and others, *The World at Work: An International Report on Jobs, Productivity, and Human Values: A Joint Report of the Public Agenda Foundation and the Aspen Institute for Humanistic Studies* (Octagon Books, 1985).

24.   See chart I-1 in Yankelovich and others, *The World at Work*, p. 41.

25.   Yankelovich, Clancy, Shulman for *Time*, April 1986.

26.   See Yankelovich, Skelly, and White for *Time*, March 1988, registered voters; and Gallup, December 1981.

27.   Louis Harris and Associates for Pier 1 Imports, college educated, August 1987.

28.   *Los Angeles Times*, December 1989, April 1985, and July 1980 (the 1980 survey was conducted with registered voters).

29.   DYG SCAN^SM, 1991, pp. 3.104–05.

30.   Peter Hart Research Associates for *Rolling Stone*, 18 to 44 years old, 1987.

31.   Mellman and Lazarus for Massachusetts Mutual, June 1989.

32.   Hart and Teeter Research/NBC News/*Wall Street Journal*, July 1990.

33.   See National Opinion Research Center, February 1986, February 1988, February 1989, and February 1990.

34.   Yankelovich, Skelly, and White for *Time*, registered voters, July 1977.

35.   Yankelovich, Clancy, Shulman for *Time*, January 1987.

36.   Daniel Yankelovich and John Immerwahr, "A Perception Gap," *Health Management Quarterly*, vol. 13, no. 3 (1991), pp. 10–13.

37.   John Immerwahr, Jean Johnson, and Adam Kernan-Schloss, "Faulty Diagnosis: Public Misconceptions about Health Care Reform" (New York: Public Agenda Foundation, 1992).

38.   DYG SCAN^SM, 1991, pp. 3.158–59.

Culture, Incentives, and the Underclass

James Q. Wilson

Policy elites, liberal and conservative, usually explain the problems of the urban underclass as the result of misguided incentives. Liberals may blame poverty and dependency on a lack of benefits and opportunities while conservatives may blame it on overly generous benefits offered without corresponding obligations, but the argument is about benefits. Liberals may blame crime on poverty or joblessness and conservatives may blame it on indefinite or lenient criminal sanctions, but the dispute is about rewards and penalties.

This is not the way ordinary citizens see the matter. Though acknowledging that schooling may be poor, jobs scarce, and the criminal justice system ineffective, they tend to stress the overriding importance of the attitudes of the permanently poor and the habitually criminal, attitudes formed in the family (or, increasingly, the nonfamily) and reinforced by culture. Those attitudes are characterized as a belief in rights but not in responsibilities, an emphasis on "me" and a neglect of "we," a preference for immediate gratification over investments for the future, and an expectation that if one is lucky or clever enough one can get something for nothing.

The public believes that whatever incentives or problems a family may face, it has a choice as to how to respond. A good family will respond by inculcating constructive habits and decent principles in its children. In recent years, however, these habits and principles have become less common in part because the family has become weaker and in part because rivals for its influence—notably television and the movies—have become stronger. More and more children are being raised by one parent, who is typically a teenage girl. Parents overall are spending less time with their children and disciplining them less. Overwhelmingly, Americans think that it is better for children if one parent stays home, even if it means having less money.[1]

Elite views, not popular views, tend to drive public policy. This is the case because the former have clear policy implications while the latter have vague ones, because changing the former acknowledges individual autonomy while changing the latter seems preachy or invasive, and because one can marshal countless facts bearing on the incentives issue but not many bearing on the culture one. We debate incentive effects by measuring unemployment rates, poverty levels, crime trends, welfare payments, and arrest probabilities and feeding these numbers into equations. By contrast, we debate cultural effects by shouting slogans, offering anecdotes, and interpreting history.

In this chapter I hope to do two things. First, I want to argue that some significant part of what is popularly called the "underclass problem" exists not simply because members of this group face perverse incentives but because they have been habituated in ways that weaken their self-control and their concern for others. Second, I want to speculate about what, if anything, can be done to change that pattern of habituation so that, given whatever incentives people face, they will be more likely to behave in a morally correct fashion.

Before going on, let me clarify some terms, admit to some uncertainties, and respond to some preemptive criticisms. I use the term *habituation* to refer to the process whereby people acquire a constant, often unconscious, way of doing something, a regular inclination to behave in ways that are either impulsive or reflective, self-indulgent or other-regarding, decent or indecent. Not all behavior, of course, is habitual, but to say that someone has a "good" or "bad" character means that, as opportunities arise, that person ordinarily behaves in a good or bad way.

I do not wish to deny the importance of incentives, such as jobs, penalties, or opportunities, but I do wish to call attention to the fact that people facing the same incentives often behave in characteristically different ways because they have been habituated to do so. That habituation was shaped in large part by the incentives confronting people earlier in their lives. "Incentives" and "culture" are different explanations of behavior at any one time, but if we trace back someone's life history, we shall surely discover that what we now call culture was instilled by incentives (for example, parental admonitions or peer-group expectations), and those earlier incentives were offered to a person because those doing the offering were, in part, culturally disposed to do so, and they in turn were so disposed because of incentives that they had once encountered, and so on. A complete explanation of human development, were that possible, would make the customary distinction between incentives and culture rather unclear, however important it may be to any contemporary policy debate. For policy purposes I am simply asserting that changing incentives will not alter the behavior of poorly habituated persons as much as we would like, at least in the near term.

I write unabashedly about "morally correct" or "moral" behavior. In this context, I mean simply that moral people do not lie, cheat, steal, rape, assault, murder, or abuse drugs. Immoral people do these things regularly and often without remorse.

Though I am here arguing for the importance of culture, I have elsewhere argued for the importance of incentives. In 1975 I published a book in which I took issue with the effort of criminologists to ground crime-control policies on an understanding of the root causes of crime.[2] At that time, those causes were thought to be the attitudes, values, and aspirations of criminals—in short, their culture. I suggested that our understanding of these cultural factors was so poor and our capacity to alter them by plan so weak that any crime-reduction policy based on them was bound to fail. I argued instead for a policy based on the assumption that would-be offenders were rationally self-interested. Given that view, the most effective response to crime would be to reduce its net benefits relative to legitimate work by increasing both the certainty of sanctions and the availability of jobs.

Lest any readers think that I am here repudiating my previous view, let me remind them that at the end of the book I suggested that an incentives-based attack on crime would be fortunate if it led to even a 20 percent reduction in the rate of serious crime. A reduction larger than this was unlikely because, while sanctions had become less certain, crime had become less shameful. One of the main reasons it had become less shameful—that is, less likely to be inhibited by internal constraints—was because of the weakening of the family.[3] Since the book was published in 1975, the probability of going to prison, given an arrest, has risen, though the time served in prison has declined, and prison has increasingly been reserved for serious career criminals instead of petty or one-time offenders. These changes probably contributed to the decline in victimization rates that has taken place since the early 1980s. But while the criminal justice system has become somewhat tougher, the family unit has become much weaker. This helps explain why the average young person is much more likely to commit a crime today than in the 1950s.[4]

What Incentives Cannot Explain

The rise in the number of out-of-wedlock births and participation in the program of Aid to Families with Dependent Children (AFDC) cannot be explained by economic conditions or the level of welfare benefits. Irwin Garfinkel and Sara McLanahan estimate that rising government benefits accounted for no more than about 14 percent of the increase in the prevalence of unwed mothers that occurred between 1960 and 1974.[5] Robert Moffitt has reviewed the evidence on the effects of welfare benefits on work and family structure and concluded that, while benefits make a difference, they do not explain more than a modest amount of the decline in work levels or the increase in single-parent families.[6] One of the reasons that welfare benefits do not correlate with welfare participation is that for some people participation carries a stigma. The fear of losing self-respect or social esteem helps explain why in 1970 only 69 percent of the families eligible for AFDC enrolled in it. One explanation of the increase in the percentage of eligibles who actually enroll to over 90 percent may be a change in the stigma attached to participation.

We have become accustomed to the sight of inner-city males on the streets, out of school and out of work, but this was not always the case. Black and white teenage unemployment rates were much lower in the 1950s than they were in the 1980s. There has been a dramatic increase in the percentage of young urban males who are not in the labor force and in the proportion who report no income,[7] an increase that has occurred during a period of generally rising incomes and educational levels and a decline in the proportion of children failing to complete high school.[8] The number of jobs has grown faster than the population. Despite this growth a large fraction of inner-city residents have dropped out of the labor force.

Some scholars, such as William Julius Wilson, explain the paradox of rising inner-city unemployment in the midst of long-term job growth by the spatial mismatch theory. In this view, jobs have moved out of the inner city and the people living there have been unable to follow. This mismatch may discourage labor force participation, especially if it lasts for several generations.[9] But evidence for the mismatch theory is not clear. Christopher Jencks and Susan E. Moyers conclude that the evidence supporting mismatch suggests that it has some effect, but "the support is so mixed that no prudent policy analyst should rely on it."[10] Wilson has responded vigorously to these criticisms with a different reading of the evidence.[11]

In my view, mismatch probably explains part of the rise in idleness, but not all. In particular it cannot explain the fact that many inner-city jobs go unfilled because of what appears to be a high reservation wage,[12] nor can it explain why Latinos (including recent immigrants) have had greater success in finding and holding inner-city jobs than have blacks, even though both groups tend to live in impoverished neighborhoods and Latinos have less formal education than blacks.[13] The black-Latino contrast is noteworthy in another respect. Though Latinos in California have very high poverty rates, Latino children are much more likely than black children to grow up in a two-parent family, Latino adults are much more likely than black adults to be in the labor force, and poor Latino families are only one-fifth as likely as black families to receive AFDC payments. So marked is this contrast that the scholars reporting these findings question whether California Latinos should be considered part of the urban underclass at all.[14] Nationally, from 1977 to 1991, when the percentage of white and black men with no income was going up, the percentage of Latino men in that predicament was going down.[15]

Finally there is the case of crime. I do not propose to give a full explanation of why either individuals or societies differ in their rates of crime. Richard Herrnstein and I have tried to provide such an explanation.[16] I will say nothing about gun ownership, television viewing, peer pressures, or some of the other possible influences on crime rates. I omit them in part because the concept of habituation already embraces most of them: millions of people watch television, own guns, or have friends, but the vast majority do not regularly commit crimes.

The increase in crime cannot be explained fully by changes in the objective features of the situation. The rate of street crime is today much higher—by three to four times—than it was in the late 1950s and early 1960s. This increase has occurred despite, some might say because of, a dramatic increase in per capita income and average educational attainment, a decrease in the proportion of students dropping out of high school, and a substantial growth in government expenditures aimed at preventing delinquency and controlling crime. Nor can this increase in crime rate be explained by the changing age structure of the population. Scarcely any expert believes that the increase in the number of young people can account for more than half of the increase in crime, and many estimate the proportion of explained variance to be as low as one-fourth.[17] If the age-specific crime rate (that is, the number of crimes committed per person of a given age, say, eighteen) had remained constant during the 1960s and 1970s, violent crime would have increased by about 8 percent. In fact it doubled.[18] A study of the officially recorded criminality of two groups of Philadelphia boys—those born in 1945 and those born in 1958—found that the group born in 1958 was three times more likely to commit violent crimes and five times more likely to commit robberies than the group born in 1945.[19]

Part of the crime increase was the result of the drop in its costs: the magnitude of punishment discounted by its probability was lower in 1980 than it had been in 1960. During the early years of the crime boom, the aggregate probability of imprisonment for a reported crime declined. In 1960 there were sixty-two prison commitments per 1,000 serious offenses; by 1970 there were only twenty-three per 1,000 serious offenses.[20] ("Serious" crimes are those that the FBI includes in its uniform crime reports (UCR): murder, rape, assault, robbery, burglary, and auto theft.) The length of time served in prison for the median inmate also declined from twenty-one months in 1960 to seventeen months in 1981.[21] The combined effect of fewer and shorter imprisonments was a drop in the expected days of imprisonment per UCR crime from ninety-three in 1959 to fourteen in 1975. This drop in the deterrent and incapacitative potential of prison was, I believe, partly responsible for the sharp increase in the crime rate.

Beginning around 1974, the absolute number of prison inmates began to rise at an accelerating rate. Between 1974 and 1989, it more than tripled. Contrary to what many people believe, this increase was not the result of prisoners serving longer sentences—on the average, time served continued to decline—or a vast influx of drug offenders—changes in drug arrest and imprisonment rates explain only 8 percent of the increase in prison populations. The growth in prison populations was mostly explained by the fact that beginning in the mid- to late 1970s, arrests were more likely to lead to imprisonment. In 1974 an arrested robber had about one chance in five of going to prison; by 1986 he had more than one chance in four.[22] By 1986, the expected days of imprisonment per UCR offense was nineteen, a third higher than it had been in 1975 but still less than a fifth of what it was in 1959. At the same time, in the years following 1974 there was a flattening out and even a decline in the rate of most crimes, at least as measured by victimization surveys.

These national data are consistent with the view—though clearly they do not prove it—that between 1960 and 1974 society may have unintentionally encouraged the idea that crime paid. This view may help explain why the age-specific crime rate increased during this period. Since 1974, society has been trying, with limited success, to unteach that lesson.

The linkage, if any, between the changing probabilities of punishment and the offense rate of any given young male is not known and probably unknowable. Even if society were willing to pay for further increases in the expected days of imprisonment per crime (a big assumption), we can only speculate on whether it would lower the age-specific crime rate, especially since the people we most wish to affect are not the small number of high-rate, hard-core criminals but the much larger number of moderate-to-low-rate offenders. We want to affect the latter because they constitute a more numerous group and because high-rate offenders already spend a very large fraction of any given year in prison. One study estimates that the average high-rate robber in California, Michigan, and Texas spends

216 days out of the typical year in prison. In compensation, he earns about $9,500 per year for the time he is free on the street.[23] Not a very attractive deal, but that is exactly my point: high-rate offenders have such poor impulse control that they are neither very rational about how they spend their time nor very likely to notice small shifts in the costs of committing a crime. This probably helps explain why changes in the unemployment rate and the business cycle have so weak a connection with the crime rate.[24]

The total amount of variance in crime rates explained by cross-section regression equations with the relevant objective factors entered—age, income, unemployment, and the probability and severity of sanctions—is relatively modest.[25] Some unknown, but I suspect large, fraction of the unexplained variance can be attributed to changes in tastes, preferences, and attitudes toward risk.

We have rather little direct evidence of such changes. One of the few tests of changes in impulsiveness compared the time preferences (that is, the willingness to postpone gratification) of a group of Rhode Island delinquents in 1959 with a similar group studied in 1974 and concluded that the latter had become much more present-oriented.[26] This finding, while indicative of a change, suffers from sample selection bias and other problems. The existence of a cultural explanation for crime must rest largely on inference, particularly on the inference that high rates of criminality and drug usage cannot easily be reconciled to any theory that people are maximizing their incomes. If criminals in prison are like those on the street, crime pays very little to its practitioners. If repeated thefts can be explained at all, it is only on the assumption that for some people the prospect of a small, immediate gain dominates the prospect of a later, larger benefit. Similarly, drug abusers sooner or later come to a crossroad where they would like to reform their lives, but the lure of drugs outweighs the benefits of abstinence, whatever the cost of continuing the drug-abuser lifestyle.[27] In short, many criminal offenders and drug abusers are very impulsive and (in the case of crime) have a low regard for the rights and well-being of others. It is likely that impulsivity has become more common in our society (and in most industrialized societies) in recent decades.

The evidence linking criminality with weak impulse control and lack of empathy with others is very strong.[28] If impulsiveness and self-regardingness are highly predictive of criminality, and if rates of criminality have increased far beyond what can be explained by the expected utility of their material returns, we are left with a presumptive case for a change in the degree to which habitual self-control and sympathy rule our lives.

Familial Habituation

Familial habituation is the chief method by which every society induces its members to exercise a modicum of self-control and to assign a reasonable value to the preferences of others. There is a broad consensus among developmental psychologists as to the parental practices that are most likely to achieve these goals. They involve a combination of affection and discipline such that the child's attachment to the parents is strong and the rules of everyday behavior are clearly understood and consistently enforced.[29] This vital socializing task, which is the foundation of human society, would be impossibly difficult were it not for two facts: babies are biologically eager for attachment and predisposed to socialization, and parents love their babies and invest without compensation in their rearing.

But individuals differ in the extent to which they have (or reveal) prosocial impulses, and so some babies are difficult and some parents are incompetent. Unfortunately, since temperament is to a significant degree under genetic control, there is an elevated probability that difficult babies will be born to incompetent parents. At one time, natural selection worked against any dysgenic trends by exposing marginal families to higher infant mortality rates. Nobody wants dead babies to be a solution to socialization failures. But these failures, if uncorrected, can breed, literally, more failures. Crime, alcoholism, and impulsive, sensation-seeking behavior run in the family.

Matters become worse if families cease to exist or are transformed into pseudofamilies. Poverty has now become a children's problem owing chiefly to the fact that an increased proportion of children live for long periods—sometimes for their entire childhood—in mother-only families, a large fraction of which are also poor. There is mounting evidence that mother-only families do not do as well as two-parent families.[30] For example, in 1988 the Department of Health and Human Services surveyed the family arrangements and personal problems of more than 60,000 children living in households all over the country. The results were striking. At every income level save the very highest (more than $50,000 a year), for both sexes and for whites, blacks, and Latinos, children living with never-married mothers were substantially worse off than those living in two-parent families. Children living with never-married mothers were more likely to have been expelled or suspended from school, to display emotional problems, and to engage in anti-social behavior.[31]

Sara McLanahan at Princeton and Gary Sandefur at Wisconsin have been analyzing the best available data—the National Longitudinal Study of Youth, the Panel Study of Income Dynamics, the High School and Beyond Study, and the National Survey of Families and Households. Their preliminary findings are that, even after controlling for race, income, and education, being a child in a mother-only family decreases a child's chances of graduating from high school, increases a girl's chances of becoming a teenage mother, and increases a boy's chances of being idle (that is, neither working nor in school).[32]

If the family is headed by a teenage mother, the risks are even greater. Children of teenage black mothers compared to those of older mothers are less able to control their impulses, have a lower tolerance for frustration, are more likely to be hyperactive, have more difficulty in adapting to school and, if boys, are more likely to be hostile, assertive, and willful.[33] If the single, teenage mother is a heavy user of drugs or alcohol, the risks increase catastrophically.

The average American fully understands this without benefit of scientific studies. As Daniel Yankelovich points out in this volume, Americans believe by overwhelming majorities that families have become weaker in ways that severely threaten human well-being and by large majorities think that this weakening results from parents spending too little time with their children. It stands to reason that one parent spends less time than two and two working parents less time than one working and one nonworking parent.[34]

What Is Culture?

To the extent that certain bad behaviors—criminality, drug abuse, welfare dependency, producing illegitimate children—are in part the result of cultural factors, one must clarify what one means by "culture" before asking whether it can be changed. The term has at least three meanings that are relevant to these behaviors. First, culture refers to a widely shared integrating perspective or world view by which people interpret their experiences, a perspective that is passed on from one generation to the next by precept, myth, and ritual and accepted by most, if not all, of society. A culture in this sense is what gives a particular society its identity and meaning; it will change very slowly, if at all, and never by plan. We have this meaning in mind when we speak of "American," "Southern," or "Yankee" culture.

A culture can also be a subjective adaptation to the circumstances of one's life. If one is poor, and the poverty extends over several generations, one might adapt to that reality by being fatalistic and pessimistic or by increasing the value one attaches to immediate pleasures at the expense of long-term investments. This is what many people have in mind when they speak of the "culture of poverty." Presumably this culture would change, albeit slowly, if objective reality changed.

Finally, a culture can be the set of standards and values held up and prized by some social elite: the rich, the powerful, the beautiful, the celebrated. These values are an elite endorsement of certain ways of acting and thinking, an endorsement that acquires causal power insofar as people seek to emulate those ways of acting and thinking. Because elites are sometimes divided, there may be more than one such culture. Beginning in the 1960s there was a conflict between bourgeois culture, with its emphasis on propriety, property, and progress, and the counterculture, with its emphasis on sincerity, spontaneity, and self-expression. This kind of culture is capable of relatively rapid change because it entails an element of fashion.

Cultural interpretations of the underclass involve a competition among all three meanings. Those who believe that the underclass consists mainly of marginal people—the indolent, the impulsive, the drug-dependent, the thrill-seekers—feel that there will always be an underclass, it will always be a small fraction of the whole society (because people in it are at the extremes of the distribution of impulse control), and the main problem is to prevent it from getting out of hand.[35] The disreputable poor have always been among us; we pay more attention to them today because they are centrally located, heavily armed, and threats to those institutions, for example, schools, in which they now participate. One can only cope with the symptoms of the underclass—its location, firepower, and institutional involvement. In this view, such people ought to be segregated or dispersed so as to reduce their numbers at any one location below a critical mass, disarmed or incarcerated, and kept out of mainstream institutions or put in specialized ones.

Those who believe in the culture of poverty have, of course, a very different view. If circumstances are changed, culture will change. The magnitude of the change varies with the radicalism of the author. For some it means simply more jobs, better schooling, and less discrimination; for others it means wholesale and fundamental changes in the economic system.[36]

Those who believe that the fault lies with elite culture call attention to the vast shift that has occurred in the mores conveyed by judges, political leaders, the mass media, and popular entertainment. It is a shift away from an ethic of self-reliance, self-control, and delicate modesty and toward one of social dependence, self-expression, and the celebration of alternative lifestyles. People holding this view interpret the underclass as simply that group in our society most vulnerable to false prophecies. For all its idiosyncratic inflections, underclass culture is, in the words of Myron Magnet, a "dialect" of the elite culture that celebrates personal liberation, denounces conformity, values the avant-garde, and regards the core traditions of the republic as nothing more than a camouflage for repression and greed. Elite culture is a curse inflicted by the haves on the have-nots.[37]

Changing Culture

It is very difficult, perhaps impossible, to choose which among these theories is the most accurate. Cultural explanations by their very nature defy experimental or mathematical tests. The best one can do is ask what we have learned from efforts to act on one or the other theory.

By that standard the news is fairly grim. The first theory implies that change is impossible. The third suggests that it is all but impossible, the logic being that if elites are the problem, and elites like their culture, and elites—by definition—control social and political resources, then there is not much chance that this culture can be changed. The second theory is easier to test, but the tests are not encouraging. The growth of the underclass during a period of unparalleled prosperity does not disprove the possibility that changing incentives will induce a change in behavior, but it does make one pessimistic about the chances of any planned improvement. Since society can only manipulate incentives in the aggregate, and cope, by lecturing and example, with culture as a whole, the likelihood of altering individual preferences by plan in the face of powerful, long-term forces operating in the opposite direction seems remote. If the underclass culture grew despite prosperity, then it stands to reason that only a radical change in the economic and social order would break the culture; however, radical changes are by definition unlikely ones. But perhaps those who hold this view have overlooked the interaction between culture and poverty: though poverty may create its own culture, that culture may perpetuate poverty. Perhaps what is needed is a concerted effort to change the fatalistic or self-indulgent attitudes of the poor so that they will take better advantage of whatever opportunities are available to them.

There is nothing in principle wrong with such a view; indeed, it is the governing assumption of every religious and of many secular efforts that attempt to help social outcasts such as alcoholics, drug abusers, and school dropouts. There are countless success stories to be found among these spiritual and worldly enterprises. The problem arises when one tries to imagine a program that by plan and in the hands of ordinary managers achieves this necessary personal redemption for large numbers of people.

Efforts to do this on a large scale and by bureaucratic processes have not, on the whole, proven very successful. Though here and there one can find promising projects, most efforts to rehabilitate large numbers of delinquents or criminals have met with more failures than successes.[38]

Using the military to improve the character of the most disadvantaged has not been a very promising solution either. In 1966, Secretary of Defense Robert McNamara began Project 100,000 as a way of contributing to the War on Poverty. Over a five-year period, 320,000 low-aptitude recruits entered military service. From 1976 to 1980, as a result of the misnorming of the military enlistment test, low-aptitude individuals were inadvertently recruited. These two occasions provided a natural, quasi-experiment in the use of intensive training and strict discipline as means of improving the self-control and expanding the other-regardingness of difficult boys.

To evaluate these quasi-experiments, investigators studied veterans of Project 100,000 and of the misnorming episode, comparing their economic, educational, and family status to that of persons of similarly low aptitude who had never served in the military. When interviewed, a majority of the low-aptitude veterans said that their military experience had been good for them, primarily because it taught them discipline and made them more mature. Unfortunately, the belief did not correspond to the reality. Project 100,000 veterans were worse off in employment status, educational achievement, and income than those presumably similar persons who had never been in the military; misnormed veterans were no better off than their nonveteran counterparts. The veterans were more likely to be divorced than the nonveterans. (There were, of course, no data on crime for the two groups.) The authors of the study concluded that "the military doesn't appear to be a panacea for struggling youth."[39]

Altering the time preferences or improving the achievements of temperamentally difficult or low-aptitude youth is not easily done if one waits until they have reached their teens or become young adults. Evidence from criminal rehabilitation programs and military experiences is not very encouraging. Evidence from early childhood programs is more encouraging but still very fragmentary and in some cases inconsistent.

These familiar facts are what give so much impetus to efforts to find supplements for family care, such as day care and preschool education. There is no governmental program more popular today than Head Start, nor any for which more inflated claims have been made. This is not to say that Head Start or similar preschool education programs for three- and four-year-olds have no effect. After it was shown that there were no lasting improvements in cognitive abilities (specifically, in IQ) resulting from Head Start participation, attention shifted to whether such participation facilitated a child's entry into kindergarten and the first grade. The evidence seems clear that it does.[40]

But the long-term effect of preschool education is not so clear. The strongest evidence of a positive effect comes from one program, the Perry Preschool in Ypsilanti, Michigan, which was not a Head Start project. It enrolled 123 poor black children, half of whom were living in mother-headed households, randomly assigned them to a preschool program or to a control group, and followed them for many years. Those in the preschool program were less likely to drop out before finishing high school, less likely to go on welfare, more likely to be working after leaving school, and less likely to have been arrested.[41]

No other preschool program has produced evidence of such dramatic long-term effects. Evaluations of the many Head Start projects (few of which were as carefully done as the Perry evaluation) fail to find school completion rates as high as those in Perry, and there is hardly any evidence on the effects of Head Start programs on such matters as pregnancy, welfare, and crime. In a 1989 review of Head Start evaluations, Ron Haskins, a staff member of the House Ways and Means Committee, was only able to locate a handful of studies that measured the long-term effects of Head Start on crime, teen pregnancy, and welfare dependency. The two studies that looked at pregnancy found no effect; the two that examined crime found some effect; and the two that considered welfare came to inconsistent conclusions.[42]

Why did the Perry program (and possibly a few other programs) do so well? One reason is that they were model programs conducted by capable people who had received extensive training and ample budgets. At Perry Preschool there was one teacher for every five or six pupils. Another reason is that the Perry project was not limited to providing children with preschool experiences for twelve-and-a-half hours a week; it also involved an extensive program of home visits conducted once a week by the teacher who would visit with the mother for about one-and-a-half hours in her home. There is evidence that such home visitations improve child development.[43]

Something akin to the Perry results, albeit, thus far, only for the short term, has been reported by the Infant Health and Development Program. This program provided an intensive array of services to nearly 1,000 premature, low-birth-weight infants in eight cities. Such babies have been found to be at risk for intellectual retardation, behavioral problems, and learning difficulties. As in Ypsilanti, these infants were randomly assigned to treatment and control groups. The infants and parents in the experimental groups were given three services: weekly (later biweekly) home visits by trained counselors, attendance at child development centers five days a week by babies after they had reached their first birthday, and biweekly meetings at which parents were given information and could share experiences. At age three, the babies in the experimental group had significantly higher measured IQs and significantly fewer behavioral problems than those in the control groups, and the gains were greatest for infants who had the most disadvantaged mothers.[44] It will be some years before we know whether these gains persist.

Suppose that the long-term results from the premature baby project parallel those of the Perry Project. What lessons can we infer? The most obvious and, to some, perhaps the most troubling is that intervention programs produce more benefits the more deeply they intervene. For at-risk children, the more the programs either assume parental functions or alter the behavior of parents (by home visits, parent training, and close preschool supervision), the greater the benefit to the child.[45]

Another possibility, albeit one that has as yet only fragmentary evidence, is that long-lasting interventions are likely to make more of a difference than short-term ones.[46] Children cannot be inoculated against behavioral problems as they are against smallpox. Yet beginning at age five or six the only intervention program aimed at children and generally under government control is the school, a state of affairs that continues until they enter the labor force, are arrested for a crime, or enlist in the armed services.

The central role of the school has led Americans to focus their hopes for character formation on it, hopes that receive some support from studies suggesting that the schools doing the best job of educating children are also, and of necessity, those that do the best job of controlling their behavior.[47] Learning is easier when students are more orderly. But in the past, the problem of improving the character of what we delicately term antisocial people was never left wholly to the schools but was given in addition to a host of home visitation and mothers' aid societies that were charged with instructing mothers on how to raise their children.[48] We do not know what effect these efforts had on family life, but we do know that the most successful contemporary programs aimed at young children include home visits and parental training. Missouri, followed by other states, has built on this insight with its Parents as Teachers plan that makes available in-home training for parents and babies.

Families with the necessary financial resources have always had boarding school as an important way of coping with hard-to-socialize children or of escaping their responsibility for socializing them. The current movement to give parents a meaningful choice among schools may help address many educational problems, but even the best public school occupies a child only six hours a day, half the days of the year.

Schools are character-forming enterprises; public schools were created first and foremost for moral instruction. But even the best school cannot offset the threats of disorderly streets, the neglect of absent parents, or the discord of unhappy homes. Boarding schools are not for everyone, but they are better for some.

If boarding schools were established as a way of shaping character, what would they do? I have a set of guidelines in mind. In the elementary years, a boarding school would simply extend the number of hours the child was under school rather than parental supervision. School might become an all-day affair, breakfast and dinner served and supervised after-class play opportunities provided in addition to regular instruction. In the extreme case of a child with no competent parent at all, sleeping quarters would be provided. As the child got older—say in the junior high years—boarding school would be full time with home visits arranged by mutual agreement. The schools would be operated, I would hope, by private more often than by public agencies; enrollment would be voluntary but encouraged for at-risk children. The object would be to provide a safe, consistent, and enjoyable mechanism for the habituation of the child—that is, for the inculcation of the ordinary virtues of politeness, self-control, and good social skills. What was taught would be less important than the regular and supportive routine by which it was taught. Character is formed by habitual action more than by memorized precepts.

Boarding schools may be especially important for boys growing up in fatherless families. Much has been said about the economic and psychological costs borne by such children. But something also must be said about the equally important communal costs. Neighborhood standards may be set by mothers but they are enforced by fathers, or at least by adult males. Neighborhoods without fathers are neighborhoods without men able and willing to confront errant youth, chase threatening gangs, and reproach delinquent fathers. Mercer Sullivan, in his study of poor neighborhoods in New York, notes that the absence of fathers, especially in black areas, deprives the community of those little platoons that informally but often effectively control boys on the street.[49]

I do not know of any way whereby this generation of errant fathers can be required to take up their responsibilities. The reach of the law has been lengthened, but we should not be optimistic that this will result in more than a modest increase in the size of family support payments received by some mothers, much less any increase in the extent to which fathers would help care for children. Our main goal ought to be reducing the number of errant fathers produced by the next generation. To that end, history supplies presumptive evidence of the value of using public resources to enable families in underclass neighborhoods voluntarily to enroll their children beginning at an early age in boarding schools. These schools then must have as a goal either placing their students into college or qualifying them for entry into an occupation by means of an apprenticeship program.[50]

Perhaps better homes can be supplied without leaving matters entirely to chance or voluntary participation. Suppose that unmarried mothers seeking welfare were given a choice: as a condition of receiving financial aid, they must either live with their parents or in group homes (shelters) where they would be instructed in child care, receive a regular education, and conform to rules governing personal conduct and group responsibilities.[51] The key elements in this idea are threefold: Welfare should not be used to subsidize independent but dysfunctional households, mothers of small children should not work outside the home, and the best and most structured start in life for the next generation of babies is of utmost importance.

Implications

The great puzzle for a free society is how it can encourage those traits of character on which the wise exercise of freedom depends. Our Constitution is silent on this matter, and so were, for the most part, the deliberations of the founders. Creatures of the Enlightenment, these men took for granted the existence of sufficient virtue among the people to make free government possible; victims of what they regarded as the excesses of centralized government, they were in no mood to create a strong central government here, much less to endow it with authority to shape character.

From the time of the founding until well into the twentieth century, their assumptions were reasonable ones. Village life, by its daily routines and face-to-face contacts, was sufficient to reinforce the normal processes of familial habituation; where the latter was lacking, villagers found ample ways to encourage the slack and punish the errant. As large cities were formed, the informal but intimate ties of village life were replaced by the formal and anonymous relationships of urban life, with the result that young men more easily escaped social control or found like-minded companions with whom they could indulge licentious impulses. But society was not powerless to counter this process nor was it inclined to use the government as its principal tool. Apart from state temperance laws that became commonplace after the middle of the nineteenth century, most efforts to inculcate self-control were made under voluntary auspices.

These efforts—temperance meetings, child care programs, home visitations, and YMCAs—involved large numbers of adults and children. There was nothing like a modern program evaluation technology available at the time, and so we can only guess at the effect of these efforts. But, as I have argued elsewhere, it is hard to explain the decline in alcohol consumption and criminality in the face of rapid urbanization, large-scale industrialization, and massive immigration on any basis other than the speculation that these efforts at inducing self-control made a difference.[52]

It is apparent today that many such programs still operate, though rarely with the religious zeal that once gave them such energy. Moreover, neighborhoods can still exist in big cities, and some of the habituation that was once achieved by small towns is now achieved by informal social controls in urban communities. Parents must assume not only individual responsibility for their own children but some measure of collective responsibility for everyone's children, at least when they are at play in public places.

It is a truism that we have transferred to the market or the government many of the responsibilities once exercised by families and neighborhoods. The family, once the chief organization for production, education, self-defense, health care, and welfare, is now an entity limited to procreation, child-rearing, and affectional ties, and it is losing ground in the performance of even these rudimentary tasks.[53] Much has been gained by the decline of the family—greater personal freedom, more economic mobility, enhanced opportunities for women, and the advantages of the division of labor. But something has been lost.

A fundamental change in family structure illustrates what has been lost. At one time children needed parents for care, affection, and nurture, and parents needed children for agricultural or pastoral labor and for support when they were sick or elderly. Today children still need parents but parents do not, in any material sense, need children. Thus the incentive some parents have to care for children has been weakened. (That it has not been weakened to the point of extinction is a measure of the power of elemental love.) When children had economic consequences, the need to care for them, up to a point, was self-enforcing. Now that children are a net economic burden, there is no material incentive to care for them.

This shift has, of course, affected men more than women. A mother's attachment to a child—call it the maternal instinct—is strong enough to insure some level of care. But there is not an equally strong attachment on the part of the father, made clear by the fact that the overwhelming majority of single-parent families are headed by women.

The goal of public policy and private effort should be to reinforce the obligation, which once was supplied by economic necessity, to care responsibly for children. We do not have a good idea of how to accomplish this. The Family Support Act of 1988 and comparable state laws have placed the government clearly on the side of mothers trying to collect support payments from absent fathers. But getting more money, while important, is far less important than getting more affection and supervision.

Better methods for socializing young men must be discovered. My general view is that this must be done, if it is to be done at all, in the first ten years of life, and perhaps even sooner. We need to know whether some combination of parent training programs, home visitations, preschool education, boarding schools, parental accountability laws, mother-child group homes, and criminal sanctions will make a significant—and above all, a lasting—difference in the probability of an at-risk boy growing up to be a decent citizen and a responsible father.

It is important that jobs be available for such men, but I see little reason for believing that job creation programs (assuming—a whopper—that the government can do this efficiently) will be enough. Not all reliable workers will find jobs in a free market, but it is my general view that good people are scarcer than good jobs.

Our object ought to be to increase the number of urban young men who marry and remain married. Of all the institutions through which people may pass—schools, employers, the military—marriage has the largest effect. For every race and at every age, married men live longer than unmarried men and have lower rates of homicide, suicide, accidents, and mental illness. Crime rates are lower for married than unmarried men and incomes are higher. It is less likely for drug dealers to be married than for young men who are not dealers.[54] Infant mortality rates are higher for unmarried than for married women, whether black or white, and these differences cannot be explained by differences in income or availability of medical care. So substantial is this difference that an unmarried woman with a college education is more likely to have her infant die than is a married woman with less than a high-school education.[55]

Though some of these differences can be explained by female selectivity in choosing mates, I doubt that all can. Marriage not only involves screening people for their capacity for self-control, it also provides inducements—the need to support a mate, care for a child, and maintain a home—that increase that capacity.

Throughout history, the institutions that have produced effective male socialization have been private, not public. Today we expect "government programs" to accomplish what families, villages, and churches once accomplished. This expectation leads to disappointment, if not frustration. Government programs, whether aimed at farmers, professors, or welfare mothers, tend to produce dependence, not self-reliance. If this is true, then our policy ought to be to identify, evaluate, and encourage those local, private efforts that seem to do the best job at reducing drug abuse, inducing people to marry, persuading parents, especially fathers, to take responsibility for their children, and exercising informal social control over neighborhood streets.

The federal government is a powerful but clumsy giant, not very adept at identifying, evaluating, and encouraging individuals who need help. It is good at passing laws, transferring funds, and multiplying regulations. These are necessary functions, but out of place in the realm of personal redemption. A government program to foster personal redemption will come equipped with standardized budgets, buy-America rules, minority set-asides, quarterly reporting requirements, and environmental impact statements and, in all likelihood, a thinly disguised bias against any kind of involvement with churches.

There may be a better way: public funds sent to private foundations that in turn do the identifying, evaluating, and encouraging, all on the basis of carefully negotiated charters that free these intermediaries from most governmental constraints. I have no example to cite, but people who wish to think seriously about changing the culture of poverty had better start inventing one.

Notes

1.   Evidence for these beliefs can be found in chapter 1 and in the poll data reported in "Public Opinion and the Demographic Report," *American Enterprise*, vol. 3 (September–October 1992), pp. 85–86.

2.   James Q. Wilson, *Thinking About Crime* (Basic Books, 1975), chap. 3.

3.   Ibid., pp. 199, 204–7.

4.   The rise in the probability of imprisonment is measured in Patrick A. Langan, "America's Soaring Prison Population," *Science*, March 1991, p. 1572. The increase in the incidence of crime among young male cohorts is established in Paul E. Tracy, Marvin E. Wolfgang, and Robert M. Figlio, *Delinquency Careers in Two Birth Cohorts* (Plenum, 1990), p. 276.

5.   Irwin Garfinkel and Sara S. McLanahan, *Single Mothers and Their Children: A New American Dilemma* (Washington: Urban Institute Press, 1986). See also William A. Galston, "Causes of Declining Well-Being among U.S. Children: Data and Debates," *Aspen Institute Quarterly*, vol. 5 no. 1 (1993), pp. 52–77.

6.   Robert Moffitt, "An Economic Model of Welfare Stigma," *American Economic Review*, vol. 73 (December 1983), pp. 1023–35; Robert Moffitt, "Incentive Effects of the U.S. Welfare System: A Review," *Journal of Economic Literature*, vol. 30 (March 1992), pp. 1–61; and Robert Moffitt, "The Effect of the U.S. Welfare System on Marital Status," *Journal of Public Economics*, vol. 41 (February 1990), pp. 101–24.

7.   Douglas J. Besharov, "Poverty, Welfare Dependency, and the Underclass," paper delivered at the Conference on Reducing Poverty in America, University of California at Los Angeles, January 1993.

8.   Between 1960 and 1988, per capita disposable income (in constant dollars) increased from $6,036 to $11,337, median school years completed increased from 10.6 to 12.7, and the percentage of people between the ages of 16 and 24 failing to complete high school declined from 17.0 in 1967 to 12.9 in 1988. Bureau of the Census, *Statistical Abstract of the United States* (Washington, 1963), p. 119, and (1990), pp. 428, 133; and National Center for Educational Statistics, *Digest of Education Statistics, 1990* (Washington: Department of Education, 1991), p. 110.

9.   William Julius Wilson, *The Truly Disadvantaged: The Inner City, the Underclass, and Public Policy* (University of Chicago Press, 1987).

10.   Christopher Jencks and Susan E. Mayer, "Residential Segregation, Job Proximity, and Black Job Opportunities," in Laurence E. Lynn, Jr., and Michael G. H. McGeary, eds., *Inner-City Poverty in the United States* (National Academy Press, 1990), p. 219.

11.   William Julius Wilson, "Public Policy Research and *The Truly Disadvantaged*," in Christopher Jencks and Paul E. Peterson, eds., *The Urban Underclass* (Brookings, 1991), pp. 460–81.

12.   Richard B. Freeman and Harry J. Holzer, eds., *The Black Youth Employment Crisis* (University of Chicago Press, 1986), p. 16.

13.   W. J. Wilson has acknowledged the black-Latino difference. See Wilson, "The Plight of the Inner-City Black Male," *Proceedings of the American Philosophical Society*, vol. 136 (September 1992), p. 321.

14.   David E. Hayes-Bautista and others, *No Longer a Minority: Latinos and Social Policy in California* (UCLA Chicano Studies Research Center, 1992). See also Aida Hurtado and others, *Redefining California: Latino Social Engagement in a Multicultural Society* (UCLA Chicano Studies Research Center, 1992).

15.   Besharov, "Poverty, Welfare Dependency, and the Underclass," p. 15.

16.   James Q. Wilson and Richard Herrnstein, *Crime and Human Nature* (Simon and Schuster, 1985).

17.   Jan M. Chaiken and Marcia R. Chaiken, "Crime Rates and the Active Criminal," in James Q. Wilson, ed., *Crime and Public Policy* (San Francisco, Calif.: Institute for Contemporary Studies, 1983), pp. 18–21; James Alan Fox, *Forecasting Crime Data: An Econometric Analysis* (Lexington Books, 1978); Theodore N. Ferdinand, "Demographic Shifts and Criminality: An Inquiry," *British Journal of Criminology*, vol. 10 (April 1970), pp. 169–75; and Darrell J. Steffensmeier and Miles D. Harer, "Is the Crime Rate Really Falling? An 'Aging' U.S. Population and its Impact on the Nation's Crime Rate, 1980–1984," *Journal of Research in Crime and Delinquency*, vol. 24 (February 1987), pp. 23–48.

18.   Christopher Jencks, "Is the American Underclass Growing?" in Jencks and Peterson, *The Urban Underclass*, p. 81.

19. Paul E. Tracy, Marvin E. Wolfgang, and Robert M. Figlio, *Delinquency Careers in Two Birth Cohorts* (Plenum, 1990), p. 276.

20. Robyn L. Cohen, *Prisoners in 1990* (Washington: Bureau of Justice Statistics, 1991), p. 7; Mark A. R. Kleiman and others, "Imprisonment-to-Offense Ratios," Working Paper 89-06-02, Program in Criminal Justice Policy and Management of the John F. Kennedy School of Government (Harvard University, 1988). I am indebted to John J. DiIulio, Jr., and Charles Logan for bringing the calculations in this paragraph to my attention.

21. Stephanie Minor-Harper and Lawrence A. Greenfeld, *Prison Admissions and Releases, 1982* (Washington: Bureau of Justice Statistics, 1985).

22. Patrick A. Langan, "America's Soaring Prison Population," *Science*, March 1991, p. 1572.

23. James Q. Wilson and Allan Abrahamse, "Does Crime Pay?" *Justice Quarterly*, vol. 9 (1993), pp. 359–78.

24. Wilson and Herrnstein, *Crime and Human Nature*, chap. 12; and James Q. Wilson and Philip J. Cook, "Unemployment and Crime: What Is the Connection?" *Public Interest*, no. 79 (Spring 1985), pp. 3–8.

25. For example, when Barbara Boland and I estimated the effects of socioeconomic conditions and police arrest rates on robbery rates in thirty-five cities, we were able to explain only 74 percent of the variance; see James Q. Wilson and Barbara Boland, "The Effect of the Police on Crime," *Law and Society Review*, vol. 12 (Spring 1978), pp. 367–90.

26. Anthony Davids, Catherine Kidder, and Melvyn Reich, "Time Orientation in Male and Female Juvenile Delinquents," *Journal of Abnormal and Social Psychology*, vol. 64 (March 1962), pp. 239–40; Anthony Davids and Bradley B. Falkof, "Juvenile Delinquents Then and Now: Comparison of Findings from 1959 and 1974," *Journal of Abnormal Psychology*, vol. 84 (April 1975), pp. 161–64.

27. See, for example, Richard J. Herrnstein and Drazen Prelec, "A Theory of Addiction," in G. F. Lowenstein and Jon Elster, eds., *Choice Over Time* (New York: Russell Sage Foundation, 1992), pp. 331–60; and Thomas Schelling, "The Intimate Contest for Self-Command," *Public Interest*, no. 60 (Summer 1980), pp. 94–118.

28. The evidence is reviewed in Wilson and Herrnstein, *Crime and Human Nature*, chap. 7; Terrie E. Moffitt, "Juvenile Delinquency and Attention Deficit Disorder: Boys' Developmental Trajectories from Age 3 to Age 15," *Child Development*, vol. 61 (June 1990), pp. 893–910; and David P. Farrington, Rolf Loeber, and W. B. Van Kammen, "Long-term Criminal Outcomes of Hyperactivity-Impulsivity-Attention Deficit and Conduct Problems in Childhood," in Lee N. Robins and Michael Rutter, eds., *Straight and Devious Pathways from Childhood to Adulthood* (Cambridge University Press, 1990), pp. 62–81.

29. For summaries, see William Damon, *The Moral Child: Nurturing Children's Natural Moral Growth* (Free Press, 1988); and Wilson and Herrnstein, *Crime and Human Nature*, chaps. 8, 9.

30.   Sheppard G. Kellam, Margaret E. Ensminger, and R. Jay Turner, "Family Structure and the Mental Health of Children," *Archives of General Psychiatry*, vol. 34 (1977), pp. 1012–22.

31.   Deborah A. Dawson, "Family Structure and Children's Health: United States, 1988," National Center for Health Statistics, *Vital and Health Statistics*, series 10, no. 178 (Hyattsville, Md.: Department of Health and Human Services, June 1991).

32.   Sara McLanahan and Gary Sandefur, *Uncertain Childhood, Uncertain Future* (Harvard University Press, forthcoming). See also James Q. Wilson, "The Family-Values Debate," *Commentary*, vol. 95 (April 1993), pp. 24–31.

33.   J. Brooks-Gunn and Frank F. Furstenberg, Jr., "The Children of Adolescent Mothers: Physical, Academic, and Psychological Outcomes," *Developmental Review*, vol. 6 (September 1986), pp. 224–51; and Frank F. Furstenberg, Jr., J. Brooks-Gunn, and Lindsay Chase-Lansdale, "Teenaged Pregnancy and Childbearing," *American Psychologist*, vol. 44 (February 1989), pp. 313–20.

34.   See Sylvia Ann Hewlett, *When the Bough Breaks: The Cost of Neglecting Our Children* (Basic Books, 1991), chap. 3, and the studies summarized therein.

35.   On time horizon as the defining characteristic of the urban poor, see Edward C. Banfield, *The Unheavenly City: The Nature and Future of Our Urban Crisis* (Boston: Little Brown, 1970).

36.   An example of the more radical view is Michael Harrington, *The Other America: Poverty in the United States* (Macmillan, 1962).

37.   Myron Magnet, *The Dream and the Nightmare: The Sixties' Legacy to the Underclass* (William Morrow, 1993), esp. pp. 16–17, 220.

38.   Wilson, *Thinking About Crime*, chap. 8. For some promising leads, see Paul Gendreau and Robert R. Ross, "Revivification of Rehabilitation: Evidence from the 1980s," *Justice Quarterly*, vol. 4 (1987), pp. 349–407.

39.   Janice H. Laurence, Peter F. Ramsberger, and Monica A. Gribben, *Effects of Military Experience on the Post-Service Lives of Low-Aptitude Recruits: Project 100,000 and the ASVAB Misnorming*, Final Report 89-29 to the Office of the Assistant Secretary of Defense for Force Management and Personnel (Alexandria, Va.: Human Resources Research Organization, 1989), p. 170. Veterans' names were selected from among participants in the National Longitudinal Survey, run by Ohio State University for the Department of Labor. There are several limitations to this study that the authors properly note. It was very difficult to locate veterans, and so there may be some sample selection bias (though if the hard-to-find were worse off than the easy-to-find, the bias means that the study underestimated how badly off the veterans were). Low-aptitude recruits who left the military may have been worse off than those who stayed in. Another evaluation of these careerists found that, on the whole, they performed reasonably well, but the authors could only locate about 8,000 such men; since they accounted for only 2.4 percent of the low-aptitude recruits, it is impossible to

generalize from their success to the success of the program. See Thomas G. Sticht and others, *Cast-Off Youth: Policy and Training Methods from the Military Experience* (Praeger, 1987), pp. 38, 56–60.

40.　Ruth Hubble McKey and others, *The Impact of Head Start on Children, Families, and Communities: Final Report of the Head Start Evaluation, Synthesis, and Utilization Project*, no. OHDS 85-31193 (Department of Health and Human Services, 1985); and Ron Haskins, "Beyond Metaphor: The Efficacy of Early Childhood Education," *American Psychologist*, vol. 44 (February 1989), pp. 274–82.

41.　John R. Berrueta-Clement and others, *Changed Lives: The Effects of the Perry Preschool Program on Youths Through Age 19* (Ypsilanti, Mich.: High/Scope, 1984); L. J. Schweinhart, "Can Preschool Programs Help Prevent Delinquency?" in James Q. Wilson and Glenn C. Loury, eds., *From Children to Citizens: Families, Schools, and Delinquency Prevention* (Springer-Verlag, 1987), pp. 135–53.

42.　Haskins, "The Efficacy of Early Childhood Education."

43.　Phyllis Levenstein, John O'Hara, and John Madden, "The Mother-Child Home Program of the Verbal Interaction Project," in Consortium for Longitudinal Studies, *As the Twig is Bent: Lasting Effects of Preschool Programs* (Hillsdale, N.J.: Erlbaum Associates, 1983), pp. 237–63.

44.　The Infant Health and Development Program, "Enhancing the Outcomes of Low-Birth-Weight, Premature Infants," *Journal of the American Medical Association*, vol. 263 (June 13, 1991), pp. 3035–42.

45.　I say "for at-risk children" because it is not clear that there are any benefits for normal children. Jay Belsky, "Infant Daycare: A Cause for Concern? *Zero to Three*, vol. 6 (September 1986), pp. 1–7, has suggested that day care for normal children may have some deleterious effects. This is disputed by other scholars. See Tiffany Field, *Infancy* (Harvard University Press, 1990), chap. 5. The issue cannot be regarded as resolved. In the low-birth-weight baby project, the improvements in IQ and infant behavior were greatest for the most disadvantaged children.

46.　Edward Zigler and Nancy Hall, "The Implications of Early Intervention Efforts for the Primary Prevention of Juvenile Delinquency," and J. David Hawkins and others, "Delinquency Prevention through Parent Training: Results and Issues from Work in Progress," in Wilson and Loury, *From Children to Citizens*, pp. 154–85 and 186–204.

47.　James S. Coleman, Thomas Hoffer, and Sally Kilgore, *High School Achievement: Public, Catholic, and Private Schools Compared* (Basic Books, 1982).

48.　For accounts in England, see Gertrude Himmelfarb, *Poverty and Compassion: The Moral Imagination of the Late Victorians* (Alfred A. Knopf, 1991), especially chap. 13; for accounts in America, see Paul S. Boyer, *Urban Masses and Moral Order in America, 1820–1920* (Harvard University Press, 1978).

49.　Mercer Sullivan, "Crime and the Social Fabric," in John Hull Mollenkopf and Manuel Castells, eds., *Dual City: Restructuring New York* (New York: Russell Sage Foundation, 1991), pp. 225–44.

50.   The preceding two paragraphs were taken from James Q. Wilson, "Human Nature and Social Progress," a Bradley Lecture delivered to the American Enterprise Institute, May 9, 1991.

51.   The proposal is made in Magnet, *The Dream and the Nightmare*, pp. 141–42.

52.   James Q. Wilson, *On Character* (Washington: AEI Press, 1991), chap. 3.

53.   David Popenoe, *Disturbing the Nest: Family Change and Decline in Modern Societies* (Aldine de Gruyter, 1988).

54.   Arthur S. Kraus and Abraham M. Lilienfeld, "Some Epidemiologic Aspects of the High Mortality Rate in the Young Widowed Group," *Journal of Chronic Diseases*, vol. 10 (1959), pp. 207–17; Walter R. Gove, "Sex, Marital Status, and Mortality," *American Journal of Sociology*, vol. 79 (July 1973), pp. 45–67; Alicia Rand, "Transitional Life Events and Desistance from Delinquency and Crime," in Marvin E. Wolfgang, Terence P. Thornberry, and Robert M. Figlio, eds., *From Boy to Man, From Delinquency to Crime* (University of Chicago Press, 1987), pp. 134–62; Peter Reuter and others, *Money from Crime: A Study of the Economics of Drug Dealing in Washington, D.C.* (Santa Monica, Calif.: Rand Corporation, 1990). I am indebted to Professor David Courtwright of the University of North Florida for directing my attention to some of these references.

55.   Nicholas Eberstadt, "America's Infant-Mortality Puzzle," *Public Interest*, no. 105 (Fall 1991), pp. 37–38.

The Family Condition of America

Cultural Change and Public Policy

David Popenoe

Throughout its history the United States has depended heavily, for both social order and economic success, on the relatively self-sufficient and nurturing family unit—a childrearing unit that is crucial for the survival and development of children, a social unit that attends to its members' socioemotional needs, an economic unit that contains efficiencies derived from the specialization of labor and shared consumption, and a welfare unit that cares for the sick, injured, handicapped, and elderly. Yet in each of these respects the family condition of America has become problematic; by many quantitative measures, American families are functioning less well today than ever before, and less well than in any other advanced, industrialized nation, especially in regard to children. The evidence is strong that today's generation of children and youth is the first in our nation's history to be less well-off—psychologically, socially, economically, and morally—than their parents were at the same age. Much of the problem, suggests the evidence, lies with what has happened to the family.[1]

It is hard to conceive of a good and successful society without reasonably strong families—multigenerational, domestic groups of kinfolk that effectively carry out their socially assigned tasks. No socially assigned task is more important than that of raising children to become adults who are able to love and to work and who are

81

committed to such prosocial values as honesty, respect, and responsibility. Successful civilizations heretofore have been based on a family foundation, one that assured that children were taught the values, attitudes, and habits of the culture and became, as adults, reasonably well integrated into society. Indeed, many scholars have viewed civilizational collapse as at least partly a problem of family decline.[2] When a nation's families show signs of disarray, therefore, it surely is reasonable to view these signs as symptoms of a broader social failure.

Biosocial Bases of the Family

Childrearing has long been the family's main biosocial (biological and sociological) function or purpose. The family probably arose because of the paramount need for adults to devote a great amount of time to rearing children. Because human offspring come into the world totally dependent, they must, for a larger portion of their lives than any other species, be cared for and taught by adults. And human childrearing is much more complex than its animal counterpart; without life-guiding instincts, humans must deliberately be taught the "functional alternative" to instincts—culture. To a unique degree, human beings nurture, protect, and educate their offspring.[3]

The mother-child dyad is probably the strongest social bond in the higher animal kingdom, including humans, and it is the typical childrearing structure among most animal species. Certainly the human mother alone can accomplish childrearing; all available evidence shows that children need, at minimum, one adult to care intimately for them. "Survivors" or "resilient children," for example, children from deprived socioeconomic backgrounds who nevertheless grow up successfully, tend to have the common denominator of one adult who gave them inordinate attention.[4]

Yet given the complexities of the task of human childrearing, in all human societies to date the task has been shared by other adults. The institutional bond of marriage between the biological parents, an essential function of which is to tie the father to the mother-child dyad, is a panhuman institution, found in virtually every society; in no society has nonmarital childbirth or the single parent been the cultural norm. In all societies the biological father is identified, and in almost all societies he is important to his children's upbringing, although often indirectly as protector and breadwinner. In most of the world's societies childrearing has involved many more persons than the biological parents; typically members of the broader kinship group share childrearing, but sometimes other community members have participated too.[5] It may well be true, as anthropologist Raoul Naroll has concluded, that "the main point of human social structure in its evolution over the past 5 or 6 million years has been its special care for women and their children."[6]

Cultural Change: Collectivism to Individualism

To fully understand what has happened to the institution of the family in the modern period, one must look at broader cultural change in the values and norms that influence everyday choices. Most societies of the past were highly collectivist (I am using this term with a cultural and not a political meaning); collective goals took precedence over individual ones. "Doing one's duty" was far more important than "self-fulfillment"; or, in the words of Ralf Dahrendorf and Daniel Yankelovich, "social bonds" were more important than "personal choice."[7] The cultures of most developing and developed societies today, however, are moving or have moved toward individualism. Attributes such as strong social hierarchy, in-group harmony, and individual behavior strongly regulated by group norms are giving way to the primacy of personal over social goals, emotional detachment from the group, and an emphasis on self-reliance, personal autonomy, and competitiveness. Indeed, this shift toward individualism seems to be one of the fundamental motivating forces in modern history.[8] This shift has been associated with movement toward a system in which the nuclear family, consisting of parents and their children, becomes structurally separated (sociologists sometimes say isolated) from other social units, including the larger kinship group.[9]

Societies marked by an individualistic culture, with the individualistic nuclear family form, rank higher than collectivist societies in political democracy, individual development, scientific achievement, and (with the important exception of the newly advanced and relatively collectivist Asian societies of the Pacific Rim) economic advancement.[10] Advanced societies accord the highest priority to these goals. Among its many other advantages, the nuclear family is well suited to the development of autonomous individuals and thus to the growth of human freedom—the supreme value of individualistic societies.[11] But the shift from collectivism to individualism entails social costs as well as human gains. Along with political democracy and economic advancement, individualistic societies tend to have high rates of individual deviance, juvenile delinquency and crime, loneliness, depression, suicide, and social alienation. In short, individualistic societies have a greater number of free and independent citizens, but a weaker social order. There is far more social disorder in the United States, for example, than in the relatively more collectivist nations of northwestern Europe, and more disorder in European nations than in the still more collectivist societies of East Asia.

Two factors can be singled out as the dominant generators of the historical trend toward individualism: economic development and cultural complexity, the fundamental components of the master social trend often called modernization. Economic development leads to material affluence, especially personal economic security. Because affluent individuals and families need not directly rely so much on others for economic support, their personal and social autonomy concomitantly increases.[12] Through relying on market goods and services and on state-provided welfare, individuals in affluent societies are able to distance themselves from those intimate social structures and community groupings that have long been the basis for personal security. As these structures of "civil society" thereby weaken, so does the social order.

I will leave to economists any discussion of the sources of economic development. Within a single culture, cultural complexity—the second of the two factors—is generated mainly by the growth of science and technology, mass education, bureaucracy, urban living, and the mass media. Cultural complexity is compounded, of course, when separate cultures based on race, religion, or national origin come together to form a culturally heterogeneous nation or multicultural society. Faced with the weakening of a widely shared and stable culture—with new, different, and often conflicting norms, values, and world views—people's decisions about appropriate behavior must be based more strongly on personal attitudes than on traditional cultural standards. This new fact of life in culturally complex societies is reflected in the socialization process: children are taught to rely more on themselves than on the group if they are to adapt successfully to the world around them. One indication of this emphasis is a notable shift from "obedience" to "independence" as a dominant goal of childrearing over recent decades in the United States.[13]

It is important to stress that collectivism is found in many social forms, from huge, totalitarian states to small, isolated groupings of coreligionists. Also, the issue of collectivism generating social order depends greatly on one's geographic perspective. That strong in-group social order can lead to antipathy toward outgroups, resulting in social strife and warfare among groups, is a sociological truism. One very narrow form of collectivism, for example, in which collective social order extends no further than the extended family and local kin group, was labeled "amoral familism" in a classic work by Edward Banfield.[14] In the southern Italian setting of his study, the social world outside the kin group (but still within the local community) was one of general disorder. And, contemporary North Korea—a totalitarian dictatorship and one of the world's last communist nations—has maximized internal order but expresses a powerful military posture toward outsiders.

Indeed, the historical trend toward individualism, although generating some internal disorder, has led to the diminution of disorder among groups and societies—certainly in the form of major world wars. This result is partly because group and national allegiances in individualistic societies are weaker, making it more difficult to mobilize people to fight external conflicts. Whatever the reasons, and they are many, the rise of relatively individualistic and economically advanced societies may have put an end to the era—consisting of all recorded human history—when "it was taken for granted that all nations were inherent rivals, seeking to conquer one another unless prevented from doing so."[15]

Individualism comes in many forms. Many people have written of the civic and utilitarian strains of individualism in American life, the individualisms on which this nation was founded.[16] Civic individualism is rooted in the belief in human rights and the sanctity of the individual, with the individual seen as part of a common civic endeavor. Utilitarian individualism is the individualism of personal achievement and the marketplace. Both developed as a reaction to historical forms of collectivism.

A new form of individualism has emerged in advanced, industrial societies—"radical" or "expressive" individualism that is devoted to "self-aggrandizement." In this form of individualism people become narcissistic, hedonistic, and self-oriented, showing concern for groups and for the public good only insofar as these matters directly affect their own well-being.[17] In turn, the traditional groupings that make up civil society—neighborhoods, local communities, voluntary associations, religious organizations—become weakened. Strong elements of radical individualism have been discerned in many highly advanced societies today, but they are especially apparent in the United States. And abundant evidence from many nations shows that the constituent groupings of civil society are in decline.[18]

As a foundation of civil society, the family is by no means exempt from this phenomenon of the deinstitutionalization or decline of civil society. The trend toward radical individualism can be perceived as movement beyond the nuclear family and toward a "postnuclear" family system. The gradual deinstitutionalization of the family, or "family decline" (which in the past has involved the shift from extended to nuclear families and the gradual loss of such family functions as economic production and formal education), consists of an increasing dissociation between pair-bonding, sexual activity, and procreation.[19] These three activities are effectively combined in nuclear family systems, and their dissociation has serious negative social consequences, especially for children.

Family decline highlights the role of affluence in driving individualism. Contrary to the popular notion that economic insecurity is the main cause of family decline, those societies that have moved furthest in a postnuclear family direction are characterized by relative economic security based on some combination of market-distributed personal affluence and welfare-state supports. Such societies have high and increasing rates of marital dissolution and nonmarriage, single-parent families, voluntary stepfamilies, single-person households, and nonmarital births. Judged by these measures, the most "postnuclear" societies in the world today are Sweden and the United States, the one having the world's greatest state-generated economic security and the other having the world's greatest market-generated consumer affluence.

Advanced Societies Today: Cultural Trade-Offs

It is useful to examine cultures by scrutinizing the trade-offs they have made between individualism and collectivism—between emphasizing personal autonomy and self-fulfillment on the one hand, and social order and cultural harmony on the other. A society that has moved too far toward individualism faces problems of personal alienation from the social order, with high rates of depression, eating disorders, suicide, and drug and alcohol abuse, and a breakdown in the social control of individual behavior, with high rates of crime and delinquency. A society that is too collectivist faces problems of political or cultural tyranny, endless warfare with out-groups, and the suppression of individual rights and initiative, all widespread problems that have plagued human history. Neither extreme collectivism nor extreme individualism is socially desirable. The good society is one that strikes a balance between the two poles, providing reasonable personal autonomy, a stable social order, and peace with neighbors.

In the West, my favorite good societies—ones that have struck the best balance between individualism and collectivism—are Iceland and Norway among the Nordic lands, and Switzerland among the nations of continental Europe. These nations are noted for their historical individualism, but at the same time they have highly intact and integrated cultures, strong social orders, economic prosperity, and with the partial exception of Norway, a long history of peace with their neighbors. They also have relatively intact families and communities and low rates of crime and personal pathology. The citizens of these nations, not incidentally, rank very high on cross-national "happiness" surveys.[20]

What is the secret of these societies? In part, they have just been lucky. They are demographically homogeneous (Switzerland is multicultural, but not in the American sense) and geographically in a position of relative isolation from the world around them. And these nations have instituted ways to become wealthy yet minimize the negative consequences of modernization, specifically the trend toward radical individualism. They are less urban than most other advanced nations, for example, and less dominated by the commercialism of the mass media. Culturally, these nations combine individualism with a moderate collectivism; we can refer to them with the phrase "communitarian individualism."[21] Individual goals are important, but they are blended with strong communal concerns and feelings of national solidarity. Self and community are in better balance than in other highly developed nations, especially the United States.

The advanced society today that has shifted least in the direction of radical individualism and postnuclear familism is Japan. Of the advanced societies, Japan ranks highest on "doing one's duty" collectivism and lowest on "self-fulfillment" individualism; in turn, Japan has the highest degree of internal social order and Japanese citizens have the lowest degree of personal autonomy.[22] This cultural situation can be attributed mainly to Japan's tremendous cultural homogeneity and very recent affluence, and because Asian cultures have traditionally been much more collectivist than Western cultures. Nevertheless, by all indications Japan is moving in the individualistic, postnuclear direction, showing signs of both growing personal autonomy and increased social disorder, including family breakup.

And the recent experience of Japan and other Pacific Rim nations has put to rest one proposition long held in the West—that a high degree of cultural individualism is necessary for economic advancement. This proposition certainly was validated by much of the Western experience, the classic example being individualistic England's (and later America's) pioneering role in the Industrial Revolution. Most of the great scientific and technological discoveries and inventions associated with that revolution came from relatively individualistic nations. Recent events suggest, however, that even in strictly economic terms, the trend toward cultural individualism can proceed too far. The most economically successful nations today, and probably in the future, are those that are able to maintain a fairly cohesive social order through the collectivist attribute of a group identity and commitment that encourages honesty, respect for authority, and a sense of personal responsibility. One thinks of nations like Japan, Taiwan, Singapore, and Korea, but it is also likely that—

partly because of their relatively stronger collectivism—most European nations will come to overshadow the economic achievements of the United States.

The Problem of America: Overindividualism

The United States has long been known as the world's most individualistic society. Yet in its heyday, over most of the past 150 years, a strong belief in the sanctity and importance of social units, such as local communities, religious organizations, voluntary associations, and the nation as a whole, tempered this individualism.[23] People's identities were rooted in such social units, and their lives were directed toward social goals that these units espoused. At the same time a cultural hegemony existed, dominated by a mostly Anglo-Saxon elite. Newcomers to the nation quickly assimilated, for the most part, to the norms and values that had been brought by the founding settlers (albeit somewhat modified in the new surroundings). Thus the United States has been marked for much of its history by a strong communitarian individualism, precisely the balance that has led to social success in other Western societies.

As the nation has become more affluent and the culture ever more diverse, however, and as self-expression and self-development have become life's dominant purposes, this situation has changed dramatically. People's faith and trust in social institutions, and their willingness to have their identities linked to them, have weakened enormously. Social units of all types, including the family, are increasingly viewed, with skepticism, as somewhat "illegitimate." [24] Especially since the 1950s, significant informal relationships, social networks, and social supports have been declining. There has been a decline in people being married, visiting informally with others, and belonging to voluntary associations, and an increase in living alone.[25] Nationally, the sense of cultural solidarity has become a pale shadow of its former being; it still can be activated through jingoist appeals in brief wars like that in the Persian Gulf but seemingly can no longer be invoked to solve such outstanding social problems as those of the inner city.

America today has all the earmarks of an overly individualistic society, with failing families, rising crime, declining interpersonal and political trust, growing personal and corporate greed, deteriorating communities, and increasing confusion over moral issues. These are all dimensions of what is increasingly felt to be "social decline." The average American seemingly has become more fearful, anxious, and unsettled. Tempers have become shorter, life's little satisfactions less frequent, and the emotional feel of life less secure. These trends are a recipe for social disaster. The push for self-fulfillment, when carried to the extreme, leads not to personal freedom and happiness but to social breakdown and individual anguish.[26]

By no means, it is important to add, has every aspect of America deteriorated in recent decades; in several key areas, indeed, this nation has seen rapid social progress. For instance, we are a much more inclusive society today—segregation and racism have substantially diminished, and blacks and other minority groups are now more fully accepted into the mainstream. The legal, sexual, and financial emancipation of women has become a reality as never before in history. With extraordinary advances in medicine, the end of many infectious diseases, and changes in life-style, we have greater longevity and, on the whole, better health. And our average material standard of living, especially in the possession of consumer durables, has increased significantly.

America's fundamental problem today is cultural disintegration, a weakening of the ties that bind. The tendency toward individualism and self-fulfillment has become too powerful; we have become, in David Riesman's phrase, an "over-optioned" society.[27] Postnuclear family decline is heavily implicated in this trend, but of course the family reflects changes in the larger sociocultural environment. To make matters worse, this cultural trend is now associated with relative economic decline and the likely deterioration in our status as a world political power.[28]

What has generated this overindividualistic social breakdown? In accordance with the theoretical propositions presented above, two factors stand out: our extreme cultural heterogeneity and our great personal wealth. Of all the advanced nations, the United States is by far the most culturally heterogeneous and complex on virtually all measures. Like Canada, Australia, and New Zealand, we were originally a nation centrally made up of immigrants from various European nations. But in two aspects of cultural complexity we are unique among advanced nations: our close proximity to the third world nations of Latin America and the originally involuntary presence of a large number of African Americans. Ours is a grand social experiment, and cultural pluralism has greatly enriched American life. Yet it has also fostered, over time, a weakening sense of common culture and national identity, and accelerated the trends toward radical individualism. When people can not agree about what values they share and which social authorities they recognize and respect, they naturally fall back on more individualistic attitudes and patterns of living.

The United States may no longer be the world's wealthiest nation on a per capita basis, but it is probably still the wealthiest nation measured by the average material living standard of households, as determined by such indices as size of domicile and ownership of consumer durables. Personal wealth is high because more of our wealth remains in private hands; we rank lowest among the advanced nations, for example, in government receipts as a percentage of gross domestic product.[29] Such personal wealth enhances the ability of Americans to pursue an individualistic, privatized life style, apart from the larger community. (Our heavy reliance on the market distribution of wealth, relatively untempered by government regulation, creates additional problems through generating inequalities; income and wealth are more unequally distributed in America than in other advanced nations, and our tax structure is relatively regressive.)

Restoring Civil Society in America

If overindividualism is the problem, and it is caused fundamentally by affluence and cultural complexity, what could possibly be the solution? There is no way to undo our affluence and cultural complexity; nor would that necessarily be desirable. But ways do exist by which the negative consequences of affluence and complexity can be minimized. In general, people require two essential things for their social well-being: close personal attachments and good community relationships. To have a society in which these are enhanced, we must seek to restore a cultural balance between individual autonomy and community needs.[30] With an ideology of communitarian individualism, our goal should be to promote families that can perform their assigned tasks, communities that can provide support to such families, and a larger society bound together by a culture of shared values. In the remainder of this paper I will deal mainly with strategies that could alleviate the problem of family decline. But because all of the dimensions of social decline are so interrelated, it is useful briefly to share some thoughts on the strengthening of local communities and the promotion of national solidarity.[31]

A major deterrent to selfish individualism is the "natural communities" that exist throughout human life, communities based on free association and sets of relational networks, on primary groups and voluntary associations, on families and local neighborhoods—communities where people have both a sense of cultural identity and a feeling of belonging. These are the locale of civility—courtesy, politeness and decency toward others, cooperation and self-restraint—on which so much of "the good life" depends. Unfortunately, such fundamental and essential social formations can readily be upset and displaced by both the market and the state. Indeed, the social environment in this respect should be thought of as every bit as fragile, and as worth preserving, as the natural environment, with its similarly intricate and easily damaged ecological network. Despite the many benefits they generate in economic growth and in social justice, both the market and the state reduce our direct reliance on others and thus tend to weaken the community fabric.[32]

State displacement of civil society has most painfully been evident in the history of the formerly communist states of Eastern Europe,[33] but it can also be seen to some degree in the strong welfare states of Western Europe. (The decline of the institution of the family in these nations has been comparable to the decline in America, although—owing to welfare measures—without such devastating consequences.) In America, contrary to what most conservatives argue, it is the untrammeled market and not the state that has done the most damage to civil society. We have the weakest state sector by far among the advanced nations, and the most unregulated market. Through advocating a social structure in which consumer choice and pleasurable consumption are the highest values, through promoting high rates of mobility, a gambler's mentality, income inequality, and materialism, the market is certainly no friend of civil society. Daniel Bell was probably right when he noted the "cultural contradiction of capitalism," that capitalism tends to undermine the very values—such as honesty and hard work—on which its ultimate success depends.[34]

The reinvigoration of civil society in America depends in part on shifting away from our current preoccupation with individual rights. Strong local communities necessarily set a framework within which people will live, which involves making fundamental moral judgments about how they should live. The assumptions that all rights rest with the individual, and that local government should be morally neutral, are antithetical to the continued existence of such communities. A new agenda of "group rights" is not what is called for; few agendas are better suited to intergroup conflict to say nothing of group tyranny—the oppression of the individual by the majority. "What we need," as Mary Ann Glendon says, "is not a new portfolio of 'group rights' but a fuller concept of human personhood and a more ecological way of thinking about social policy."[35]

We are clearly at an early stage of development in our public policy thinking about how best to support positively (and avoid damaging) viable natural communities, while protecting the fundamental rights of individuals. There are the obvious concerns about racial and ethnic discrimination. And our impulses to support community can sometimes run awry, as was the case with the "community action" programs of the 1960s. Many community development efforts of that time, aimed at ending the War on Poverty, are considered to have been a failure.[36] But just as we now require environmental and family impact statements for pending legislation, so should we be thinking in similar terms about the impact of public policies on functioning local communities and civil society in general.

An important caveat is that many existing communities in America could hardly be called natural. They are artificial, market-generated, income and life-style enclaves that function mainly to preserve property values; or depressed areas, found in both urban and rural settings, from which everyone who could afford to has long since fled. The issue of which communities should garner public support is a profound one. Nevertheless, in general, public policies should seek to protect local neighborhoods against the unnecessary intrusion of outsiders, promote community identity and solidarity through local social, educational, cultural, and religious organizations, and deeply respect the wishes and concerns of each subcultural grouping.

While we are shoring up natural communities, however, we must be equally concerned about maintaining national solidarity. No nation can survive without a framework of common values.[37] A "natural-communities policy" is a different strategy than the one followed successfully for the first two hundred years of our nation, which typically was oriented to promoting rapid assimilation to the dominant European-based culture. Because the dark side of strong, in-group solidarity tends to be bigotry, prejudice, and violence against out-groups, the community strategy, if carried to the extreme, could lead to the tribalization and breakdown of America as we have known it. Utmost care will be necessary, therefore, to avoid the furtherance of moral exclusiveness in local communities. A natural communities policy must be counterbalanced by strongly fostering those common values and traditions that have held us together at the national level. If these shared values and traditions were to be lost, we as a nation would be bound together solely by the market and its ally, the mass media. What could be called amoral communalism would then reign supreme over the land.

This concern for national solidarity is all the greater because of the new conditions under which we now live. As a culturally heterogeneous society from the beginning, the United States has been profoundly fortunate in having had a great amount of uninhabited space. If Americans did not wish, or were not able, to fit into the cultural mainstream, they could go off and live somewhere by themselves. Although many such isolated subcultures still exist in this country, the possibility today of geographic and cultural isolation has greatly diminished. Not only is usable space a diminishing resource, but modern transportation and communication technologies and economic forces bind the nation ever closer together in a network of interaction. And the widespread and continuing growth of metropolitan areas, despite the attempts of suburbanites to isolate themselves, compounds the connections that we all have. It is no longer possible or feasible for natural communities to exist in splendid isolation.

Apart from our governmental and legal institutions, the social institution that has played the most important role in enabling the nation to remain somewhat unified over the past centuries is probably education. The schools have taught patriotism, common values, and most importantly, a common language. Although local schools must remain, under a natural communities policy, as strong, community-led institutions, they should also continue to heavily promote national identity and solidarity. I suggest, for example, along the lines advocated by Chester Finn, that a strong, uniform national curriculum be incorporated into our primary and secondary schools, not only in such fundamental subjects as math, science, and writing, which are so necessary for economic success in the modern world, but also in our Western traditions.[38] I suggest further that our colleges and universities, which draw in a larger percentage of citizens than in any other world nation, should also heavily stress our common Western values.

Just as moral exclusiveness is an issue at the local level, so also must it be a concern at the national level. Americans have gradually been developing a more cosmopolitan and global frame of mind. Efforts to promote national solidarity should not impede that development. While the society and the polity remain national in scope, the economy is increasingly international. It would be especially counterproductive if national solidarity were to be promoted in the age-old fashion of jingoism—through focusing attention on some presumed external threat, either political or economic. With the end of the cold war and the globalization of the economy, maintaining national solidarity without inventing a new enemy will become a national test of character.[39]

Nuclear Families: The Vital Factor

At the heart of civil society lies the family.[40] In 1973, Margaret Mead told a Senate Committee, "as families go, so goes the nation."[41] She might have been more precise. The market and the state seem to go on despite everything, but it is increasingly clear that "as families go, so goes civil society." A symbiotic relationship exists between the family and civil society. The family in an unfriendly surrounding culture is precarious; the stresses can be overwhelming. And civil societies depend on families to inculcate those civic values—honesty, trust, self-sacrifice, personal responsibility—by which they can thrive. In this sense, families can be thought of as "seedbeds of civic virtue." Such civic values are taught in the home, or they virtually are not taught at all. The school can try to teach these values—as it must—but if they are not taught within the home, early in a child's life, it is usually too late.

What family structure, under the conditions of industrial, liberal-democratic nations, is best able to produce offspring who grow up to be both autonomous and socially responsible, while also meeting the adult needs for intimacy and personal attachment that become ever more compelling in an increasingly impersonal world? Based on all available empirical evidence, as well as the lessons of recent human experience, the family structure that unquestionably works best is the nuclear family. I do not necessarily mean the traditional nuclear family, characterized by male dominance and a stay-at-home wife, that has been the predominant family form of the past 150 years (historians often refer to this as the modern family). I refer instead to the nuclear family in more general terms—consisting of a male and female living together, apart from other relatives, who share responsibility for their children and for each other.

Consider the fate of other family forms. There is no advanced, Western society where the three-generation extended family is very important, and where it is not also on the wane. Among advanced, industrial societies, Japan is the exception, but with the passing of the pre-World War II generation and the movement of women into the labor force, the days of the extended family there appear numbered. In the United States, it is the hope of some of my female college students that their mothers will come to live with them at the birth of their child, enabling these young women happily to stay on in the workplace. But such an arrangement on a widespread basis is hardly in the offing; for one thing, the mothers in question are now themselves in the labor force. Some scholars suggest that a new extended family is to be found in the trend toward step- and blended families. "Isn't it nice," they say, "that we now have so many new relatives around!" The final verdict is not yet in on stepfamilies, but preliminary evidence from the few empirical studies that have been done sends quite the opposite message, and it is a chilling one. The National Child Development Study in Great Britain, a longitudinal analysis of 17,000 children born in 1958, found that the chances of stepchildren suffering social deprivation before reaching 21 are even greater than those left living after divorce with a lone parent. Similar findings are turning up in the United States.[42]

Another alternative, somewhat similar to extended families, is the bunching together of mostly unrelated individuals in a group setting. This was the dream of the 1960s flower children, and the ideal of some of their scholarly allies. But virtually all of the communes have been notoriously unsuccessful (where are they today?). And even in their heyday, one of their most distinguishing characteristics was few or no children. Their main purpose was adult fulfillment, not generational continuity.

At the other extreme from the extended family are such postnuclear alternative family forms as the single-parent family. Here, accumulating evidence on the personal and social consequences of this family type paints a grim picture indeed. A recent survey found, for example, that children from single-parent families are two to three times more likely to have emotional and behavioral problems than children from intact families, and by no means is reduced family income the sole factor involved.[43]

If we rule out these family alternatives, we are left with the nuclear family—children raised by their biological parents. Just as the international emergence and growth of liberal democracy may proclaim the "end of history," or at least the "end of ideology," I suggest that the nuclear family proclaims something similar in the family field. Family history comes to an end in this elemental, essential unit of human procreation.[44] As liberal democracy does the best job of resolving what Hegel referred to as peoples' "struggle for recognition," so the nuclear family is best at producing the kind of adults who can both promote and benefit from liberal democracy. Other family forms are not only possible but optimal in other cultural settings, but in advanced societies the nuclear family best combines the nurture of children with the strong need for emotional intimacy and the sexuality of parents. It is the family form for the modern world and, moreover, the family form that people in modern societies favor. The overwhelming majority of young people today put forth as their major life goal a lasting, monogamous, heterosexual relationship that includes the procreation of children.[45]

Let us explore more fully the benefits that strong nuclear families bring to an affluent and high-achieving, individualistic, democratic society; the reasons why nuclear families are worth tremendous social efforts to support and maintain. First, monogamous marriage—the basis of the nuclear family—brings enormous benefits to the adults involved. It is ironic in this age of self-fulfillment, when people are pulling themselves away from marriage, that a happy marriage seems in fact to provide a powerful source of self-fulfillment. By virtually every measure, married individuals are better off than single individuals; quite clearly, marriage is good for one's physical and mental health.[46] Based on the evidence, nothing would benefit the nation more, perhaps, than a national drive to promote strong marriages. Studies of depression, probably the most pervasive mental health problem in America today (particularly among young people) and one that by some estimates has increased as much as tenfold in the past two generations, indicate this point. These studies make clear that having an emotional confidant is probably the single best inhibitor of (unipolar) depression; not just any emotional confidant, but especially one that involves a stable relationship with the opposite sex. By the same token, "happiness" and "subjective well-being" have also been shown to depend, more than anything else, on ties with spouse, family, and friends.[47]

Whichever sex personally gains the most from being married, and scholars are in conflict about that issue, society certainly gains enormously from having a high percentage of men who are married. Unmarried women can take pretty good care of themselves, but unmarried men have difficulty in this regard. In general, as James Q. Wilson has stressed, every society must be wary of the unattached male, for he is universally the cause of numerous social ills.[48] The good society is heavily dependent on men being attached to a strong moral order centered on families, both to discipline their sexual behavior and to reduce their competitive aggression. Men need the moral and emotional instruction of women more than vice versa; and family life, especially having children, is a considerable civilizing force for men.[49] (It is not uncommon to hear men say that they will give up certain deviant or socially irresponsible patterns of life only when they have children, for then they feel the need to set a good example.)

Yet men today spend more time apart from family life than at probably any other time in American history. About a quarter of all men ages 25–34 (18.6 percent of all men aged 18 or older) live in nonfamily households, either alone or with an unrelated individual. Indeed, for Americans as a whole, just as the 1950s was a high watermark of family involvement, today is a low watermark. The proportion of the average American's adult life spent with spouse and children in 1960 was 62 percent, the highest in our history; today it is about 43 percent, the lowest in our history.[50] This trend alone probably helps to account for the high and rising crime rates over the past thirty years, a period in which the number of violent crimes per capita, as reported to authorities, increased by 355 percent. (And it should at least give us pause before wholeheartedly endorsing such movements as "single parents by choice," with its message that "women should not have to marry men to have babies.")[51]

Many recent empirical studies and investigations by social scientists have focused on those elements of nuclear family childrearing that produce autonomous yet socially responsible adults. Of fundamental importance for the child, as Urie Bronfenbrenner has long pointed out, is the presence of "one or more persons with whom the child develops a strong, mutual, irrational, emotional attachment and who is committed to the child's well-being and development, preferably for life."[52] There can be little doubt that the biological parent, usually the mother, is best suited to this role, although many other kinds of people obviously have had success in special situations.

The principal issue is what is called attachment. Most of the voluminous literature on attachment theory focuses on the need for a child to have a strong, emotional attachment with an adult. The theory has garnered solid empirical support. A growing body of findings indicates that infants who do not have a strong attachment, especially in the first year of life but probably longer than that, have intellectual, emotional, social, and moral problems in later childhood. Moreover, according to recent evidence, these problems may carry over to adulthood.[53] Adult attachments (especially sustained pair bonding), as already noted, seem to be as important to personal well-being as child attachments, and they are shaped to a significant degree by the attachment experiences of childhood. For example, in a recent study of middle-aged adults who had satisfying marriages, maintained close friends, and were happily engaged in their work, the most important single explanatory factor was having had warm and affectionate parents when they were very young. In fact, the much-discussed decline of trust in American life today, especially in interpersonal relationships, could well be related to childhood attachment-type problems, including the distrust and loss of confidence in parents that often is a consequence of divorce.[54]

It is highly relevant that the traditional family role of men in almost all societies has been that of protector and provider, precisely so that mother and infant could be closely attached. In the absence of a husband or other helping relative, mother-infant attachment obviously becomes problematic. Today, however, childrearing women are more isolated from others than at any other time. Some American men are directly involved in childrearing, others are providing more help to mothers than their own fathers did, but many men, through the avenues of out-of-wedlock births or divorce, have abandoned their children entirely. The state and the market can give some help to the abandoned mothers, as they should, but they can not provide the emotional attachment that is the basis of good childrearing.

An inescapable benefit of high male involvement in childrearing concerns the resource of time. Good childrearing takes time, and two parents can devote more attention to a child than a single parent. The significance of time in childrearing is highlighted by empirical findings on the promotion of "prosocial behavior" in children. The development of prosocial behavior—which includes helping, sharing, and concern for others—has been shown to stem from early attachment experiences, from the modeling by children of their parents' prosocial behavior, and from good nurturing, especially the way children are disciplined. At heart, prosocial behavior is based on strong feelings of empathy for other people. The type of discipline that best promotes the development of empathy in children is that which involves reasoning with the child, clearly pointing out the consequences of the child's actions on others. Discipline that relies on physical punishment, in contrast, often fails to develop empathy and, in any event, mainly teaches what is wrong rather than what is right.[55] (It has often been noted that families who have prosocial children, yet rarely use physical punishment, do not have to rely on punishment; as the result of lengthy interaction between parent and child, the child knows just what the parent is thinking and will adjust his or her behavior accordingly.) Discipline with reasoning and explanation is time intensive, especially compared with physical punishment. Today, when the time devoted to parent-child interaction is decreasing, especially in the father-absent family, it is likely that the teaching of empathy correspondingly suffers.

To make matters worse, no discipline at all—permissiveness—takes even less time. Parents who lack time and who also disavow physical punishment, a typical combination today, are shifting their childrearing techniques in the permissive direction. This path may be the worst of all, leading at best to a nation of anxious, aimless, and depressed youth who become troubled, self-indulgent adults.

Rebuilding the Nest

For all of the above reasons, our nation is well advised to establish as a para. unt national goal the promotion of intact, nuclear families that can successfully raise children. If we had such a goal, what would be the most worthwhile public policies to achieve it? Two broad efforts should be uppermost—the promotion of long-term, monogamous marriages, especially when children are involved; and the provision of additional resources to the parents of young children so that parents will be able to do a better job of childrearing.

The marriage question is the most difficult one. A massive cultural decline has occurred in the ideal of marital permanence, even when children are involved. For example, while 51 percent of Americans in 1962 said that "parents who don't get along should not stay together because there are children in the family," in 1985 the figure was 82 percent.[56] Social stigma against divorce has all but disappeared, and with the divorce rate remaining very high (latest estimate: 60 percent probability of divorce for first marriages; higher for second marriages),[57] it is likely that any remaining stigma against divorce will be further diminished. A recent study found that individuals who have experienced parental divorce as children, or who have experienced divorce in their own marriages, have more favorable attitudes toward divorce than do those persons who have not had such experiences.[58] This could change, however, as the children of the "divorce revolution"—who are painfully aware of the consequences of divorce—become adults.

With the United States having the industrial world's highest divorce rate, one might have expected a national commission, or at least a congressional investigation, to study the problem. But, unlike the case with almost every other national social problem, no such national study or investigation has ever been undertaken. Nor is there much likelihood of one. The basic reason is that it would step on too many toes; divorce has become a legal and moral right, and in most states divorces can be secured today with little cost or effort and no moral disapproval. Moreover, often led by the cultural and intellectual elite, national sentiment tends to accept a high rate of divorce as inevitable. As Frank F. Furstenberg, Jr., and Andrew Cherlin concluded in their recent book on the consequences of divorce, "we are inclined to accept the irreversibility of high levels of divorce as our starting point for thinking about changes in public policy."[59]

Few wish to return to the era of no divorce; some divorces are clearly desirable. The central problem is the so-called individualistic divorce when children are involved—typically one partner departs in order to achieve self-fulfillment, leaving the children in the lurch. The number of such divorces has greatly increased. Neither the state nor the market probably can do very much to remedy the problem; at best, they should avoid exacerbating the situation. Longer waiting periods for divorcing couples with children would probably help, combined with mandatory marriage counseling. Perhaps we should institute a two-tier system of divorce law; marriages between adults without minor children would be relatively easy to dissolve, but marriages between adults with children would not. Properly conceived family life and sex education in the schools might help. Rigorously enforcing economic child support from divorced fathers and stigmatizing "deadbeat dads" would probably yield more male responsibility, as well as marginally more money for children.

But the problem is at heart cultural, not political or economic. Married couples must increasingly come to believe that they live in a society where marriage and marital permanence are valued, and where divorce is to be undertaken only as a very last resort. And for that to occur, our cultural values must change. It is hard to imagine, for marriage and divorce, the kind of attitudinal and value changes that have occurred in recent decades with respect to gender roles, minority rights, the environment, and smoking, but changes in those areas certainly point out that rapid and relatively deep cultural change is possible. In our overmedicalized society, perhaps it would help to cast divorce as a health problem.[60] Data could probably be gathered easily showing that divorce is a more serious threat to public health than, for example, smoking.

How to get men to marry the mothers of their children in the first place is no less daunting a task than lowering the divorce rate. It rests on a combination of having fewer unplanned births through widespread birth control, and finding ways to lock the father into the union (at least when the child is young). The message to men must be loud and clear: if you father a child, you are obligated to provide economic, social, and emotional support both to the child and to the child-caring mother.

One of the few institutions still pushing today for strong nuclear families is religion, but even there the message has become compromised to appear more sensitive to "nontraditional" and "alternative" family forms. Liberals and especially feminists often support such compromises, partly in fear that society will shift back to the traditional nuclear family, with all of its rejected moral baggage. But there need be little fear of that; the real fear is how to prevent our society from culturally deconstructing into a sea of individualistic chaos, for that is the direction in which the trends of the past few decades have been carrying us.

Even when fathers and mothers marry and remain together, however, their problems may have just begun. Children are no longer valued by our culture at the highest level of priority, as they have been for most of our history. Parents are economically falling behind nonparents; they have enormous problems meshing their family and work lives and are faced with a local environment that is hardly conducive to childrearing. So effectively has the children-first cultural message been suppressed in favor of a do-your-own-thing individualism for adults, especially by the advertising and entertainment industries, that many parents speak of their own life-styles today in countercultural terms; it is them against the rest of the world.[61]

The income of families with young children has remained relatively stagnant for almost two decades, despite a doubling of women in the labor force. Whatever economic gains have been achieved for children stem mostly from having two parents at work and from the decrease in family size, both of which have now about reached their limits.[62] At the same time, the economic situation of the elderly has markedly improved. This anomaly is largely because the elderly have been handsomely rewarded through income redistribution (especially social security and medicare), while children have not. According to Peter Peterson and Neil Howe, who estimate that eleven times more benefit dollars per capita go to those over 65 than to those under 18, Americans have decided to socialize much of the cost of growing old, but very little of the cost of raising children.[63] By another estimate, 22.9 percent of the federal budget in 1987 went to support the elderly, while only 4.8 percent supported children.[64] Any serious consideration of equity or national interest underlines the need of childrearing families for economic assistance, and several ways to provide such assistance are currently on the national table. Many proposals involve a child allowance or tax credit/exemption for children, such as the $1,000 refundable child tax credit proposed by the bipartisan National Commission on Children, headed by Governor John D. Rockefeller IV.[65]

Parents of young children need time, however, even more than money. For children in America today there is a national time-famine, brought about mainly by father absence and by both husband and wife being in the labor force. Moreover, the arrival of a new baby instigates the most stressful period in the life course of most marriages. Having more time to adjust to the radically changed family situation would be beneficial not only to the child but to the marriage.[66]

Contrary to the predictions made earlier in this century, new evidence suggests that adults in their prime work years are spending more time on the job than ever before.[67] Estimates of the thirty-year decline in the time that parents spend with their children run as high as 40 percent.[68] As the working world currently is organized, a fundamental problem is the assumption that someone is home taking care of the kids. We should enact policies that make work more family-friendly, including parental leave, flexible hours, compressed work weeks, more part-time work (with benefits), job sharing, and home-based employment opportunities. Another possibility is more "career sequencing," in which parents deliberately postpone careers to provide more time for young children.[69]

Finally, many of the local environments in which children are being raised today are saturated with crime, materialism, and the loss of neighborliness, leading parents to despair.[70] Such problems can only be resolved, in the final analysis, by a reinvigoration of civil society.

The New Familism: A Hopeful Trend

One bright spot on the national scene is what some of us have called "the new familism," a growing belief by Americans that, yes, the family really is of central importance and worth preserving.[71] There are two groups primarily involved in this cultural minishift: the maturing baby boomers, now at the family stage of the life cycle and family oriented as never before, and the "babyboom echo" children of the divorce revolution, now coming into adulthood with a troubled childhood to look back on and a new resolve not to go down the same path their parents took. Spurred by growing evidence that recent family changes have hurt children, the middle-aged, child-rearing, baby boomers clearly have shifted the media in a more profamily direction. Only time will tell, however, about the echo-children of the 1970s. Some evidence suggests that the will to change is there: they tend to favor marital permanence more than their parents did, for example, perhaps because they do not take the family as much for granted as their parents (the children of the familistic 1950s) did.[72] But do they also have the psychological wherewithal to change, or will their insecure childhood remain personally damaging to them for the rest of their lives? Studies of the long-term effects of divorce and other recent cultural changes on children and adolescents provide no solace in regard to this question.[73]

A few other sociocultural factors and trends seem to be working in a profamily direction. One is AIDS, which has now demonstrably slowed the sexual revolution; as one entertainment figure recently said (with obvious dismay), "dating in Hollywood just isn't what it used to be." Neither is dating on the college campus, but the changes so far have not been remarkable. Possibly a more important factor, working paradoxically in a profamily direction, is the economic downturn. Just as affluence breeds marital breakup, so moderate economic decline may generate more family solidarity. The problem is that economic decline has two conflicting consequences on the family. One is the hunker-down attitude that is good for marital permanence; people look to their social ties for support, and they have fewer options to break apart from those ties. But the other is unemployment and the misery it brings, no one's prescription for a happy marriage.

Social theorists might add another explanation for the profamily trend. Cultural change is often dialectical and cyclical, and some cycles of change are patterned in generational terms.[74] Not all cultural values can simultaneously be maximized, and one generation comes to value, because they have less of it, what their parents' generation rejected. This may be happening today in the family, a shift away from individualism and choice and toward family and other social bonds. Pessimists might say that the new shift, if it really exists, will be short-lived. The long-run effects of affluence and cultural complexity on the promotion of individualism seem highly compelling. But the fact is, no one is able to predict the future, even something as relatively simple as foretelling the collapse of communism a year before it occurs.[75]

The strong belief that a cultural shift is occurring, away from radical individualism and toward collective values, might become a "culture-fulfilling prophecy." Certainly, public policy should posit such a shift as an overriding goal and do everything possible to encourage it. If my analysis is correct, this encouragement would mean measures to curtail the negative effects of affluence and cultural complexity, programs to foster nuclear families and natural communities while protecting them from unnecessary incursions of both the market and the state, and efforts to maintain national solidarity and a common culture. This is a tall order, to be sure, but one that is rooted in the fundamental nature of our predicament.

Notes

1.   National Commission on Children, *Beyond Rhetoric: A New American Agenda for Children and Families* (Washington, 1991); National Commission on America's Urban Families, *Families First* (Washington, 1993); Select Committee on Children, Youth, and Families, *U.S. Children and Their Families: Current Conditions and Recent Trends, 1989*, 101 Cong. 1 sess. (Government Printing Office, 1989); Isabel V. Sawhill, "Young Chil-

dren and Families," in Henry J. Aaron and Charles L. Schultze, eds., *Setting Domestic Priorities* (Brookings, 1992), pp. 147–84.

2.   See, for example, Pitirim A. Sorokin, *Social and Cultural Dynamics* (American Books, 1941).

3.   Pierre L. van den Berghe, *Human Family Systems: An Evolutionary View* (Prospect Company Heights, Ill.: Waveland Press: 1990/1979); Jane B. Lancaster and Chet S. Lancaster, "The Watershed: Change in Parental-Investment and Family Formation Strategies in the Course of Human Evolution," in J. B. Lancaster and others, eds., *Parenting Across the Life Span: Biosocial Dimensions* (Aldine de Gruyter, 1987), pp. 187–205.

4.   Urie Bronfenbrenner, "Discovering What Families Do," in David Blankenhorn, Steven Bayme, and Jean Bethke Elshtain, eds., *Rebuilding the Nest* (Milwaukee, Wis.: Family Service America, 1990), pp. 27–38; on survivors, see Emmy E. Werner, "Children of the Garden Island," *Scientific American*, vol. 206 (April 1989), pp. 106–08; and Emmy E. Werner and Ruth S. Smith, *Overcoming the Odds: High-Risk Children from Birth to Adulthood* (Cornell University Press, 1992).

5.   Kingsley Davis, ed., *Contemporary Marriage: Comparative Perspectives on a Changing Situation* (New York: Russell Sage Foundation, 1985); Martin Daly and Margo Wilson, *Sex, Evolution, and Behavior*, 2d ed., (Belmont, Calif.: Wadsworth, 1983); Mary Maxwell Katz and Melvin J. Konner, "The Role of the Father: An Anthropological Perspective," in Michael E. Lamb, ed., *The Role of the Father in Child Development* (John Wiley, 1981), pp. 155–85; and Ruth Busch, *Family Systems: A Comparative Study of the Family* (Peter Lang, 1990).

6.   Raoul Naroll, *The Moral Order: An Introduction to the Human Situation* (Beverly Hills, Calif.: Sage, 1983) p. 343.

7.   Ralf Dahrendorf, *Life Chances: Approaches to Social and Political Theory* (University of Chicago Press, 1979); and Daniel Yankelovich, "The Affluence Effect," in this volume.

8.   Francis Fukuyama, *The End of History and the Last Man* (Free Press, 1992), emphasizes this point, drawing on Hegel's notion that history is driven by "a struggle for recognition"–the intense desire of human beings to have their inherent worth acknowledged and respected.

9.   A cross-cultural analysis by Harry C. Triandis and others found that a family measure accounted for more variance between collectivism and individualism than any other. "The Measurement of the Etic Aspects of Individualism and Collectivism," *Australian Journal of Psychology*, vol. 38 (1986), pp. 257–67.

10.   Harry C. Triandis, "Cross-Cultural Studies of Individualism and Collectivism," in John J. Berman, ed., *Nebraska Symposium on Motivation, 1989*, vol. 37 (University of Nebraska Press, 1990), pp. 41–133.

11.   Brigitte Berger and Peter L. Berger, *The Wall over the Family: Capturing the Middle Ground* (Anchor Press/Doubleday, 1983); C. C. Harris, *The Family and Industrial Society* (George Allen and Unwin, 1983); Lawrence Stone, *The Family, Sex and Marriage in England 1500–1800*

(Harper and Row; 1979); Emmanuel Todd, *The Explanation of Ideology* (Basil Blackwell, 1985); and Emmanuel Todd, *The Causes of Progress: Culture, Authority, and Change* (Basil Blackwell, 1987).

12.   Margaret Mooney Marini, "The Rise of Individualism in Advanced Industrial Societies," University of Minnesota, 1991.

13.   Duane F. Alwin, "From Obedience to Autonomy: Changes in Traits Desired in Children, 1924–1978," *Public Opinion Quarterly*, vol. 52 (Spring 1988), pp. 33–52.

14.   Edward C. Banfield, *The Moral Basis of a Backward Society* (Free Press, 1958).

15.   Ronald Ingelhart, *Culture Shift in Advanced Industrial Societies* (Princeton University Press, 1990), p. 424.

16.   Robert N. Bellah and others, *Habits of the Heart: Individualism and Commitment in American Life* (University of California Press, 1985); and Bellah and others, *The Good Society* (Alfred J. Knopf, 1991).

17.   This is not the same as Ronald Ingelhart's well-known concept "postmaterialism," which involves the rejection of materialism. See *The Silent Revolution: Changing Values and Political Styles among Western Publics* (Princeton University Press, 1977); and Inglehart, *Culture Shift*.

18.   Christopher Lasch, *The Culture of Narcissism: American Life in an Age of Diminishing Expectations* (W.W. Norton, 1987); Bellah and others, *Habits of the Heart*; and Herbert Hendin, *The Age of Sensation* (Norton, 1975). On the decline of civil society, see Allan Wolfe, *Whose Keeper? Social Science and Moral Obligation* (University of California Press, 1989); Amitai Etzioni, *The Spirit of Community: Rights, Responsibilities, and the Communitarian Agenda* (Crown, 1993); and Philip Selznick, *The Moral Commonwealth: Social Theory and the Promise of Community* (University of California Press, 1992).

19.   David Popenoe, *Disturbing the Nest: Family Change and Decline in Modern Societies* (Aldine de Gruyter, 1988), chap. 13.

20.   Based on quantitative "quality of life" measure, Raoul Naroll determined Norway to be the world's best society. Naroll, *The Moral Order*, chap. 3. On happiness surveys, see Fritz Strack, Michael Argyle, and Norbert Schwarze, eds., *Subjective Well-Being: An Interdisciplinary Perspective* (Pergamon Press, 1991).

21.   Triandis, "Cross-Cultural Studies," p. 105.

22.   See, for example, Robert J. Smith, *Japanese Society: Tradition, Self, and the Social Order* (Cambridge University Press, 1983).

23.   America's civic individualism was stressd by the first analyst of American individualism, Alexis de Tocqueville, *Democracy in America*, ed. Richard D. Heffner (Penguin, 1956).

24.   Louis Harris, *Inside America* (Vintage Books/Random House, 1987).

25.   James S. House, "Social Support and the Quality of Life," in Frank M. Andrews, ed., *Research on the Quality of Life* (University of Michigan Press, 1986), p. 267, comparing adults in the 1950s with those in the 1970s.

26.   Andrew Oldenquist, *The Non-Suicidal Society* (Indiana University Press, 1988).

27.   David Riesman, "Egocentrism," *Encounter*, vol. 55 (August–September 1980), pp. 19–28.

28.   Paul Kennedy, *The Rise and Fall of the Great Powers: Economic Change and Military Conflict from 500-2000* (Vintage Books/Random House, 1987); and Bennett Harrison and Barry Bluestone, *The Great U-Turn: Corporate Restructuring and the Polarizing of America* (Basic Books, 1988).

29.   The 1989 data from the Organization for Economic Cooperation and Development show the U.S. figure to be 30.9 percent in 1989, compared with 38.5 percent in Britain, 47.8 percent in France, and higher still in the Nordic countries. *OECD Economic Outlook*, vol. 53 (June 1993), p. 216.

30.   This is the credo of communitarians. See Michael Sandel, *Liberalism and the Limits of Justice* (Cambridge University Press, 1982); Etzioni, *The Spirit of the Community*; and the journal *The Responsive Community*.

31.   This issue is explored more fully in David Popenoe, "The Social Roots of Declining Civic Virtue: Family, Community and the Need for a 'Natural Communities' Policy" (New York: Institute for American Values, 1992).

32.   The "natural communities" concept is closely related to the concept of protecting "social capital" in James S. Coleman, *Foundations of Social Theory* (Belknap Press, 1990), and of protecting "mediating institutions" advanced by Peter L. Berger and Richard J. Neuhaus, *To Empower People: The Role of Mediating Structures in Public Policy* (Washington: American Enterprise Institute for Public Policy Research, 1977).

33.   Zbigniew Rau, "Human Nature, Social Engineering, and the Reemergence of Civil Society," *Social Philosophy and Policy*, vol. 8 (1991), pp. 159–79.

34.   Daniel Bell, *The Cultural Contradictions of Capitalism* (Basic Books, 1976).

35.   Mary Ann Glendon, *Rights Talk: The Impoverishment of Political Discourse* (Free Press, 1991), p. 137.

36.   Nathan Glazer, *The Limits of Social Policy* (Harvard University Press, 1988).

37.   Arthur M. Schlesinger, Jr., *The Disuniting of America: Reflections on a Multicultural Society* (W.W. Norton, 1992).

38.   Chester E. Finn, Jr., *We Must Take Charge: Our Schools and Our Future* (Free Press, 1991). The difficulties in reaching agreement on "American values," of course, are considerable. See James Davison Hunter, *Culture Wars: The Struggle to Define America* (Basic Books, 1991).

39.   Robert B. Reich, *The Work of Nations: Preparing Ourselves for 21st-Century Capitalism* (Alfred A. Knopf, 1991).

40.   Moira Eastman, *Family, The Vital Factor: The Key to Society's Survival* (North Blackburn, Victoria: CollinsDove, 1989).

41.   Cited in Walter F. Mondale's foreword to Edward F. Zigler, Sharon Lyn Kagan, and Edgar Klugman, eds., *Children, Families, and Government* (Cambridge University Press, 1983), p. xi.

42.   Kathleen E. Kiernan, "The Impact of Family Disruption in Childhood on Transitions Made in Young Adult Life," *Population Studies*, vol. 46 (1992), pp. 213–34. See also National Commission on Children, *Speaking of Kids: A National Survey of Children and Parents* (Washington, 1991).

43.   Nicholas Zill and Charlotte A. Schoenborn, "Developmental, Learning, and Emotional Problems: Health of Our Nation's Children, United States, 1988," in National Center for Health Statistics, *Advance Data*, no. 190, November 16, 1990.

44.   Family history comes to an end just about where it started. As sociologist Pierre L. van den Berghe has noted, "Advanced industrial societies have recreated, through a long evolutionary path, much the same kind of mobile, seminomadic, nuclear, bilateral family . . . as existed in the simplest, smallest societies." *Human Family Systems: An Evolutionary View* (Prospect Heights, Ill.: Waveland Press, 1990/1979), p. 132.

45.   Richard A. Easterlin and Eileen M. Crimmins, "Recent Social Trends: Changes in Personal Aspirations of American Youth," *Social Science Research*, vol. 72 (July 1988), pp. 217–23.

46.   Walter R. Gove, Carolyn Briggs Style, and Michael Hughes, "The Effect of Marriage on the Well-Being of Adults: A Theoretical Analysis," *Journal of Family Issues*, vol. 11 (March 1990), pp. 4–35; and R.H. Coombs, "Marital Status and Personal Well-Being: A Literature Review," *Family Relations*, vol. 40 (January 1991), pp. 97–102.

47.   On the health effects of the nuclear family, see Leonard A. Sagan, *The Health of Nations* (Basic Books, 1987). On depression, see Gerald L. Klerman and Myrna M. Weissman, "Increasing Rates of Depression," *Journal of the American Medical Association*, vol. 261 (April 1989), pp. 2229–35. On social supports, see Nan Lin, Alfred Dean, and Walter M. Ensel, *Social Support, Life Events and Depression* (Orlando, Fla.: Academic Press, 1986). On subjective well-being, see Fritz Strack, Michael Argyle, and Norbert Schwarze, eds., *Subjective Well-Being*.

48.   James Q. Wilson, "Culture, Incentives, and the Underclass," in this volume.

49.   George Gilder, *Men and Marriage* (Gretna, La.: Pelican, 1986).

50.   Susan Cotts Watkins, Jane A. Menken, and John Bongaarts, "The Demographic Foundations of Family Change," *American Sociological Review*, vol. 52 (June 1987), pp. 346–58.

51.   See Barbara Dafoe Whitehead, "Dan Quayle Was Right," *Atlantic* (April 1993), pp. 47–84.

52.   Urie Bronfenbrenner, "Discovering What Families Do," in Blankenhorn, Bayme, and Elshtain, *Rebuilding the Nest*, pp. 27–38.

53.   John Bowlby, *Attachment and Loss*, 3 vols. (Basic Books, 1969, 1973, 1977); and Willard W. Hartup, "Social Relationships and Their De-

velopmental Significance," *American Psychologist*, vol. 44 (February 1989), pp. 120–26; Cindy Hazan and Phillip R. Shaver, "Love and Work: An Attachment-Theoretical Perspective, *Journal of Personality and Social Psychology*, vol. 59 (1990), pp. 270–80; Mary D. Salter Ainsworth, "Attachments beyond Infancy," *American Psychologist*, vol. 44 (April 1989), pp. 709–16; Robert S. Weiss, "The Attachment Bond in Childhood and Adulthood," in Colin Murray Parkes, Joan Stevenson-Hinde, and Peter Maris, eds., *Attachment across the Life Cycle* (London: Tavistock/Routledge, 1991), chap. 4; Phillip R. Shaver and Cindy Hazan, "Adult Romantic Attachment: Theory and Evidence," in D. Perlman and W. Jones, eds., *Advances in Personal Relationships* (London: Jessica Kingsley, 1993), chap. 4.

54. Carol E. Franz, David C. McClelland, and Joel Weinberger, "Childhood Antecedents of Conventional Social Accomplishment in Midlife Adults: A 36-Year Prospective Study," *Journal of Personality and Social Psychology*, vol. 60 (1991), pp. 585–95; and John Nordheimer, "For Lovers, No. 1 Activity These Days Is Worrying," *New York Times*, February 12, 1992, p. C10.

55. Nancy Eisenberg and Paul H. Mussen, *The Roots of Prosocial Behavior in Children* (Cambridge University Press, 1989).

56. Norval D. Glenn, "The Family Values of Americans," Working Paper 2 (New York: Council on Families in America, Institute for American Values, 1991), p. 6.

57. Larry L. Bumpass, "What's Happening to the Family? Interactions between Demographic and Institutional Change," *Demography*, vol. 27 (November 1990), pp. 483–98.

58. Paul R. Amato and Alan Booth, "The Consequences of Divorce for Attitudes toward Divorce and Gender Roles," *Journal of Family Issues*, vol. 12 (September 1991), pp. 306–22.

59. Frank F. Furstenberg, Jr., and Andrew Cherlin, *Divided Families: What Happens to Children When Parents Part* (Harvard University Press, 1991), p. 105.

60. Thanks to Barbara Dafoe Whitehead for making this observation.

61. Barbara Dafoe Whitehead, "Maryland Focus Group Report on Family Time," Working Paper 6 (New York: Council on Families in America, Institute for American Values, 1991).

62. "Families on a Treadmill: Work and Income in the 1980s," A staff study prepared for the use of members of the Joint Economic Committee of the U.S. Congress, January 17, 1992; Frank Levy and Richard C. Michael, *The Economic Future of American Families: Income and Wealth Trends* (Washington: Urban Institute Press, 1991); Frank Levy, *Dollars and Dreams: The Changing American Income Distribution* (Basic Books, 1987); and Diane J. Macunovich and Richard J. Easterlin, "How Parents Have Coped: The Effect of Life Cycle Demographic Decisions on the Economic Status of Pre-School Age Children, 1964–87," *Population and Development Review*, vol. 16 (June 1990), pp. 301–25.

63.   Peter G. Peterson and Neil Howe, *On Borrowed Time: How the Growth in Entitlement Spending Threatens America's Future* (San Francisco, Calif.: ICS Press, 1988), p. 11.

64.   Sylvia Ann Hewlitt, *When the Bough Breaks: The Costs of Neglecting Our Children* (Basic Books, 1991), p. 14.

65.   National Commission on Children, *Beyond Rhetoric: A New American Agenda for Children and Families* (Washington: Government Printing Office, 1991); and Elaine Ciulla Kamarck and William A. Galston, *Putting Children First: A Progressive Family Policy for the 1990s* (Washington: Progressive Policy Institute, 1990).

66.   Carolyn Pape Cowan and Philip A. Cowan, *When Partners Become Parents: The Big Life Change for Couples* (Basic Books, 1992).

67.   Juliet B. Schor, *The Overworked American: The Unexpected Decline of Leisure* (Basic Books, 1992).

68.   William Mattox, Jr., "Running on Empty: America's Time-Starved Families with Children," Working Paper 5 (New York: Council on Families in America, Institute for American Values, 1991).

69.   For a wide range of useful child policies, see Hewlitt, *When the Bough Breaks*. For sequencing, see Arlene Rossen Cardozo, *Sequencing* (Collier Books, 1986); and Felice N. Schwartz, *Breaking with Tradition: Women, Management, and the New Facts of Life* (Warner, 1992).

70.   See Richard Louv, *Childhood's Future* (Houghton Mifflin, 1990).

71.   David Popenoe, "Fostering the New Familism," *Responsive Community*, vol. 2 (Fall 1992), pp. 31–39.

72.   Kristin A. Moore and Thomas M. Stief, "Changes in Marriage and Fertility Behavior: Behavior Versus Attitudes of Young Adults," Washington, Child Trends, 1989.

73.   Judith S. Wallerstein and Sandra Blakeslee, *Second Chances: Men, Women, and Children a Decade after Divorce* (Ticknor and Fields, 1989); and Peter Wilson, "The Impact of Cultural Changes on the Internal Experience of the Adolescent," *Journal of Adolescence*, vol. 11 (1988), pp. 271–286.

74.   Zvi Namenwirth and Robert Weber, *Dynamics of Culture* (London: Allen and Unwin, 1987); and William Strauss and Neil Howe, *Generations* (William Morrow, 1991).

75.   Timur Kuran, "'Now Out of Never,' The Element of Surprise in the East European Revolution of 1989," *World Politics* (December 1991), pp. 7–48.

Multiculturalism and Public Policy

Nathan Glazer

What central questions for the relationship between public policies and values does the present conflict over multiculturalism raise? If one is guided by the intensity of the response among leading scholars and public figures, and major organs of public opinion, then clearly many people feel that the recent proposals for more multicultural content in school and college curricula threaten to change, in some important ways, how we conduct our democracy and public affairs, how we live together in a common nation, and how we manage a productive economy. In each case, the threat is one of divisiveness overcoming and superseding a healthy diversity. No one argues against diversity: neither Arthur Schlesinger, Jr., nor Diane Ravitch, the educational historian and former assistant secretary of education, nor Albert Shanker, president of the American Federation of Teachers, nor the writers of cover stories for *Time* and *Newsweek*.[1] All have been critics of the well-publicized, more extreme trends in multiculturalism. They see a threat of disunity politically, of "fraying" culturally, or of greater interethnic and interracial conflict among students and citizens generally.

More than disunity is feared, however, though that is the first and central concern. The critics also see a fatal disregard for truth, for the mechanisms by which agreement on reality—call it "the scientific method"—is reached. In the insistence of multiculturalists that the role of the West—Western thought, Western philosophy, Western achievements—has been exaggerated, and that this exaggeration has damaged those whose origins are not in European countries, critics see a challenge to the means by which rational men and women agree on the nature of reality and the truth. They ask, is not a mechanism for reaching agreement on truths, science, the chief heritage of the West?

The fears are real, the alarm is great, and the consequences for America can be substantial. The proponents of multiculturalism, however, argue that diversity is the greatest strength of America and that further recognition of this diversity and its ever greater reach will not harm polity, culture, or economy—quite the contrary, America will be strengthened by it. The more vociferous proponents claim that the injustice of racial discrimination is being perpetuated in the curriculum and that they do not challenge the truth—they rather seek to establish a truth that has been ignored, hidden, the more extreme say "stolen."

Quite a bit is wrapped up in this brief, initial effort to describe what is at stake for values in the argument over multiculturalism. The potential outcomes for America are not the only issue in the debate over multicultural education. Less debated, but equally important, is the question of what has changed in the values of Americans or in large segments of the American population, that has led to this call for what seems to be a radical overhaul in the way our children are educated? Multiculturalism, whatever it is, or will be, has consequences for values, but multiculturalism itself arises from value change. Both sides have to be addressed, and both sides are significant for public policy.

This chapter will not be equally responsive to every part of this broad-ranging debate. The discussion will be limited to the key institutional area in which it is most sharply raised, education, and even there will be limited. Thus, one might consider the mix of students, racially and ethnically, an issue in multiculturalism, but we generally use the terms "segregation" and "integration" to consider this issue. A changing mix of students need have no effect on curriculum or on the culture of school and college. Certainly it was not expected, in those distant days when the United States first set out on the effort to desegregate schools, that one consequence would be a change in curriculum. Blacks hoped to have schools just like whites, in facilities, in finances, in textbooks, in curricula, and in achievement. I believe the same was true in the first efforts to integrate colleges. Today we know the changing mix of students does have consequences for curriculum, and so to some extent this issue arises in a discussion of multiculturalism.

Nor will the chapter consider much, as an issue of multiculturalism, the selection, placement, and promotion of staff, teachers, principals, faculty, and administrators. These issues are generally raised under the rubric of discrimination and affirmative action. But just as in the case of the changing mix of students, these issues do have consequences for curriculum, for multiculturalism. More black teachers, it is argued, are needed because they will change the way the school and college go about their business. Even if such teachers have no intention of changing curriculum and school and college atmosphere, the mere fact they are black, raised in a somewhat different setting and culture, will make them different from white teachers. Whether they are more empathetic or understanding, or stricter and more demanding, how they act will stem from some interaction between their black background and how they see and respond to black students.

The rules under which schools operate, especially in issues of discipline, raise issues of culture and multiculturalism, but they are not the central arena for the present severe dispute. That central arena deals with how history and the social studies and the humanities are to be taught. These issues have fueled debate over the rewriting of curricula and the creation of new textbooks in New York, California, and nationally and are the central focus of this chapter.

The Central Challenge of Multiculturalism: Identity and Effectiveness

The largest question multiculturalism raises is how we are to understand our nation and its culture. This understanding does have specific policy consequences in areas far from education, for example, immigration policy. As Daniel Yankelovich has pointed out in this volume, one of the most striking changes of the past thirty years has been the increasing acceptance of pluralism as a central American value—the acceptance of all races, both sexes, and different lifestyles as being equally good and deserving of respect and of protection against discrimination. Nevertheless, one finds struggling against this massive change in attitudes and accompanying policies some attitudes, somewhat repressed, and held by a minority, that this country should remain primarily a white, or Christian, or Anglo-Saxon, nation.

The discussion of multiculturalism cannot evade this key issue of American identity. The issue is being thrashed out most openly in the field of education. There we see a substantial movement to change what has been done in the past, an effort that in the eyes of many is already remarkably and unfortunately very successful, with possibly significant effects on the children and students subjected to it.

As a result, numerous threats are foreseen. The central one, I have pointed out, is the threat of disunity, but this danger has to be specified. What kind and how much unity does a nation need and for what purposes? The threat is not seen, it would be generally agreed, as one of dangerous disaffection in war or sympathy with potential enemies. (This was the chief concern in World War I and led to the near eradication of German as a subject of instruction in school. It was a concern in World War II and led to the incarceration of the Japanese-American population.) The threat of disunity is seen as one of *internal* disaffection and conflict. The image is not that of the Germans in World War I or the Japanese in World War II, but the Croatians and Serbians, the Armenians and Azerbaijanis, the Russians and Ukrainians today—or the French- and English-speaking Canadians. Of course our disunity cannot take precisely these forms, if only because our ethnic and racial groups are not as sharply concentrated geographically as any of these contending groups, but one can envisage a dangerous degree of conflict among intermingled groups.

Perhaps numerous Americans, particularly those who are poor and have been subjected to discrimination, will receive an education that attributes blame for their condition to the white or European majority, thus contributing to political and social splits along racial and ethnic lines even more severe than those we see today. Students could become hostile to the major institutions of state, economy, and culture, which they will see as designed to hold them down. "Oppression studies," as proponents label multiculturalism, will lead not only to disunity but to an active hostility among some minorities to the key institutions of state and society, making effective government, as well as the rise of such groups economically, more difficult. Disunity, distrust, disharmony, sum up the first group of possible effects of multiculturalism.

A second set of effects, linked to this first one, is of a somewhat different order. Opponents of multiculturalism worry about the effectiveness of an education with a strong multicultural content. By "effectiveness" I mean, will it raise the educational achievement of minority students who are the chief concern of multicultural advocates? Will multicultural studies make them more effective students and participants in the economy? We know little about the answers to these questions.

And a third issue, does multiculturalism teach untruths? We have seen a great deal of attention to Afrocentrism, one variant of multiculturalism, which argues that there are deficiencies in the education of blacks and whites because of the neglect or worse of Africa. Afrocentrist advocates charge that Africa's achievement in civilization has not only been neglected but has been hidden because of active prejudice and malice, and even further has been "stolen." Now one question here is about truth, a sound understanding of the past. Truth is an absolute value, whatever its effects. (But as will be seen, whether truth is an absolute value in elementary and secondary school is open to question. In a school setting other values such as socialization and the instilling of good citizenship may be considered important enough to lead authorities to shade the truth.)

Teaching students distortions of the truth or even absolute lies cannot be good. But this issue of truth is mixed up with a fourth question, that of self-esteem among students and its relationship to their capacity to learn. The opponents of multiculturalism argue that the proponents are willing to tolerate or advocate the teaching of distortions and lies to prop up the self-esteem of students from groups doing poorly, in particular African Americans. The proponents say that distortions and lies have already undermined the students' self-esteem, and they want to restore this esteem through unveiling a concealed and empowering truth.

The role of truth as an absolute value must be considered when we take up multiculturalism. In some areas, there is no argument about truth—or hardly any. Whatever the African contribution to mathematics, and regardless of whether our system for numbers is originally Indian, Arabic, Babylonian, or African, there can be no admittance of different conclusions on the basis of culture as to how to use numbers for practical ends. The reasons that bridges stand are undoubtedly the same, whether in Asia, Africa, or Europe.

One possible threat of multiculturalism is the simple depreciation of studies, such as mathematics and science, that are essential to economic effectiveness and participation in a modern technical society, and that do not lend themselves easily to multicultural adaptations. Among extreme Afrocentrists there is an effort to adapt even those parts of the curriculum, apparently to make them more user-friendly to black students. But these subjects have never been taught from the point of view of their history or their origins or their great contributors: they are taught as truths or skills divorced from origins, sources, or individual contributors.

In view of the nature of the tests that states and independent testing organizations create for certifying high-school completion or capacity for college work, I doubt that such adaptations will ever enter in large measure into such tests and affect teaching very much. (I may be wrong, as some efforts by some advocates have already been made to affect the tests.) Some attempts are being made to explore deficiencies that are common among blacks and perhaps other groups in their understanding of mathematics. Should teaching methods adapted to address these deficiencies be called multiculturalism? Such teaching certainly involves a sensitivity to various subcultures. Eleanor Wilson Orr's fascinating book, *Twice as Less: Black English and the Performance of Black Students in Mathematics and Science*, discusses these questions.[2] But whatever Orr's efforts to understand why some black students understand and try to solve mathematical questions differently, her aim is to get them to the one, correct, result. Roger Brown's commendation on the back flap of the book jacket describes it as a discussion of "the possibility that subtle nonstandard understandings, . . . of prepositions, conjunctions, and relative pronouns, can impede comprehension of basic concepts in mathematics and science."

One problem in multiculturalism not much discussed is its effect on the "majority," however conceived. Minorities as commonly understood—blacks, Hispanic Americans, Asian American, Native Americans—make up only a quarter of the country. In large stretches of the country—the suburbs, the small towns, the Great Plains—minorities are not much in evidence. One already hears from teachers that some nonminority students grumble over multicultural emphasis. This reaction points to a perhaps more serious problem of potential disunity and conflict than that evoked by the unlikely scenarios of the threat of an American Quebec or Yugoslavia. Multiculturalism is a movement of the cities, a response to problems in the education of minorities, particularly blacks. Blacks are concentrated in the large central cities, whose school systems now consist overwhelmingly of black and Hispanic students. By contrast, other school systems have few minority students.

Clearly the pressures for multicultural education in the large central cities, whose school superintendents and school boards are dominantly from minority groups, will be greater than elsewhere. In the worst case, one can imagine one kind of education in the social sciences and humanities for the cities and another kind of education for the rest of the country. This prospect is not a happy one. Avoiding it clearly requires some compromise—more education about minorities and minority viewpoints and perspectives in the curricula of schools where minorities are little in evidence, while students in the central cities are taught that there is a larger nation out there, different from the central cities with their huge minority populations. These problems of racial separation are of course far beyond the capacity of schools alone to settle.

Dominating orientations toward this issue among many participants in the debate is the memory of a school system that at one time tried to create unity out of difference and apparently did so very effectively. Immigrant students in the tenements of Manhattan learned that George Washington and Thomas Jefferson were their forefathers, sang of amber waves of grain they had never seen, and learned about Indian predecessors who could track game and enemies soundlessly. Education need not be immediately "relevant." We know of many successes of classic and traditional education in inner cities. Homer and Shakespeare and Hiawatha can be as absorbing to black and Hispanic-American students as they were to Irish or German or Jewish or Italian predecessors in those same schools. One must admire and support such enterprises. But I do not believe we can avoid the demand for "relevance" in our transformed central city schools. Demands arise primarily because of demographic change but also because so much else in society has changed, such as our views of authority, of the relations between children and teachers and principals, of sex, and of the very nature of the United States and its place in the world.

We must continue to be concerned about the divisiveness a more responsive education introduces: divisiveness among groups, between cities and the rest of the country, and the possibility of backlash. We already see a backlash in the rise of Christian schools, which are responding less to multicultural education than to the elimination of public education's commitment to traditional values.

Yet other conflicts attest to another interesting problem: the ever-expanding scope of multiculturalism. The explosion against the multicultural curriculum "Children of the Rainbow" in New York City in 1992-93 was less against its principal aim of teaching about racial and ethnic minorities than against the inclusion of gays and lesbians among the groups entitled to equal respect. The conflation of gays and lesbians with ethnic and racial minority groups—as in the debate over gays and lesbians in the army—raises many difficult questions. Parents who were willing to accept a multicultural curriculum dealing with ethnic and racial minorities rebelled against enrolling gays and lesbians as part of the multicultural spectrum. To them they were minorities defined by morally deviant practice, not by morally neutral race and ethnic difference.

It is hard to estimate how successful this attempt to expand multiculturalism will be. Notably, the most radical change in the curriculum in social sciences and humanities in recent decades has been the inclusion of women and women's issues. The women's movement has transformed texts and tests to a greater degree than has multiculturalism strictly considered. Critics of multiculturalism will often grumble about this change too, but it has nothing to do with race and ethnicity, nor does it raise the questions about potential divisiveness that multicultural education strictly considered does. But the surprising success of the women's movement should alert us to the possibility that the gay-lesbian movement may yet affect curriculum.

These arguments over curriculum convey how difficult it is to settle these issues by an appeal to truth, or, what truth becomes in the social sciences and humanities, the best judgment of scholars. The scholars themselves diverge and divide; many of them today in the universities attack with great influence the notion of the primacy of an unchallenged truth or interpretation in our understanding of the history and present state of the world and the nation. They question the usefulness or value for education of what have been considered classics and deemed essential for the curriculum for every child.

Issues of identity are central in education: we are supposed to form the child and his sense of himself. Yet so much modern social and literary theory dissolves or destroys any notion of identity. Even while these theories loosen or destroy traditional (or, to use their language, "privileged") notions of identity, they privilege some ident-ities over others: sexual and ethnic and racial over national and religious and (often sex-linked) occupational identities. And yet the latter have been central in education. How will they survive the onslaught of multicultural educational reform? Should they?

Certain end-values, we could call them, are not much in dispute: higher educational achievement for all groups, a measure of civil harmony, concern for the nation as a whole, at least to some extent, as against the interest of one's own group alone, competence in performing the tasks that are basic to economic productivity, all of which require other supporting values—truthfulness, punctuality, ability to communicate, fulfilling agreements and contracts, and so on. It is not easy to separate these end-values, or objectives, from the values that support them, but we generally feel that in some ways our capacity to effectively fulfill these end-values has been undermined by failures in education. The evidence for this failure is not overwhelming, but popular opinion blames the increasing looseness of school requirements, school discipline, and school cur-ricula of the end of the 1960s and the 1970s with a decline in the effectiveness of American education. So we have seen recently, in the 1980s, an increasing emphasis on new tests intended to monitor progress or attest publicly that students have reached some level of achievement and a shift to more required and uniform courses in the curriculum (though by no means a reversion to the practices of the 1950s and earlier). We are concerned about how multicultural-ism in education is changing both the end-values to which education has been directed and the subordinate values that assist in reaching any end in education.

A New Word for an Old Problem

Multiculturalism is a new word for an old problem in American public education. The problem is how public education is to respond to and take account of the religious, ethnic, and racial diversity of public school students. Public education in the United States, at least that part of it in our major cities, has never been free of this issue. With the origins of urban public education in the 1840s, the first of the "great school wars," as Diane Ravitch calls them in her history of New York City public education, broke out.[3] It centered on the demands of Catholic leaders for something like equal treat-ment for Catholic students. As historians have pointed out, a prin-cipal aim of urban public education, which was the creation of re-formers of Protestant religious background, was the socialization of children into the Protestant moral and religious world of the mid-nineteenth century. Catholic religious leaders objected in particular to readings from the Protestant King James Bible. Why not the Catholic Douay translation? (No one dreamed, in those distant days, that the First Amendment to the Constitution, with its prohibition of an "establishment of religion," would in time be used to ban all bible reading in schools and even to prohibit a moment of silence if its motivation had some taint of religion about it.) The outcome of the conflict was that Catholics decided to establish their own schools, to the degree their capacities allowed, and they did create a sepa-rate, Catholic system of education in the major cities of the country.

In the 1880s and 1890s, we again find serious public disputes that today we would call multicultural. They centered on the rights of German children to receive instruction in German. Teaching in German was widely established in Cincinnati, St. Louis, and elsewhere, to the discomfort of nativists and those concerned with the assimilation of immigrants. In 1889, the historian David Tyack tells us, Illinois and Wisconsin "tried to regulate immigrant private and parochial schools by requiring that most instruction be conducted in English. As in the case of Protestant rituals in the schools, the contest over instruction in languages other than English became a symbolic battle between those who wanted to impose one standard of belief and those who welcomed pluralistic forms of education."[4]

The First World War, with its encouragement of a fierce national (or was it ethnic?) chauvinism, finished off the acceptance of German as a language of instruction in public schools. Nevertheless, during the buildup to entry into the war, and in response to the attacks on "hyphenated Americanism" by Woodrow Wilson and Theodore Roosevelt, the first serious arguments for multiculturalism in American education were set forth. Hyphenated Americanism meant to its attackers less than undivided loyalty to the United States.

"Cultural pluralism" was the term Horace Kallen, a student and follower of John Dewey, used to describe a new kind of public education, in which a variety of cultures besides that of England would receive a significant place in American public education. His essay, "Democracy versus the Melting-Pot," appeared in *The Nation* in 1915. Randolph Bourne, a young journalist of the time, who had written a book on the progressive, Dewey-influenced, Gary schools, and who was admired by Van Wyck Brooks and Lewis Mumford, among others, about the same time made a similar case in the *Atlantic Monthly*, in an essay titled "Transnational America."[5] John Dewey himself in 1916, speaking to the National Education Association, took up the cudgels for cultural pluralism.

> Such terms as Irish-American or Hebrew-American or German-American are false terms, because they seem to assume something which is already in existence called America, to which the other factors may be hitched on. The fact is, the genuine American, the typical American, is himself a hyphenated character. It does not mean that he is part American and that some foreign ingredient is then added. It means that . . . he is international and interracial in his make-up. He is not American plus Pole or German. But the American is himself Pole-German-English-French-Spanish-

Italian-Greek-Irish-Scandinavian-Bohemian-Jew—and so on. The point is to see to it that the hyphen connects instead of separates. And this means at least that our public schools shall teach each factor to respect every other, and shall take pains to enlighten us all as to the great past contributions of every strain in our composite make-up.[6]

So spoke the exemplary American philosopher from Burlington, Vermont, in 1916. But if Dewey, Kallen, and Bourne influence the history of multiculturalism, they do so only as advocates without any direct effect on the schools. The wave of postwar chauvinism that led to the deportation of East Europeans to Bolshevist Russia in the postwar "Red Scare," to the banning of mass immigration in 1924, and to the revival of the Ku Klux Klan in the 1920s was too strong. In 1919 Nebraska banned the teaching of any foreign language before the eighth grade (the Nebraska courts exempted Greek, Latin, and Hebrew, all presumed safely dead). In the 1920s Oregon tried to ban any private schools at all. Both laws were overturned by the Supreme Court.[7] In the public schools, Americanization was the order of the day and prevailed without a check through the 1920s, 1930s, and 1940s, while the children of the last great wave of European immigration were being educated.

I attended the schools of New York City from 1929 to 1944 (I include the public City College of New York in that stretch), and not a whiff of cultural pluralism was to be found. The public schools of New York City were then two-thirds or more Jewish and Italian in student composition, but no Jewish or Italian figure was to be found in our texts for reading or writing, for literature, for social studies, or for history. This background, which many older Americans have experienced, of a strong, unself-conscious, self-confident Americanization, in which all cultures but that of the founding English and its American variant were completely ignored, and in which students were left to assume, if they thought about the matter at all, that the cultures of their homes and parental homelands were irrelevant or inferior, is crucial in the current debates over multiculturalism. For many protagonists in this debate, the creation in conflict of the Catholic parochial school system, the abolition of German-language public schools, and the arguments for multiculturalism in the age of mass immigration are all a murky prehistory, wiped out in a flood that deposited a uniform silt over our past, leaving only fossil remains of that earlier diversity and those earlier conflicts. This is true for both the advocates and opponents of multiculturalism today. Advocates often do not know they had forebears, opponents often do not know that the education they experienced was the expression of an age singularly free of conflict over issues of cultural pluralism or multiculturalism.

The arguments for cultural pluralism began to emerge again in World War II, and the motivating force was Hitler. If he argued that one race and one people were superior and should be dominant, if he spread hatred of Jews and Negroes, and if we were at war with him, then it was in the interest of the war effort to teach the opposite: all peoples were equal, and tolerance must be extended to all. In the 1940s, a modest movement for intercultural education sprouted. Its aim was to teach something about the various ethnic and racial groups that made up America and to teach tolerance. Just how extensive it actually was in the schools is not clear, but neither the word nor the movement survived the fifties.[8]

The issues of the 1950s and 1960s pushed cultural pluralism aside. Educators had to deal with the shock of Sputnik, and after 1954 the issue of desegregation and the overcoming of legal segregation in the South and de facto segregation in the North.

There was something of a contradiction between desegregation, as then envisaged, and cultural pluralism. Black and liberal civil rights leaders wanted to provide the *same* education for all. Blacks would now get the education that whites had previously received. The education of white students had precious little of cultural pluralism or multiculturalism in it. Why should that be changed for blacks? The black objective, through the entire course of the struggle in the courts in the 1940s and 1950s for equality, was assimilation. Blacks should not be treated differently because of being black.

But that aim was transmuted very rapidly into the demand of many militants that blacks must get something different because they are black. By the late 1960s a black power movement, black Muslims, and other manifestations of black nationalism were already challenging the assimilationist civil rights leadership, black schools were started in black communities, and some were even established under the aegis of liberal public school systems (as in Berkeley). Mexican Americans and Puerto Ricans raised their own grievances against the public school system, and political activists in particular demanded the recognition of Spanish. Civil rights laws that guaranteed equality were interpreted by the Supreme Court to mean that equality for those speaking a foreign language could require instruction in that language; liberal states passed laws giving a limited right to instruction in one's native language, and federal laws and regulations and court decisions made that instruction a requirement in many school systems.

Bilingualism is not the same thing as multiculturalism, but it was taken for granted that instruction in one's native language for those speaking Spanish also meant some instruction in Puerto Rican or Mexican culture and history. Through the 1970s, bilingualism and the acknowledgment of distinctive group cultures and histories in social studies and history spread and established themselves in the public schools.

Multiculturalism in the 1970s and 1980s no longer was much concerned with European immigrants or ethnic groups. European mass immigration never recovered, even after immigration reform in 1965. Immigration became overwhelmingly Asian, Latin American, and Caribbean. Assimilation had radically transformed the children and grandchildren of European immigrants. If a few voices were raised in the 1970s from representatives of these groups, claiming "us, too!", there was very little response, and quite properly, from the public schools. One can find Russian and Italian bilingual classes in New York, Portuguese in Fall River, Armenian in Watertown, but these classes are understood to be temporary adaptations. No one expects that full-scale bilingual and bicultural programs for European groups will be established. The issue of multiculturalism today affects primarily the Spanish-speaking groups from Latin America and the Caribbean, whose numbers have grown hugely in the 1970s and 1980s. But above all it affects blacks.

One might well ask, why did multiculturalism become such an important issue in the early 1990s? At least twenty years ago public schools started adapting to the presumed cultural distinctiveness and interests of two major groups in the public schools, blacks and Hispanics, by modifying textbooks, introducing new reading materials, changing examinations, and instructing non-English-speaking students from Spanish-speaking families in Spanish for a few years.

What has happened to put the issue on the agenda today, not only in the public schools, but in colleges and universities, public and private?

I believe the basic explanation is that we have seen in the late 1980s a buildup of frustration in the black population over the failure of civil rights reforms to deliver what was expected from them. In the colleges, affirmative action, well established as it is, has not increased markedly the number of black instructors or the number of black students who can qualify for the more selective institutions without special consideration. In the public schools, we have seen some modest improvement in black achievement as measured by National Assessment of Educational Progress scores, Scholastic Aptitude Test scores, and high school completion rates. But the gaps between black and white achievement remain large. Blacks on the whole do worse than Hispanic groups, even though one might expect the achievement of Hispanics to be lowered by the very large numbers of non-English-speaking immigrants of recent years. Blacks score far below the various Asian groups. One can record a substantial measure of black achievement in politics, in the armed forces, in the civil service, and in the gaining of some high positions in the private economy, but alongside these successes has been a continuance of a host of social problems afflicting a large part of the black population, problems that by some key measures have grown, not declined, in the past twenty years.

One might have expected the multicultural debate to be fueled by the large new immigration (not by any means as large as the immigration of the first two decades of this century) of the past twenty years. But that is really not the moving force. The Asian immigrants, who make up half the total number of immigrants, seem quite content with the education they get. If there are demands for more Asian recognition or Asian content in the curriculum, they come from assimilated and native-born militants, not from immigrants and their representatives. What has agitated the Asians is not the absence of their native cultures and languages from school curricula but rather the discrimination they have detected in recent years in admission to selective colleges and universities. Most seem content with a Eurocentric curriculum, as multiculturalist activists call it. The science and mathematics to which Asians are often drawn as offering the best opportunity for them to display their assiduity and talents and provide access to good jobs is the same in all languages.

The Hispanics or Latinos—the preferred term is shifting from the former to the latter—consist of at least four major groups, each with somewhat different interests and orientations. Mexican Americans, the largest, consist of some people that have been settled in the United States for some time, some for centuries, and large numbers of new immigrants. In time the immigrants learn English and lose interest in Mexico. While it is premature to say their development will be similar to that of older European immigrant groups, that is not an unlikely prospect. Their assimilation is affected by the continuing massive immigration from Mexico, their geographical closeness to Mexico, and the prevailing atmosphere of grievance that is encouraged for all so-called minority groups by the media, militant leaders, and indeed by the legal advocacy of rights to bilingualism and multiculturalism. All these circumstances will slow their assimilation. Yet I do not think their demands on the public school system mean any radical change is needed. They would like to see their children do better in school and to have more of them graduate. But there is no strong commitment among Mexican immigrants to the idea that this objective will be enhanced by more teaching in Spanish or more Mexican cultural and historical content in their children's studies. Some activists call for this change. But that is not the prevailing view. If the Mexican Americans do poorly, they can explain it by their class position and the predominance of new immigrants. Both will change over time.

The Puerto Ricans, concentrated in New York, do even worse economically and perhaps educationally than Mexican Americans. One reason is their frequent movement back and forth between Puerto Rico and the mainland. As citizens they are not required to break from the homeland and make the commitment to a new land and language that immigrants must make. Puerto Rican leaders do call for more bilingualism and more Puerto Rican content in the curriculum. Even so, they do not approach the militancy of black advocates.

Cubans now dominate Miami and Dade County, politically and educationally; they have power to influence the schools there. What they want seems to be a sound education with a large admixture of culturally distinctive content in the curriculum. Other Latin Americans—they are now as numerous as Puerto Ricans in New York City—seem very much like earlier immigrants. They want to get ahead through the schools and see no special need to transform them culturally.

Blacks are the chief proponents of multiculturalism. Some black educational leaders have also developed a variant of multiculturalism, Afrocentrism, which is perhaps the most alarming development to those who are skeptical about multicultural education. Just as the black pride movement of the late 1960s and early 1970s led to imitation among other groups, so does the present movement lead to imitation. I do not question the motives of Native American, Latino, and Asian educators who call for more information in the curriculum about their groups and about their cultures. But I cannot believe we would see the present uproar over multiculturalism were it not for the frustration among blacks over widespread black educational failure, which leads them to cast about for alternatives, new departures, new approaches, anything that might help, including special schools for black boys featuring an Afrocentric education.

Much has been and might be said about the new multicultural thrust in the colleges and universities—the replacement of a required Western civilization course at Stanford by somewhat different courses with more focus on minorities, third world peoples, and women; the establishment of required courses on American minorities at the University of California, Berkeley, at the University of Minnesota, at Hunter College, and elsewhere; sit-ins in many institutions demanding more black faculty and more black studies. I concentrate, however, on the elementary and secondary public schools. The situation is more serious there because the issue is the content of required courses that all students must take and be tested on and that will make up their entire education in social studies and history and English. In the colleges, presumably, there will always be courses in American and European and Asian history and literature that are not affected by the political pressures stemming from America's racial situation. But the question is, will such an education be possible in the public schools in the wake of varied multicultural demands?

The New York Story

The debate over multicultural education has reached the peak of stridency in New York State, but it would be a mistake to consider the situation in New York State unique. It seems true that every issue of racial and group conflict becomes exaggerated in New York City, and multicultural education is no exception. Perhaps it is because New York City is our most diverse city (though Los Angeles by now can claim almost as much diversity), and New York State has been until recently our most diverse state (California now challenges it), or because New York City is the center of the mass media and has developed a particularly acerbic style of ideological conflict.

The New York State controversy has been exacerbated by several political errors and misjudgments by a new state commissioner of education, Thomas Sobol. His appointment disappointed black and Latino state legislators, who had hoped the time had come for a black or Latino commissioner. Perhaps to show his responsiveness to their concerns, he appointed various committees to consider issues affecting blacks and Latinos, among them a curriculum committee. This committee included primarily black and Latino educators and advocates, and it employed as one of its consultants one of the most extreme and militant Afrocentrists, Professor Leonard Jeffries, chairman of the Department of Black Studies at the City College of New York. Its report, *A Curriculum of Inclusion*, denounced "Eurocentric" education in unmeasured language, exuded hostility to what it considered European dominance, and called for a distinctive education for each racial and ethnic group (the Europeans being lumped as one), which would cover not only social studies but all fields of the curriculum. Its content and tone can be grasped from the first sentences of the executive summary: "African Americans, Asian Americans, Puerto Ricans/Latinos, and Native Americans have all been the victims of an intellectual and educational oppression that has characterized the culture and institutions of the United States and the European American world for centuries. Negative characterizations or the absence of positive references have a terribly damaging effect on the psyche of young people of African, Asian, Latino and Native American descent."[9]

The report was fiercely attacked. Leading the attack was the historian Diane Ravitch, who had long been engaged in reforming the teaching of history in order to emphasize the narrative thrust of history rather than murky social studies concepts, and in order to emphasize the more positive elements of American history, its democracy, constitutionalism, inclusiveness, and tolerance. She had recently completed work as a primary author on a revision of the California social studies curriculum that expressed the kind of emphases she felt desirable in the teaching of American history. Diane Ravitch, along with the distinguished historian Arthur Schlesinger, Jr., and joined by other leading American historians, issued a statement denouncing the report. They wrote, "The report, a polemical document, viewed division into racial groups as the basic analytical framework for an understanding of American history. It showed no understanding of the integrity of history as an intellectual discipline based on commonly accepted standards of evidence. It saw history rather as a form of social and psychological therapy whose function is to raise the self-esteem of children from minority groups."

Most of the signers of the statement attacking *A Curriculum of Inclusion* are well-known liberals. The statement insists that the signers are committed to "a pluralistic interpretation of American history and support for such shamefully neglected fields as the history of women, of immigration and of minorities." But, it asserts, "we are after all a nation—as Walt Whitman said, 'a teeming nation of nations'." (Note that even those who call for a nation-building curriculum acknowledge American diversity.)[10]

A Curriculum of Inclusion was an easy target because of its intemperateness and its espousal of very doubtful claims of African primacy in various fields. It was attacked not only by historians but by the leading newspapers of New York City and the state.

A second committee, more balanced (its members included some leading historians, such as Arthur Schlesinger and Kenneth Jackson, who were critics of the first committee report, but also a leading Afrocentrist, Asa Hilliard III, and the African political scientist Ali Mazrui), was now appointed to repair the damage of the first. I was also a member of this committee. It met during 1990–91. Its report was more moderate. It was titled *One Nation, Many Peoples: A Declaration of Cultural Interdependence.*[11] But it did not escape denunciation almost as fierce as that which greeted the first report. Battle lines had already been set by the first report, positions had been chosen, and the context in which the second committee operated made it impossible for it to produce a document that would gain acceptance among the critics of the first. Consider the political realities. The committee had to moderate the extreme positions of the first document. But to withdraw too far would lead to denunciation by black and Latino advocates, and, after all, the entire enterprise had been launched to respond to their complaints and concerns.

On the whole, the new report, wending its way in educationese through various uncontroversial themes, as is typical of all educational curricular reports, avoided inflammatory language. But the report, in its effort to move away from but not too far from the first, mainly emphasized multiple perspectives in the teaching of history. And these multiple perspectives were to be ethnic and racial: the perspectives of American Indians, blacks, Mexican Americans, Asian Americans, and others. How a common history would emerge from these perspectives, which were to be critically examined by schoolchildren, was not clear. The report did point to common elements in American history and society but rather weakly: "The social studies will very likely continue to serve nation-building purposes, among others, even as we encourage global perspectives. With efforts to respect and honor the diverse and pluralistic elements in our nation, special attention will have to be given to those values, characteristics, and traditions we share in common." The report also said, "The program should be committed to the honoring and continuing examination of democratic values as an essential basis for social organization and nation-building." When the report spoke of the Constitution and the Bill of Rights, it emphasized the struggle to achieve and realize rights, rather than celebrating these charters as guaranteeing them.

The report and the entire multicultural enterprise were attacked in a cover story in *Time* magazine, in a long editorial in *The New Republic*, and elsewhere.[12] Governor Mario Cuomo also attacked it. On the whole, its reception was hostile. One reason is the nature of press reporting on such reports. Press reporting tends to focus on who says what about a report, who attacks and who defends it. This report, because of its relative blandness, had few items the press could seize on. But in its efforts to indicate how language in syllabi or texts could be more sensitive, the report was unwise enough to suggest that the term "enslaved persons" could replace "slaves" and that Thanksgiving should be seen from the point of view of the

Indians as well as the pilgrims. These were easy objects of attack and ridicule. In general, the entire stance of press and media treatment is to emphasize differences rather than commonalities, conflict rather than areas of agreement, and to polarize issues even more than they already are by selecting or publicizing extreme statements. Multiculturalism is no exception to this pattern. Afrocentrism has many variants and could mean many things, but to the press it means only outlandish nonsense (of which there is unfortunately a good deal).

Matters did not end with the second report. Curriculum revision is a long-term enterprise. The commissioner of education and the board of regents of New York State then set a further course for curriculum revision by preparing a statement that steered the recommendations of the report, *One Nation: Many Peoples*, in a more moderate direction, and by setting up a Council for Curriculum and Assessment, with subordinate committees for each curricular area, which have been producing their own reports. (I served for a while on the committee dealing with the social studies.) There is still no new social studies curriculum for the state of New York. While the controversy has died down somewhat, the issue remains as controversial as ever, both in New York State and elsewhere. Nevertheless, American elementary and secondary school education seems to be lurching glacially toward multiculturalism, hardly cognizant of the powerful counterattacks that have been launched against the movement.

Can Truth Alone Guide Us?

What posture is one to take toward this controversy? Undoubtedly the most respectable one is defined in the statement by the historians in criticism of the first New York State report, *A Curriculum of Inclusion*. In effect, those historians say, we should teach the truth and let the chips fall where they may. The historians' statement emphasizes the autonomy and independence of history as a discipline establishing truths. It criticizes the committee that produced the first curriculum report because it included no historian. It insists on the integrity of history as an intellectual discipline based on commonly accepted standards of evidence. But it acknowledges at the same time that history has "shamefully neglected . . . the history of women, of immigrants, and of minorities."[13]

Whether the distinguished signers really believe this I am not sure; history has certainly not neglected these topics for the past twenty-five years. But the political realities made it necessary for them to say it. Having made the necessary acknowledgement, they went on to say, "We have an equal commitment to standards of historical scholarship. We condemn the reduction of history to ethnic cheerleading on the demand of pressure groups." They then state another deep concern: the "contemptuous" dismissal of the Western tradition by the New York State committee. They point out, "The Western tradition is the source of ideas of individual freedom and political democracy to which most of the world now aspires." They acknowledge that "the West has committed its share of crimes against humanity, but the Western democratic philosophy also contains in its essence the means of exposing crimes and producing reforms." Finally, they assert "little can have more damaging effect on the republic than the use of the school system to promote the division of our people into antagonistic racial groups. We are after all a nation," and they quote Walt Whitman on a "teeming nation of nations."[14]

Clearly there are two souls struggling in this statement. One soul is that of commitment to historical truth as best established at any given time by a body of professional historians, who must come to some general agreement even though much at any point remains disputed and controversial and even though agreements shift over time. But the statement cannot rest itself on truth alone. If it could, one's task would indeed be easy. Hard as it may be to define the truth, there are those best qualified to tell us what it is at any given time. One consults authorities and comes to the best judgment one can on the basis of their judgments. The criticism, however, contains political concession, as well as concern for the truth. It is careful to acknowledge "shameful neglect" of certain fields of study, even though in the past two or three decades these subjects have not been neglected at all—who can keep up with the volume of work on women's, immigrant, and minority history?

The statement also expresses concern over "the use of the school system to promote the division of our people into antagonistic racial groups." National unity is an eminently desirable objective. But what is its relationship to the primary objective of historical truth? Does it mean we will take into account in composing our truthful history whether some truths will promote divisiveness? (This consideration certainly affected the teaching of history in the erstwhile Soviet Union and Yugoslav federation. Presumably other truths will now be taught in the successor states.) Even in our democratic and open society, one can see how certain political objectives could lead us to emphasize or deemphasize various elements in our history. Do we insist on the self-corrective role of the Western liberal tradition, or do we accentuate the role of conflict, sometimes bloody conflict, and still continuing conflict, in making for correction? I know what I prefer. Yes, acknowledge the crimes, but insist that most of that is behind us and that we live in a continuously improving society that is coming ever closer to the good society envisaged by our founding documents. I think that is where the truth lies. I do not know how I could persuade someone who insists that there is still much to be done, that our freedoms and our equality are always in peril from malign forces, and that the founding promise is still unrealized.

Thus even a statement in defense of the autonomy of historical truth (the *Newsday* reprint of this statement is headed, "Don't Subject History to Political Revamping") has some political objectives and takes account of some political realities in its rhetoric and concessions. We have always had political, social, and moral objectives in elementary and secondary school education, and our teaching of history has never been free of them. We may personally prefer the history texts of the 1930s and 1940s, with their strong narrative thrust, their emphasis on the main political line of American history, their celebration of the virtues and triumphs of American society and polity, and their very modest attention to issues of race. But a good deal has happened since that time. The issues of class interest and conflict debated by the historians of the thirties have found their way to some extent into history texts, the story of immigration plays a larger role, we pay much greater attention to women, we pay much greater attention to race, and European history has been swallowed up in "global studies."

How does one persuade those convinced that reform has not yet gone far enough? How does one demonstrate that consensus and harmony have played a larger role in American history than conflict and dissent, or really any other central thesis in American history?

Of course the determination of what should be taught in history must take account of scholarship and must not teach falsehoods. But to some extent political objectives will determine the history we prefer, and different groups will have different political objectives. The only solution, in an age of dissent in which the authority of educators is much reduced, is a political solution. In the lower schools, the teaching of history is always something more than the teaching of the truth as established by the consensus of scholarship, and I do not see how we can escape that. (Even the most extreme of the multiculturalists, however, would insist that what drives them is also the search for the truth, a suppressed truth. Some of them argued the first report should have been labeled not *A Curriculum of Inclusion* but *A Curriculum of Truth*.)

In the course of this conflict over the New York State curriculum, I referred to what appeared at the time to be a much more harmonious and successful effort to reform a state social studies curriculum. In California a curriculum revision was carried through with deliberation and care by a highly professional group that included Diane Ravitch, the strongest critic of *A Curriculum of Inclusion*. I find the California proposals admirable.[15] Their major substantive goal is given as "democratic understanding and civic values," and the first specification under that goal is "national identity." The framework reads as follows.

> To understand this nation's identity, students must: Recognize that American society is now and has always been pluralistic and multicultural. From the first encounter between indigenous peoples and exploring Europeans, the inhabitants of the North American continent have represented a variety of races, religions, languages, and ethnic and cultural groups. With the passage of time, the United States had grown increasingly diverse in its social and cultural composition. Yet, even as our people have become increasingly diverse, there is broad recognition that we are one people. Whatever our origins, we are all Americans.[16]

The first subtheme under national identity is "understand the American creed as an ideology extolling equality and freedom." The only individual quoted under this theme (or indeed in the entire section on national identity) is Martin Luther King, Jr. The subthemes call for the curriculum to "Recognize the status of minorities and women in different times in American history; Understand the unique experiences of immigrants from Asia, the Pacific Islands, and Latin America; Understand the special role of the United States in world history as a nation for immigrants; Realize that true patriotism celebrates the moral force of the American idea of nation that unites as one people the descendants of many cultures, races, religions, and ethnic groups." Multiculturalism seems dominant even in a curriculum proposal that, despite general approval, was attacked for not being multicultural enough.

The excellent California *History-Social Science Framework* emphasizes narrative history, rather than fuzzy concepts in social studies or social problems. It also emphasizes positive features in American history and brings into the social studies material on the role of religion that was banned in an earlier excessively cautious effort to comply with the separation of church and state. The *Framework* was applauded widely. Initially, there were few attacks on it. Textbooks were produced in response to the framework and accepted by the California State Board of Education. California is one of the states that approves textbooks (New York does not). Nevertheless, the textbooks aroused storms of controversy as being inadequate in their treatment of the history and character of various religions and racial and ethnic groups and were rejected by the one large California city that is dominantly black, Oakland.[17]

The story is worth telling for two reasons. First, even the most balanced and professional effort to define a curriculum for students in American schools today will place a heavy emphasis on multiplicity and diversity, race and ethnicity. That is our reality today. Although there are many differences between the California framework and the second New York State report, *One Nation, Many Peoples: A Declaration of Cultural Interdependence*, a Martian, or a Frenchman, might be impressed by the similarities. Second, whatever efforts we make to include all the strands that make up American society, we will not in the present state of affairs avoid conflict. The admirable California texts will be rejected by some cities, attacked in almost all.

We are serving three masters in social studies: truth, national unity, and civil harmony. The first two seem somewhat short-changed by our concern for civil harmony.

I have been concentrating on the social studies curriculum, but similar changes are going on in the teaching of English and litera-ture and have been occurring for a long time. These changes have aroused more controversy at the college and university level than at the elementary and high-school level. Many books have been written on these controversies over the "canon," whether we need it, what should be in it, the role of Western classics in it, and the like. But changes proceed apace at the lower levels of schooling too. There the question is not as simply formulated as in the social sciences, where the critics of change have recourse to the ultimate value of truth. Can any similar value be used as the criterion to select poems or essays or books to be read? Questions of literary worth are even more debatable than questions of historical fact and judgment. But on the whole similar issues arise. "Privileged" texts are challenged and replaced by writing by women and minority authors. It is as difficult to find out how extensive these changes are in classrooms across the nation as to find out how these controversies over social studies curricula are reflected in classroom teaching.

Where Is Multiculturalism Headed?

I believe that the key issue that determines the acceptability of these curricular changes to the critics of a strong multiculturalism is a judgment about the underlying purpose of the curriculum re-form. Is it to promote harmony, acceptance of our society as good and fair? Or is it to promote a view of our society as fatally flawed by racism, irredeemably unfair and unequal, and thus to be rejected as evil? The critics of multiculturalism fear that the second vision underlies the strong multicultural position. In part, they are right. But if we look further into the objectives of those who strongly pro-mote multiculturalism and who in doing so present a somewhat lopsided view of our history, we will find that they promote it not because they aim at divisiveness and separatism as a good, not because they want to break up the union, but because they aim at a fuller inclusiveness of deprived groups. Proximately, their vision may well mean more conflict and divisiveness, but they see this outcome as a stage to a greater inclusiveness. They are no Quebec separatists, Croatian nationalists, Sikh or Tamil separatists. They seek inclusion and equality in a common society. Their view of the principles that should govern this equality may be disputed, but that brings us to such issues as affirmative action, ethnic studies, and yes, multiculturalism, not to issues of fundamental and irreconcilable division of the kind we have faced in the past.

We are quite far in the present dispute from the naive and unrealistic separatists of the late 1960s and early 1970s. Frustration at the failure to bring a larger share of blacks into the common society drives multiculturalism today.

This may appear—I know it will—to the critics of the new multiculturalism as far too benign a judgment on the underlying intentions of its proponents and on its possible effects. Undoubtedly one can point to some leading or at least notorious figures—Asa Hilliard III, Leonard Jeffries—whose intentions are not benign. Jeffries would like to accentuate the split between Jews and blacks, both would teach a racial interpretation of history, reviving the worst of nineteenth-century racist anthropology, and both would propagate fantastic views and illusions as truth. And they do have followers in the world of education, some supporting them out of a misguided view that anything to enhance black self-image is a good thing, others giving support because of white guilt over the black condition, and others, among blacks, supporting them because they are convinced that "they"—the hidden powers—are plotting to destroy blacks through drugs and AIDS—a point of view that is alarmingly widespread among the black population. These views must be fought—the racial interpretation, the excessive enhancement of the role of black Africa in world history, and the belief in malevolent plots and conspiracies.

I am not too confident about what even vigorous denunciation can do: We have not done very well in affecting the widespread view among whites (as well as blacks), and the educated as well as the uneducated, that some vast conspiracy lies behind the assassination of John F. Kennedy. Why shouldn't many blacks believe the same thing about the assassinations of Malcolm X and Martin Luther King?

But I would emphasize that we deal with a spectrum of views in multiculturalism, some reasonable enough to gain the endorsement of Diane Ravitch, Arthur Schlesinger, and Albert Shanker, and some of the extreme character of the positions of Hilliard and Jeffries. Even on the middle ground there is a good deal to argue about, especially content and presentation. Much has been made of the reference in the New York State history syllabus to the presumed fact that the framers of our Constitution were influenced by their knowledge of the Iroquois confederation (as most of us know it) on the writing of the American Constitution. (The preferred name for the Iroquois is now the Hodenosaunee, and that is how they are referred to in the syllabus.) Possibly, there is a fragment of reality around which this story is built. One wonders how great the harm is if this view is part of a high school history syllabus. If it is totally concocted, without a fragment of evidence, it might still be told as a story to grade-school children who are learning about Native American life and culture. Perhaps it would become something like the story of George Washington and the cherry tree and would do no greater harm. Curriculum writers will have to argue about this kind of decision.

History is becoming much more of a battleground than it was earlier, but there are many reasons, aside from multiculturalism, for this development. We are seeing the rise of a new history, of immigrants, of minorities, of women, and of gays and lesbians. Such trends often begin in anger but end in scholarship and in incorporation into college curricula. In time, this change begins to influence, at the margins, high school history. Another change is the generally greater sophistication with which we now view America's role in the world. The United States is not God's country anymore. We can lose wars, we can be beaten in economic competition by the Japanese, and we can become only one of several economically powerful, democratic countries, and not in every respect the best. We see the larger reality of the non-Western world. A good deal of it is sunk in poverty and political disorder, but some of it is teaching lessons in economic effectiveness to the West. Western hubris can never again be what it was in the late nineteenth and early twentieth century. In the West confidence in science and irreversible progress is declining, as is religious faith. And there are other changes.

Perhaps there is simply more debunking than there used to be, although we should all remember that debunking is an old American word. But all these trends affect the teaching of history in high schools. Attributing the changes that the teaching of history is undergoing solely to multiculturalism or Afrocentrism gives these movements too much credit.

My assessment of the possible effect of these trends may well be too benign, but I view them in light of the alarm over disunity that they have aroused. Perhaps I take too extreme an outcome (civil war among ethnic and racial groups?) as a test against which to estimate their effects. One can think of lesser effects that are serious enough. For example, greater hostility could occur between blacks and whites, and among other ethnic and racial groups. But I do not think this hostility, which was evident in the early days of desegregation, long before any multiculturalism affected school curricula, is the result of a multicultural curriculum. We should not exaggerate the effects of the content of teaching in history and the humanities. Were Americans better patriots when Lincoln and Washington were on the school walls (instead of Martin Luther King and Cesar Chavez), and if they were, was it for that reason?

There is almost no empirical evidence on the consequences of promoting multiculturalism in schools. One problem in studying such effects is that multiculturalism can mean many things, from somewhat greater attention to immigrants and blacks to the notorious Portland Baseline essays, which spout a good deal of nonsense and have been adopted as ancillary teaching materials in Portland, Oregon, and some other school districts.[18] How can we study the effects of multiculturalism? From history, we know that Catholic schools, which must have taught a rather different American history, turned out Americans as good and patriotic as those who emerged from public schools. Whatever the intentions of school curricula, American culture overwhelmingly leads to assimilation and homogenization.

One of the arguments for multiculturalism is that it will raise self-esteem, and that self-esteem will raise educational achievement. This area is as murky as most in educational research. We have no evidence that learning about one's group raises one's self-esteem or that raising self-esteem raises the educational achievement of a group, and the experience of Jews and Asians is devastating counterevidence. These groups encountered nothing in their education to raise their self-esteem as members of a minority ethnic or racial group yet did well in school.

Millions of dollars have been spent on research in bilingual education. But the objective of almost all this research is the effects of bilingual education on achievement, not on self-esteem, and not on the role of a raised self-esteem, if any, on educational achievement. Bilingual education is relevant because it is given in the home language and will almost always have some component dealing with group history and culture in a positive way. But no clear results on the effect of bilingualism on self-esteem can be drawn from the research, nor from the research on self-esteem conducted for the California Commission on Self Esteem.

Yet we should not rest there. Perhaps educational materials emphasizing heroes and role models might be helpful in raising the self-esteem of groups who have suffered radically reduced self-esteem because of their experiences. But we certainly have no evidence on the effectiveness of such an endeavor.

Regardless of the scantiness of the research results, blacks and others are going to get a good deal of multicultural content in their studies. They already do get it, and it is hard to see how the tide will be reversed in the big cities where black and Latino students form a large majority of the students, and black and Latino administrators increasingly dominate the top echelon. Our strong localistic traditions of education mean big-city school systems can and will respond to the shifting moods of educational professionals and of parent groups.

Parents are not the primary enthusiasts of multicultural education, but they are ready to try anything—uniforms, schools for black boys, Afrocentric curricula, schools of choice, or other innovations—and those who oppose these trends will not be the parents of the children in the schools or even in many places a majority of the voters. They will be an elite telling the big-city school leaders what they should do for the good of the country and how to be faithful to the truths of history. They will get a great deal of publicity for their views but will not I think win on the ground.

The teaching profession is playing the major role in institutionalizing multiculturalism in the schools. It was a sobering experience to review the computerized ERIC file (which covers a great deal of material from educational periodicals and many state and school district reports and publications) under the heading "multiculturalism." Of some 160 items in over a year and a half, there was only one piece that raised critical questions about this movement, a paper by Diane Ravitch. I do not know or understand all the reasons why educators and teachers favor multiculturalism. In our New York State committee, there was not a single teacher or administrator critical of multiculturalism. Whether from big cities or small, the ghettoes or the suburbs, they took it for granted that multiculturalism was the way to go. In our committee, the only debate on the subject was carried on by the academic members, who have no responsibility for or participation in public schools.

In view of the strength of these trends, one is left only with the hope that our nation and its unity can and will survive them. The Catholic schools, once feared as a threat to national unity, produced Americans as patriotic or more patriotic than the norm. Even Amish, Hasidic, and Black Muslim schools, while I do not know whether they produce patriots, turn out citizens as good by many measures as those produced by the public schools. Our diversity has one major binding force in the Constitution, under which we live, and which still, through the procedures it laid down and that have been developed in our history, governs at the margins what we can do and can not do in our public (and indeed private) schooling. It guarantees that the Amish need not attend schools after the age when they feel their children will be corrupted, and that the Mormons and the Black Muslims can teach their own variant of the truth, which is as fantastic to many of us as the furthest reaches of Afrocentrism. Even the most dissident call upon the Constitution for protection, and we are far from a situation in which people are ready to tear it up as a compact with the devil. This common political bond keeps us together: nationalists and antinationalists, Eurocentrists and Afrocentrists, and may continue to do so through the storms of multiculturalism.

Perhaps I am giving too much credit to our common political procedures and understanding. It would certainly be worthwhile to learn more about multiculturalism, to move the debate from curricular philosophies to the actual practice of education as it is affected by multiculturalism. Censuses of what is going on in classrooms in

American history and in literature would be desirable. What subjects are being covered? What books and essays are being read? At a more sophisticated level, we need research on the effects of various practices. Does more attention to African materials raise self-esteem among blacks? Is there any relationship between self-esteem and achievement? The longer-range effects of curricular change are of course unavailable to research. But one can ask about attitudes toward the United States, its role in the world, the degree to which it is worthy of respect or defense. In view of fears that multiculturalism produces a nation of victims, one could try to inquire whether multicultural curricula lead students to believe hard work does not matter and that their fate is dependent solely on their race or ethnic group.

We already know a good deal about what our children know (or do not know) on the basis of results from various tests. We might be able to relate overall achievement to the presence or absence of multicultural curricula. After the storm and fury of recent debate, it would be worthwhile finding out just what is going on. It is a long stretch from state curriculum committees to curriculum change, from new curricula to new texts, from texts to what the teachers actually teach, from what teachers teach to what children learn, and there is good deal of slippage at every point along the way.

But that multiculturalism has come as far as it has is not to be attributed simply to the soft-headedness of educators or the intemperance of minority advocates. America is changing. Its population is changing in racial and ethnic composition, its values are changing, its notions of the proper relation of groups and individuals to the national society are changing. It is hard to see how the educational orientations in the fields of the social sciences and humanities of the first half of this century can survive in the face of these changes.

Notes

1.   Arthur Schlesinger, Jr., *The Disuniting of America: Reflections on a Multicultural Society* (Norton, 1992).

2.   Eleanor Wilson Orr, *Twice as Less: Black English and the Performance of Black Students in Mathematics and Science* (W. W. Norton, 1987).

3.   Diane Ravitch, *The Great School Wars: New York City, 1805–1973* (Basic Books, 1974).

4.   David B. Tyack, *The One Best System: A History of American Urban Education* (Harvard University Press, 1974), p. 109.

5.   Horace Kallen, "Democracy versus the Melting Pot," *Nation*, February 18, 1915, p. 190; and Randolph Bourne, "Trans-national America," *Atlantic*, vol. 118 (July 1916), p. 86.

6.   Horace M. Kallen, *Culture and Democracy in the United States: Studies in the Group Psychology of the American Peoples* (New York: Boni and Liveright, 1924), reprints Kallen's essay and the speech of John Dewey from which the quotation is taken, pp. 131–32; Randolph Bourne's essay can be found in Randolph Bourne, *The History of a Literary Radical and Other Papers* (New York: S. A. Russell, 1956).

7.   *Meyer* v. *State of Nebraska*, 262 U.S. 390 (1923); and *Pierce* v. *Society of Sisters*, 268 U.S. 510 (1925).

8.   For a brief characterization of the movement see Nathan Glazer, *Ethnic Dilemmas, 1964–1982* (Harvard University Press, 1983), pp. 102–07.

9.   *A Curriculum of Inclusion*, Report of the Commissioner's Task Force on Minorities: Equity and Excellence (Albany: New York State Education Department, July 1989).

10.   The letter was published in a number of places, among them the New York newspaper *Newsday*, June 29, 1990, p. A15, and that is the source from which I quote.

11.   This report, which was printed, was published in June 1991. *One Nation, Many Peoples: A Declaration of Cultural Interdependence: The Report of the New York Social Studies Review and Development Committee* (Albany: New York State Education Department, June 1991).

12.   Paul Gray, "Whose America?" *Time*, July 8, 1991, pp. 12–17; and "Mr. Sobol's Planet," *New Republic*, July 15 and 22, 1991, pp. 5–7.

13.   *Newsday*, June 19, 1990.

14.   Ibid.

15.   *History-Social Science Framework for California Public Schools, Kindergarten through Grade Twelve* (Sacramento: California Department of Education, 1988).

16.   *History-Social Science Framework*, p. 20.

17.   David Kirp, "Textbooks and Tribalism in California," *The Public Interest*, no. 104 (Summer 1991), pp. 20–36.

18.   The Portland Baseline Essays, commissioned by the Portland, Oregon, public schools to provide supplementary teaching materials in various fields on the contributions of Africa and Africans, range from the fully disreputable (in science) to the competent, but they have often been cited as an example of how standards of truth and reliability are debased in multiculturalism and Afrocentrism. They are curricular materials that may be available from the Portland public schools.

Public Spirit in Political Systems

Jane Mansbridge

Were the much-maligned Sophists of ancient philosophy really the first modern political economists? Because little of the Sophists' own work remains, we must deduce primarily from Plato and other detractors that these philosophers saw the state only as an instrument for increasing the material well-being of its members. Aristotle described the Sophists as arguing that it is "the end [goal, *telos*] of the state to provide an alliance for mutual defence against all injury, or to ease exchange and promote economic intercourse." This kind of purely instrumental political association, he charged, "sinks into a mere alliance," and "law becomes a mere covenant," instead of being, "as it should be, a rule of life such as will make the members of a polis good and just."[1] At least some of the Sophists seem to have linked this view of the state as an alliance for defense and economic advancement with a view of human nature as purely or primarily self-interested. They may also have believed that political values could be reduced to self-interest: Thrasymachus argued, in Plato's formulation of his words, that justice was no more than the interest of the stronger.[2]

I would like to thank the Russell Sage Foundation and the Center for Urban Affairs and Policy Research for making available the time to write this chapter, and William Galston for helpful comments.

In the United States today the debate continues, often with the same link between a view of the state as no more than an alliance for economic advancement and the assumption that a state need be built on no more than self-interest. I will argue against this link. Even if one adopts a view of the state in which political arrangements exist only to increase material well-being, an efficient state will still require a good deal of public spirit, rather than pure self-interest, among its citizens.

Solving Problems through Public Spirit

Public spirit, the political form of altruism, produces effective solutions to the problem of cooperation in collective action dilemmas. In many situations, including the market, each individual acting self-interestedly produces a common good. In certain dilemmas, however, each individual's acting in his or her narrow self-interest makes it impossible to achieve a collective good.[3] In these situations one can institute some form of authority to punish defection and reward cooperation, or use other strategies to make cooperation "pay" in narrowly self-interested terms. Love and duty, however, also accomplish the same result. If I make your good my own through empathy (love), I will be less likely to act in ways that hurt you. If I make the collective good my own (love of nation), I will forgo my individual benefit for that good. If I am committed to a principle that for one reason or another prescribes cooperation, I will forgo self-interest for reasons of duty.

Altruistic motivation comes in these two distinguishable forms. One, which I call love, connotes an emotional attachment to another individual or collective through which an actor makes the other's good his or her own. The second, which I call duty, connotes a rational commitment to a principle or set of principles. Several scholars have independently divided altruistic motives into these two forms, each giving the pair a different set of names: affection and principle, sympathy and commitment, love and duty, empathy and morality, we-feeling and conscience, or solidary and purposive motivations.[4]

Solving collective action problems through love and duty rather than through punishment or material reward has certain costs.

Those motivations are less susceptible to compromise and negotiation than the motivation to gain material benefit. However, solutions based on love and duty, that is, altruistic solutions, are also usually cheaper, require less monitoring, and are more adaptable than solutions based solely on material sanctions. When participants in a system develop an emotional attachment or moral commitment to a cooperative goal, they will tend to adopt whatever policies they think will promote that goal, adapting themselves to situational changes rather than requiring a fixed schedule of regulations and sanctions. In the many cases where great adaptability is needed, effective monitoring is not possible, or the cost of effective sanctions is too high, altruistic solutions are the only feasible solutions to collective action problems.

Most existing forms of social organization rely on mixtures of material sanctions and altruistic motivations. The systems that produce the most cooperation often stress altruistic values in conjunction with a backup system of incrementally graded, relatively certain sanctions. Altruistic values produce most of the cooperation, while sanctions keep the purely self-interested from making suckers of the altruists.

Observers can easily underestimate the degree of altruism necessary to make a polity, or any organization, operate effectively. First, we underestimate the incidence of altruism dramatically if we define all behavior as self-interested, using the criterion of revealed preferences: if an action were not in some sense in one's interest, one would not do it. The problem here is that analytic and moral reasoning requires some distinction between self- and other-regarding actions. After defining all motives as self-interested, we then have to distinguish between self-regarding self-interest and other-regarding self-interest. But the seemingly harmless definitional move of calling all behavior self-interested on the grounds that some self decided to do it often slides into a substantive underestimation of the prevalence of "other-regarding self-interest."

Second, we underestimate the prevalence of altruism if we count as altruistic only behavior that is demonstrably opposed to self-interest. Human beings often spend considerable effort making their duty, love, and self-interest coincide. Altruism thus plays a role—sometimes a major role—in much behavior for which some self-interested explanation could be found. Although social scientists studying altruism can definitively demonstrate its occurrence only when someone acts in ways that defy any feasible interpretation of self-interest, identifying only such instances as altruistic would mean recognizing only a fraction of the altruism actually operating in social interaction.

Categorizing an act as altruistic or not is not just an academic exercise, but has practical consequences. Social psychologists have observed that, at least in the United States, modeling altruism tends to produce altruism in those who observe the model. Reducing the number of times people see or hear about others acting altruistically should, in the same way, reduce incentives to act altruistically.[5]

Private Spirit Can Lead to Political Breakdown

Not only in emergencies, when some citizens must find it in themselves to give their lives for their country, but also in an infinite number of daily individual choices, successful polities cannot work on the basis of purely private spirit. Although the "American genius for politics" has always been thought to describe designing political institutions that required only self-interested motivation, none of the framers of the Constitution believed that the Republic could survive without a healthy leaven of "virtue" in the characters of its representatives and its citizenry.[6] Without what the framers called virtue (and I here call public spirit), for example, elections would not be possible, regulatory compliance would dwindle, and Congress would self-destruct.

As B. F. Skinner pointed out, the chance that one man's vote will decide the issue in a national election "is less than the chance he will be killed on his way to the polls."[7] The odds of making a difference through one's vote are, from a rationally self-interested perspective, not worth any voter's trouble. If every voter acted only on the basis of self-interest, therefore, very few people would vote.[8]

Regulatory strategies based only on self-interest also often destroy what they hope to improve. Systems based on negative sanctions are particularly likely to foster an organized subculture of resistance to regulation. Sanctions can produce a game of "regulatory cat-and-mouse" in which regulated businesses defy the spirit of the law by exploiting loopholes, and the regulators write more specific rules to cover the loopholes. The result is often an incoherent accretion of rules, a "barren legalism concentrating on specific, simple, visible violations to the neglect of underlying systemic problems" and a system unable to adapt to new technologies and environments.[9]

In the United States Congress, it is in each individual's narrow self-interest to devote most of his or her time to constituency service, personal contact with voters in the constituency, and attracting media attention. If each individual acted this way, however, no one would do sufficient "homework" in any area of specialization to give the members of Congress enough expertise to judge the policy recommendations of their staff, the experts testifying before their committees, and the information that interest groups produce.

Similarly, it is in the interest of each individual member of Congress to blame the country's ills on the venality of Congress in general and the other members of Congress in particular, painting him or herself as the sterling exception. But the more often each member of Congress engages in this behavior, the less often voters will trust Congress as a whole or any member of that institution.

The Role of Public Spirit

Each of these dilemmas has a solution based largely on the cultivation of public spirit.

In large elections in the United States, some voters simply engage in denial, refusing to look at the odds and insisting that their vote has a large chance of being decisive. Others engage in a form of "magical thinking," implicitly assuming that their voting, and voting in a particular way, will lead others to vote, and vote in that way, as well.[10] These voters may believe they are voting for purely self-interested reasons. Yet many citizens who vote do so, at least partly, on the grounds that it is their duty to vote ("Well, it's my duty to vote. [Who is it a duty to?] Myself, my country, my family, my people"). Some act on the larger moral principle that a maxim based on their action could become a universal rule ("If everybody thought the same way, then what's going to happen with the voting? . . . you're going to have no vote at all").[11] In the aggregate, the decision to vote is correlated with other measures of social altruism, such as giving blood and being willing to serve on a jury.[12] Were it not for these millions of individual actions based in part on public spirit, the system of popular elections, which serves as the primary legitimating tool of American democracy, would collapse.

In regulatory systems, Ian Ayers and John Braithwaite argue that "the more sanctions can be kept in the background, the more regulation can be transacted through moral suasion, the more effective regulation will be." Their studies of regulatory compliance in the nursing home, pharmaceutical, and mining industries show that in these cases successful regulation requires combining a primary stress on moral suasion with the ability to draw, if necessary, on big sanctions and a graded system of lesser sanctions. The regulatory strategy must be mixed, because the motives of the regulated are mixed. Many corporate actors are both material value maximizers and concerned to do what is right, to be faithful to their identities as law-abiding citizens, and to sustain self-concepts of social responsibility. A strategy based totally on appeals to public spirit will be exploited when actors are motivated solely by self-interest, but a strategy based mostly on punishment will undermine the goodwill of those motivated by public spirit. Ayers and Braithwaite suggest a tit-for-tat regulatory strategy that begins with cooperation, prompting and expecting a cooperative (public-spirited) response, and that punishes a noncooperative response with small sanctions, keeping a set of incrementally bigger sanctions in the wings.[13]

Mixed strategies must emphasize public spirit not only to avoid the counterproductive expenditure of energy on conflicts of will and the subsequent rigidity of regulation, but also in order to avoid the well-documented phenomenon of extrinsic incentives driving out intrinsic ones. In the experiments that reveal this pattern, subjects who were given material rewards for desired behavior came to see that reward as the sole reason for their actions. When the reward was removed, they stopped acting in the desired manner—even though before any material reward was introduced they had acted in the desired way for nonmaterial reasons, including reasons intrinsic to the act itself.[14]

Yet strategies that depend primarily on public spirit also require sanctions, allowing the regulators to punish those who cheat in order to keep the public spirited from being "suckered." For example, in efficient systems in which most taxpayers pay their taxes, many taxpayers comply both because they believe that the collective objective for which they have tacitly agreed to be taxed is achieved (that is, that those who control the revenue from taxes are using it effectively for public-interested ends) and because they believe that others are also complying. Coercion is an essential condition for achieving the second goal, which assures those who contribute that they will not be exploited by the noncontributors.[15] The criminal justice system has a similar structure, in which most compliance derives from moral suasion but is supported by a graded set of sanctions.[16]

In the United States Congress, a relatively elaborate set of institutionally public-spirited norms backed by a graded series of formal and informal sanctions has traditionally encouraged members of Congress to, among other things, do their "homework" in their areas of specialization and not overly deprecate Congress as an institution. Since the 1950s, when such norms were first documented,[17] congressional reforms have undermined certain sanctions that helped uphold some of the norms, and political changes outside Congress, such as a weakening of the party structure and a greater emphasis on individual media attention, have undermined other sanctions. At the same time, nonpolitical changes, such as cheaper airfares to one's home state, lower levels of social drinking, and a greater emphasis on private family life, have weakened some of the social ties that created emotional attachments to the institution.[18]

Healthy institutions adapt to changes like these by developing functional equivalents of past norms. Although specialists in Congress have documented a decline in certain older norms,[19] no one has investigated the possible evolution of new norms serving similar functions. In light of the more permeable boundaries of today's Senate, one would want to incorporate in the network of applicable incentives, sanctions, and monitoring much that is outside the walls of Congress, taking place in the executive and judicial branches and in the media. Negative campaigning, for example, has undoubtedly contributed to the widespread public perception that "my congressman is good, but Congress itself is bad."[20] Yet the incentives for negative campaigning extend far beyond the walls of Congress, as do some of the disincentives. Permeable boundaries make it harder to control a collective action problem.

In a 1986 speech to the Institute for Humane Studies, James Buchanan repudiated analyses of legislatures based on the single motive of self-interest. He argued that both those who imagine a world of benevolent public servants following only the public interest and those who have "modelled politicians and bureaucrats as self-interested maximizers" share a "fatal flaw." Their images are partial, pulling out and accentuating one element in human behavior, while in fact each political actor combines a concern for the general interest, narrow self-interest, and other motivational elements. Buchanan pointed out that "the constraints, rules, and institutions within which persons make choices politically can and do influence the relative importance of the separate motivational elements."[21]

Buchanan concluded, with a sentiment common in American institutional thought, that constitutional design should aim at reducing overall the extent to which institutions must rely on public spirit.[22] I disagree. We do not know much yet about the way efficient organizations function, but two facts seem clear. First, public spirit is not simply a fixed and scarce resource that must be hoarded for emergencies and used sparingly. Rather, in some circumstances, the exercise of public spirit creates more public spirit, both in the actors and in those who notice their behavior.[23] Second, context is crucial. We must distinguish between the arenas of national politics in which the political system can afford to look most like a Schumpeterian marketplace, where each individual's acting according to self-interest produces relatively good aggregate results, and, conversely, the arenas in which each individual's acting according to self-interest is most likely to undermine cooperative gains. In the arenas where self-interested action is most likely to undermine the larger system, we should think consciously about which combinations of sanctions and altruistic motivation are most likely to generate cooperation. We must also then think about the structures, experiences, and cognitions most likely to produce and support those combinations of sanctions and altruistic motivation.

Creating Public Spirit in Political Systems

Although some sort of public spirit is at least functionally useful, and perhaps even necessary, in political systems, political scientists know remarkably little about how to go about creating it. I will argue that a degree of perceived justice, the experience of political partici- pation, and the experience and outcomes of political deliberation help create and maintain that spirit. This list is not intended to be exhaustive. Leadership, particularly of individuals who evoke public spirit rhetorically and model it in their own lives, and the creation or discovery of an outside enemy can galvanize collective energy, turning it to public ends for good or for ill.

Normatively, neither public spirit nor altruism in general is good in itself. The Spanish Inquisition, the Nazi Holocaust, the return of runaway slaves in the United States before emancipation, and the present war in the former Yugoslavia are all manifestations, in part, of public spirit. Public spirit must be judged by what it is directed toward. Political elites can, for example, influence perceptions of justice so that those perceptions work against the interests of sub- ordinated groups.[24] They can structure opportunities for participa- tion so that public rallies, informal political gatherings, and even the act of voting itself reinforces pro-regime sentiment.[25] They can guide the process of deliberation so that issues that might under- mine the interests of elites never appear on the political agenda.[26] Public spirit may be the result of "false consciousness"; it may be misguided; and it may be directed toward evil. The perception of justice, political participation, and political deliberation, all of which help create a sense of public spirit, may also help make that public spirit somewhat less misguided. But they are far from infallible in doing so.

Justice

Human beings hate being exploited. Although in bad situations some people can produce a degree of inner peace by convincing them- selves that all is as it should be, many people in many cultures seem to react to transgressions of justice with emotions running from irritation to rage, depending on the depth and closeness of the in- fraction. Even when more powerful groups punish the expression of these emotions, the less powerful often nourish a culture of resis- tance, expressing, legitimating, and elaborating their rejection of the dominant norms and patterns of behavior.[27] Even when they know it contravenes their rational individual self-interest, people often take revenge or bear inappropriate costs to right a perceived wrong.[28] Emotions related to the sense of injustice are perhaps functional for beings whose group cohesion rests more on learned social patterns than on the direct action of instinct. These emotions probably help sustain public spirit by providing informal sanctions against the selfish, even when no one may have a rationally self-interested reason to bear the costs of sanctioning. But these emotions also destroy public spirit among segments of the public when members of those segments do not perceive as just acts that are done in the public name.

The perception of justice, so critical to the creation and maintenance of public spirit, is linked to, but not necessarily tightly correlated with, the enactment of justice itself. What is just in any concrete instance, or even in the abstract, is often contested, so that it is not always easy for a polity simply to act justly and thus provoke public spirit. Moreover, as with any other good, expectations can outrun provision, so that even if we could speak of an absolute amount of justice increasing in a polity, such an increase would not necessarily be accompanied by an increase in public satisfaction with the degree of justice. Nevertheless, a polity whose ruling elites are trying to promote justice, even justice as they see it, is probably more likely to be able to command public spirit among its members than a polity whose ruling elites consciously view the state primarily as an instrument for their own material betterment.

Participation

One of the earliest findings from small group research was that in the United States, mothers who made a public-spirited decision (in this case, to feed their children cod-liver oil rather than orange juice in order to free existing oranges for the troops in World II) through deliberation with others in a small group and announced their decision in public within the group were more likely to change their behavior than mothers who made the same decision after hearing a public lecture.[29] Later, industrial psychologists discovered that employees who participated in making decisions that changed the conditions of their workplace were more likely than those who did not participate to stay on their jobs, working steadily, after the changes were instituted.[30] Although group leaders can manipulate these processes so that the outcomes are relatively predetermined,[31] they tend to produce a commitment to the group much like what I am calling public spirit.

In the mid-nineteenth century Alexis de Tocqueville noticed that in the United States taking responsibility for others through jury duty and other local offices produced what he saw as an unprecedented degree of sustaining, everyday public spirit.[32] Influenced by de Tocqueville, John Stuart Mill argued for extending the franchise on the grounds that taking responsibility for others, even through such a small action as voting, induced a concern for the public interest.[33] Academics who become heads of committees or department chairs often find that their new responsibility produces a greater sense of identification with the whole, which lasts after the term in office is over. The greater sense of public spirit that citizens from small towns usually experience may derive from their having held some form of small town office or, less stringently, having known that for some reason others in the town depended on them.[34] To borrow a phrase from ancient Greek democracy, they have ruled and been ruled in turn.

Deliberation

Well-designed deliberative processes have, for several reasons, the potential for fostering public spirit. Deliberation can provide information that avoids needless conflict. The process can also create feelings of solidarity and mutual responsibility among the participants. And good deliberation will often lead all but the most contrary-minded to change at least some of their preferences, sometimes producing agreement, sometimes clarifying conflict in ways that reveal what steps to take next.

Political deliberation can obfuscate as well as clarify participants' interests. Normatively, good deliberation should help those who participate understand better, emotionally and factually, what it is they most want to do.[35] It should illuminate both conflict and commonality. When interests conflict in important ways, deliberation should lead those affected by a decision to recognize and understand the character of their conflicts. When interests coincide or can be made to coincide, deliberation should lead those affected to recognize and understand the interests they have in common with others, the ways they can make the interests of others their own, and the ways in which they can change their preferences to give moral priority to what is good for most others or for the whole as they conccive it.

The deliberative process, however, is usually not neutral between the two ends of conflict and consensus. It encourages "we" rather than "I" thinking[36]—although the "we" may be a subgroup whose interests conflict with the interests of others in the larger polity. Having to persuade others tends to rule out arguments that rest solely on self-interest, unless the appeal is to a more just distribution of self-interested benefits. Moreover, because successful persuasion can appeal only to values the whole group shares, and because the more powerful groups in a society often greatly influence those values and have a more authoritative voice in public discourse, individuals and groups whose interests and identities are subordinated in the larger society need to form protected deliberative enclaves to work out their own conceptions of their interests.

Normatively, ideal deliberation should take place in an environment where power, in the sense of the use of force and threat of sanction, is absent, and only good reasons, advanced in the public interest, prevail.[37] In practice, however, deliberation will always be laced with power, and that power will tend to make the prevailing version of "public spirit" work in favor of the more powerful groups in a society. The question is not whether any existing deliberative process avoids or fully counteracts prevailing patterns of power, but whether well-designed deliberative bodies do a better job than other forms of politics in helping each group in a polity understand its desires and get more of what it wants.

Deliberative bodies designed to facilitate input from the less powerful and from minority opinion are more likely than other groups to discover objectively correct answers in experiments where such answers exist.[38] Deliberative groups constructed to include, say, an equal number of members from labor and from capital help approach conditions of relatively equal group power and an equal likelihood of making coalitions with others, so that each party's power will cancel the other out, coming closer to the ideal of removing all power from the deliberative process. Even in the context of overall conflict, good deliberative groups, like successful negotiators, can work to highlight shared interests (including interests in on-going relationships with other parties), invent options for mutual gain, recognize the multiple interests on each side, and encourage each side in the conflict to find inventive ways to meet the others' underlying needs at the lowest possible cost to their own interests.[39] Again like successful negotiators, deliberative groups can use as central foci for negotiation "objective" criteria, based on "principle," that are "independent of the wills of either side."[40] Far more than mere coordination devices,[41] these standards have legitimacy in themselves, allowing the person who advocates them to feel "fair" and "decent" and maintain a self-image as one who responds to "sound reasons" and arguments "on the merits."[42]

Steven Kelman argues cogently that participation in what he calls "cooperationist" institutions is more likely to create public spirit than participation in "adversary" institutions. By adversary institutions, he means those with a division of labor between advocates and decisionmakers, in which opposing advocates make the strongest possible case for their interests or point of view and a third party makes the actual political choice. By contrast, cooperationist institutions bring opposing parties together, often with government representatives or others who specifically represent the larger public interest, to work out conflicts among themselves.[43] In the United States, Kelman argues, institutional designers often consciously promote adversary institutions. They neglect the two main ways cooperationist institutions promote public spirit: by helping their participants to derive emotional satisfaction from their interaction and by encouraging respect for the opinions, knowledge, and feelings of the others in the group.[44] Kelman's evidence also indicates that groups produce better decisions when participants are highly committed to different positions at the outset rather than when they want simply to come to an agreement as quickly as possible.

Deliberation designed to promote public spirit will encourage minorities to develop and articulate their opinions, reduce the exercise of power, not overly disparage the articulation of self-interest, invent new options, seek consensually agreed criteria for decision, and promote listening. But simply bringing into the political process on a single issue more interested parties who do not have prior experience in working together will often produce only gridlock or a focus on narrow self-interest.[45]

When interests conflict in irreconcilable ways, deliberation should lead to recognizing conflict. But even here, the increased clarity of that recognition can point the way to appropriate nondeliberative forms of resolution, through majority vote, judicial proceedings, or, in the extreme, the naked exercise of power in war, lockout, or a strike.

In practice, in the United States and in Europe, deliberative procedures play a critical role in political life. In this process, ideas and self-interest become entangled. In using ideas to persuade others, one sometimes persuades oneself in the process. The idea becomes part of one's identity, even when its practical consequences turn out to work against one's narrow self-interest.[46]

Even interest groups, which in the American system often appear only as pressure groups designed to get more for their own members in a zero-sum game, sometimes create public spirit through deliberation. In some cases, deliberation among the rank and file creates a commitment to interests beyond their own, as when a union votes to support another union or cause. In some cases, interest groups also produce elites whose mutual deliberations generate or reinforce a commitment to the public interest as they see it.

Hugh Heclo, for example, describes the importance in United States public policy of "issue networks," whose members share knowledge on some aspect of public policy and for whom "direct material interest is often secondary to intellectual or emotional commitment." "Increasingly," Heclo concludes, "it is through networks of people who regard each other as knowledgeable, or at least as needing to be answered, that public policy issues tend to be refined, evidence debated, and alternative opinions worked out—though rarely in any controlled, well-organized way."[47] Beyond self-selection, the desire of members of the network for the respect of others in that network gives the other members the power to reward and punish their behavior, often in ways that direct it toward the public interest.[48]

In some European countries, neocorporatist negotiations among interest groups that include diffuse consumer, ecological, and other affected interests have produced outcomes that are as much, or more, in the public interest broadly defined as legislatively determined policies.[49] European policy networks may be socially struc-

tured to encourage public spirit among the elites who act as negotiators for specific societal interests, and the state-sponsored arenas
of negotiation may also provide incentives for public-interested outcomes.

In international relations, Peter Haas has documented how scientists and other environmentalists in their individual capacity as
professionals began to come together twice a year in conferences to
exchange information on how to control pollution in the Mediterranean. Through their deliberations, these particular elites became
professionally bonded, eventually came to reasonable agreement on
goals and means for reducing pollution, persuaded their respective
governments to set up environmental ministries that they then
staffed, and finally used both direct persuasion and the authority
inherent in their new ministries to persuade the relevant national
bodies to cooperate in costly antipollution plans that were sometimes not in the short-run national interest but were in the long-
run interest of all the countries around the Mediterranean. Haas
calls these networks "epistemic communities," on the basis of their
coherence around a particular way of looking at the world and the
consensual knowledge they evolved through their deliberations.[50]
They provide an international analogue to the issue networks Heclo
describes in the United States and to networks of neocorporatist
elites in Europe, in both of which the deliberative process also seems
to nurture a commitment to the common good, at least as the elites
perceive it.

Public Spirit in the United States: A Decline?

It is not clear whether United States citizens and their leaders
have become more or less public spirited over the past 50, 100, or
200 years. Traits like altruism or public spirit are not unidimen-
sional but vary greatly by context. An individual who is public spirited in one context may be extremely self-seeking in another.[51] If we
set out to measure the increases and declines in public spirit (or
"community obligation" or "public morality") over time, we would
undoubtedly find that on some dimensions public spirit had increased and on others declined.

Yet we do not require evidence of decline to justify concern with public spirit. If my arguments here are correct, improvements in material productivity, both absolute and relative to others, depend at least in part on improvements in increasing certain "efficient" forms of public spirit. As workers in more developed societies move into services, technological improvements in the production of material goods will necessarily play an ever smaller role in economic growth, just as improvements in agriculture eventually did. That means a society's overall economic success will increasingly depend on innovations in institutional design for the delivery of services and on improving the human qualities of the work force, including its capacity for public spirit.

Some indications seem to mark a decline in public spirit in the United States. We know that turnout in elections has declined markedly, as has confidence in most of the professions, confidence in the institutions of government, and feelings of efficacy and trust in government. But there are many possible reasons for these declines. It is not clear that they are caused by a general decline in public spirit. Nor is it clear that we want, for example, a return to the violently partisan conditions that promoted the highest historical electoral turnout in the United States.

Certain structural changes might have produced declines in public spirit; others might have produced increases. Fewer citizens in the United States now come from small towns, and small towns promote a sense of collective responsibility.[52] Greater demands on government ("overload") may lead more citizens to think the government is not doing its part in the tax bargain and to feel grudging in return.[53] The "me-generation" rhetoric of the Reagan years may have undermined civic concern, as may earlier disillusion with the Vietnam War and an uncertainty about values associated with the questioning of authority brought about in part by that war and in part by other rapid social changes, such as the increased availability of safe contraception and the adolescent demographic bulge of the late 1960s. However, the citizenry is becoming more educated, which on the individual level is strongly associated with public-spirited attitudes.[54] Compared with the 1950s, a higher standard of living and a stronger social safety net should allow individuals the luxury of more other-regarding behavior, although these real improvements since the 1950s might be counteracted by more recent and therefore psychologically more effective declines since the 1970s. Childrearing has also become more reasoned and less punitive, a characteristic associated at all class levels with higher altruism.[55]

Despite the good beginnings evidenced in this volume, research on public spirit is in its infancy. It will not be possible to understand more about the direction of any such trends, let alone their possible causes, until social scientists take the issue of public spirit more seriously. If they were to do so, many possible lines of investigation would present themselves. It would be worthwhile, for example, consciously to devise a set of survey questions and structured experiments to try to tap various dimensions of public spirit among citizens, legislators, and bureaucrats, both to make some sense of the concept[56] and to serve as a first timepoint for later research. Such questions should measure different dimensions of communal spirit. One would also want to replicate measures from past survey research in the United States and Europe and from past psychological experiments to create a second point in a projected time series.[57]

This chapter has pointed to several areas in which, although public spirit plays an important role in political arrangements, it remains to be adequately researched. Wolfinger and Rosenstone, for example, conclude that "a feeling that one has done one's duty to society . . . is the most common motivation to vote,"[58] but to my knowledge no political scientist has investigated empirically the content of this feeling or the incentives that promote it.[59]

Given the perception in and around Congress that the norms that preserve its functionning have eroded even more dramatically in recent years, it would be worth repeating the survey of those norms that Rohde and his colleagues did in 1973. The study could also try to determine if new equivalents of decayed traditional norms have arisen.

The processes of deliberation need research. Richard Freeman and James Medoff attribute their quantitative finding that in the United States "unions are associated with greater efficiency in most settings" to the deliberative efficiencies involved in using collective "voice" rather than individual "exit" to convey information on workers' needs.[60] But neither they nor the European neocorporatist theorists who recognize deliberation within interest groups have explored empirically the kinds of transformations in preferences that such deliberation may encourage, and which were once explored tentatively in a single prescient study of attitudes toward trade.[61]

Although several scholars have investigated the deliberative process in juries,[62] no one has used this work, or reanalyzed the original videotapes, to speculate on how public deliberation, broadly speaking, can bring opponents together, push them apart, or create public spirit for good or ill. Nor has anyone investigated empirically the contention of Alexis de Tocqueville and John Stuart Mill that serving on a jury or taking a small public office helps promote a sense of civic responsibility and public spirit.

Again, although Heclo and Haas have documented the existence of issue networks and epistemic communities motivated at least in part by public spirit, neither they nor others, as far as I know, have investigated closely the motivations and incentives faced by the professionals who constitute these highly effective communities. To understand the creation and maintenance of public spirit in different contexts, we would want to understand not only the most obvious material incentives and sanctions available, and not only how to invoke the relatively pure forms of love and duty, but also the character of the great panoply of nonmaterial, but not fully altruistic, "self-enhancing" motives that impel many political actors: the desire, for example, to leave a mark on history, to be part of a historic moment, to do a job one can be proud of, or even to finish what one has started.

Finally, rational choice analysts have begun to incorporate the motivations of love and duty in their analyses of political and organizational life. Seeking to understand the creation of trust in principal-agent relations, James Coleman has recently begun to explore briefly what I have called "love" and he calls "affine agency," in which the agent adopts the principal's interests through identification (parent with child, child with parent, citizen with the nation, and employee with firm).[63] Coleman also recognizes the importance of duty, as actors internalize norms. Yet Coleman's foray into the motivations of love and duty grounds both almost exclusively in previous rewards and punishments. His approach needs a link to work showing how perceived similarity between self and other helps produce identification and how cogent arguments help people internalize norms.

In a recent survey of Italian regions, Robert Putnam demonstrates a high correlation between "civic community" (measured by associational membership, newspaper circulation, referendum participation, and nonclientelistic voting) and institutional performance in the twenty Italian regional governments. In regions where civic community is high, the government performs well. The high institutional performance of the regions north of Rome is not created by their higher economic development. Rather, the differing economic development and institutional performances of the regions derive at least in part from the differing degrees of civic community that the regions have developed. The sense of civic community seems to be fostered by horizontal, or egalitarian, linkages among the citizenry in the north rather than by the vertical, or hierarchical, linkages that prevail in Italy's south.[64]

Putnam indicates that in Italy the origins of public spirit of the northern regions and its lack in the south can be traced back to the eleventh century. But, as an Italian reformer who read his work exclaimed, "This is a counsel of despair! If you're right, nothing I can do will improve our prospects for success. The fate of the reform was sealed centuries ago."[65] This chapter has suggested how social science, in its analytic study of game theory, experimental social psychology, and constitutional design, is poised to learn much more in the next decade about how specific institutions might encourage public spirit without magnifying elite domination.

Conclusion

Political systems are forms of "social capital," that is, networks of relations created by past effort that make present effort more productive.[66] Like many other complex social organizations, political systems usually require for efficient functioning not only good systems of monitoring and sanctioning but also a powerful leaven of the mutual trust generated through love and duty.

Evolutionary biologists posit a race between the demands of individual selection, in which individual altruism is punished (except in the case of various orders of genetic kin) by genetic extinction, and the demands of collective selection, in which individual altruism that benefits the community is rewarded by collective survival and growth. The cultural arrangements of human beings, including our political arrangements, are our primary mechanisms for promoting collective survival and prosperity in the face of individual incentives for narrow self-interest. Those cultural arrangements depend, as I have tried to show, not only on efficient arrangements for monitoring and sanctioning defection but equally critically on public spirit. We urgently need to understand more than we now do about the institutions, norms, principles, affinities, and sanctions that promote public-spirited behavior in political life, because in many instances that public-spirited behavior is precisely what makes the collective system viable.

Notes

1.   Aristotle, *The Politics of Aristotle*, 1280b, trans. Ernest Barker (Oxford University Press, 1958), pp. 118–19.

2.   Plato, *Republic*, Book I: 338, *The Collected Dialogues of Plato*, ed. Edith Hamilton and Huntington Cairns (Princeton University Press, 1961), p. 558, citing Thrasymachus in order to demolish this view. See also Plato's *Gorgias* and, more generally, Eric Alfred Havelock, *The Liberal Temper in Greek Politics* (Yale University Press, 1957).

3.   In Michael Taylor's more formal definition, "A *collective action problem* . . . exists where rational individual action by each of the members of some set of actors can lead to an inefficient or Pareto-inferior outcome" (Michael Taylor and Sara Singleton, "The Communal Resource: Transaction Costs and the Solution of Collective Action Problems," in Robert O. Keohane, Michael McGinnis, and Elinor Ostrom, eds., *Proceedings of a Conference on Linking Local and Global Commons Held at Harvard University, April 23–25, 1992* [Harvard University Center for International Affairs, 1993], p. 66). For an analysis of experiments using the prisoners' dilemma and related collective action problems, and of a variety of solutions to these problems using both material sanctions and forms of altruism, see my "On the Relation of Altruism and Self-Interest," in Jane J. Mansbridge, ed., *Beyond Self-Interest* (University of Chicago Press, 1990), pp. 133–43. Although I have avoided explicit references to prisoners' dilemmas and related problems in this article, they remain the implicit analytic focus throughout.

4.   These labels derive, respectively, from David Hume, *Essays Moral, Political, and Literary*, vol. 1, ed. T. H. Green and T. H. Grose (Longmans [1741], 1898); Amartya Sen, "Rational Fools: A Critique of the Behavioral Foundations of Economic Theory" [1978], in Mansbridge, *Beyond Self-Interest*, pp. 25–43; Jon Elster, "Selfishness and Altruism," in Mansbridge, *Be-*

166   *Jane Mansbridge*

yond Self-Interest, pp. 44–52; Christopher Jencks, "Varieties of Altruism," in Mansbridge, *Beyond Self-Interest*, pp. 54–67; Robyn Dawes, Alphons J. C. van de Kragt, and John M. Orbell, "Cooperation for the Benefit of Us–Not Me, or My Conscience," in Mansbridge, *Beyond Self-Interest*, pp. 97–110; and James Q. Wilson, *The Amateur Democrat: Club Politics in Three Cities* (University of Chicago Press, 1962). See also the contrast between concern with doing the right thing and concern with others' welfare in Ervin Staub, "Helping a Distressed Person," in Leonard Berkowitz, ed., *Advances in Experimental Social Psychology*, vol. 7 (Academic Press, 1974), pp. 293–341, and Emile Durkheim, in *Moral Education*, on the contrast between being responsible and being good (cited in Staub, p. 300). Some scholars contend that only one of the pair is genuinely altruistic. Sen, for example, argues that love (sympathy) falls in the category of egoism and duty (commitment) in the category of nonegoism, while Dawes and his coauthors argue just the reverse. Immanuel Kant maintained that only actions done from duty, not sympathy, had "true moral worth." Many feminist theorists argue that both forms have legitimate claims to the titles of altruism or nonegoism (see Mansbridge, "On the Relation of Altruism and Self-interest," pp. 132–43, and "Feminism and Democratic Community," in John W. Chapman and Ian Shapiro, eds., *Democratic Community: NOMOS XXXV* [New York University Press, 1993], pp. 357–59).

5. For evidence on modeling, see Mansbridge, "On the Relation of Altruism and Self-Interest," pp. 132–43.

6. For a critique of this relatively frequent misinterpretation, see my "The Rise and Fall of Self-Interest in the Explanation of Political Life," in Mansbridge, *Beyond Self-Interest*, pp. 3–22.

7. B. F. Skinner, *Walden II* (Macmillan, 1948), p. 265, cited in R. E. Goodin and K. W. S. Roberts, "The Ethical Voter," *American Political Science Review*, vol. 69 (September 1975), pp. 926–28, quotation on p. 926.

8. This "voters' paradox" first appeared as a formal element in democratic theory in Anthony Downs, *An Economic Theory of Democracy* (Harper and Row, 1957), nine years after Skinner's *Walden II*, and has since become a staple problem in the "rational choice" school of political analysis, whose practitioners usually take self-interest as a fundamental assumption in modeling political behavior.

9. Ian Ayres and John Braithwaite, *Responsive Regulation: Transcending the Regulation Debate* (Oxford: Oxford University Press, 1992), p. 26.

10. George A. Quattrone and Amos Tversky, "Self-deception and the Voter's Illusion," in Jon Elster, ed., *The Multiple Self* (Cambridge: Cambridge University Press, 1986), pp. 35–58.

11. Interviews with voters at the polls in the 1988 presidential election (Mansbridge, "The Moral Concerns of the Rational Voter," paper presented at the Center for American Political Studies, Harvard University, 1989). I would argue further that most of the deniers engage in denial for largely public-spirited reasons. That is, they believe it is something of a heresy,

undermining public faith in the system, even to suggest that their vote has a minuscule chance of being decisive. The political scientists who designed the early questions on voting for the American National Election Study also seem to have held this view. In Angus Campbell, Gerald Gurin, and Warren E. Miller, *The Voter Decides* (Row, Peterson, 1954), Angus Campbell and his colleagues gave the somewhat honorific label "citizen duty" to disagreement with a set of four statements that from a rational choice point of view are simply statements of fact: "It isn't so important to vote when you know your party doesn't have a chance to win." "So many other people vote in the national elections that it doesn't matter much to me whether I vote or not." "If a person doesn't care how an election comes out he shouldn't vote in it." "A good many local elections aren't important enough to bother with," p. 194.

12.   Stephen Knack, "Civic Norms, Social Sanctions, and Voter Turnout," *Rationality and Society*, vol. 4 (1992), pp. 133–56. The incorporation of several of Knack's questions in the 1992 National Election Study presages a more thorough investigation of this form of non-self-interested motivation.

13.   Ayres and Braithwaite, *Responsive Regulation*, especially, pp. 47ff.; quotation from p. 19. On the complex relationships between trust and self-interest, see also Charles Sabel, "Moebius-Strip Organizations and Open Labor Markets," in Pierre Bourdieu and James S. Coleman, eds., *Social Theory for a Changing Society* (Westview Press, 1991). On mixed motivations, see my "On the Relation between Altruism and Self-Interest," in Mansbridge, *Beyond Self-Interest*, and Neil Pinney and John Scholz, "Can Cognitive Consistency Cure Collective Dilemmas? Self-Interest versus Duty to Pay Taxes," Working Paper 28 (New York: Russell Sage Foundation, October 1992).

14.   For example, Edward L. Deci, "Effects of Externally Mediated Rewards on Intrinsic Motivation," *Journal of Personality and Social Psychology*, vol. 18 (April 1971), pp. 105–15; and citations in Ann K. Boggiano and others, "Use of the Maximal-Operant Principle to Motivate Childrens' Intrinsic Interest," *Journal of Personality and Social Psychology*, vol. 53 (November 1987), pp. 866–79. This line of research in social psychology has not addressed itself to the critical question of when extrinsic rewards and punishments can be combined effectively with intrinsic rewards. For evidence of one such successful combination, see Richard D. Katzev and Anton U. Pardini, "The Comparative Effectiveness of Reward and Commitment Approaches in Motivating Community Recycling," *Journal of Environmental Systems*, vol. 17, no. 2 (1987–88), pp. 93–111.

15.   Margaret Levi, who documents this behavior in *Of Rule and Revenue* (University of California Press, 1988), characterizes it as "quasi-voluntary" compliance. Her forthcoming *The Contingencies of Consent* analyzes other examples of "contingent consent." In *The Possibility of Cooperation* (Cambridge University Press, 1987), Michael Taylor points out that an equilibrium of cooperation in an iterated prisoners' dilemma involves "conditional cooperation," which in turn requires monitoring and sanctioning oth-

ers' actions. For another form of conditional cooperation, see John M. Orbell, Alphons J. C. van de Kragt, and Robyn M. Dawes, "Explaining Discussion-Induced Cooperation," *Journal of Personality and Social Psychology*, vol. 54 (May 1988), pp. 811–19, in which promises to cooperate in a social dilemma increased cooperation only when everyone in the discussing group promised.

16.   See James Q. Wilson, *Thinking about Crime* (Vintage, 1977), on the effects of a combination of shared agreement on appropriate standards and informal social controls.

17.   Donald R. Matthews, *U.S. Senators and Their World* (Vintage Books, 1960).

18.   See my "Motivating Deliberation in Congress," in Sarah Baumgartner Thurow, ed., *Constitutionalism in America*, vol. 2: *Constitutional Principles and the Institutions of Government* (University Press of America, 1988), pp. 59–86.

19.   Barbara Sinclair, *The Transformation of the U.S. Senate* (Johns Hopkins University Press, 1989). David W. Rohde, Norman J. Ornstein, and Robert L. Peabody, in "Political Change and Legislative Norms in the U.S. Senate, 1957–1974," in Glen R. Parker, ed., *Studies of Congress* (Congressional Quarterly Press, 1985), pp. 147–88, agree that what they call the "limited benefit norms" of apprenticeship and specialization, which they argue benefited primarily the conservative senators of the "Senate Establishment," had eroded between the late 1950s and 1973. However, they argue, the "general benefit norms" that interest us here, of legislative work, courtesy, reciprocity, and institutional patriotism, were still maintained at the time of their 1973 survey.

20.   See Richard F. Fenno, Jr., *Home Style: House Members in Their Districts* (Little Brown, 1978).

21.   James M. Buchanan, "Then and Now, 1961-1986: From Delusion to Disutopia," paper presented at the Institute for Humane Studies, November 13, 1986. Buchanan's 1986 statement, somewhat reversing the stance he took with Gordon Tullock in *Calculus of Consent* (University of Michigan Press, 1965), came in the midst of a decade in which "rational choice" analyses of Congress, such as David R. Mayhew's *Congress: The Electoral Connection* (Yale University Press, 1974) and Morris P. Fiorina's *Congress: Keystone of the Washington Establishment* (Yale University Press, 1977), which had directed the profession in the 1970s to the self-interested motives of members of Congress, were countered by legislative studies marshaling evidence of members of Congress acting in ways incompatible with self-interest, particularly reelection. See William Ker Muir, *Legislature: California's School for Politics* (University of Chicago Press, 1982); Arthur Maass, *Congress and the Common Good* (Basic Books, 1983); David J. Vogler and Sidney R. Waldman, *Congress and Democracy* (Congressional Quarterly Press, 1985); Martha Derthick and Paul J. Quirk, *The Politics of Deregulation* (Brookings, 1985); Steven Kelman, *Making Public Policy: A Helpful View of American Government* (Basic Books, 1987); and articles in Robert B. Reich, ed., *The Power of Public Ideas* (Ballinger, 1988).

22.　See also, for example, Mancur Olson, "The Role of Morals and Incentives in Society," in Joseph E. Earley, ed., *Individuality and Cooperative Action* (Georgetown University Press, 1991): "Morality is, indeed, a scarce resource. It follows that we should structure incentives so that we do not need to call on morality any more than we have to" (p. 126), and Garrett Hardin, *The Limits of Altruism: An Ecologist's View of Survival* (Indiana University Press, 1977), esp. pp. 26–27, 40–42.

23.　On use augmenting rather than diminishing supply, see Albert O. Hirschman, "Against Parsimony: Three Easy Ways of Complicating Some Categories of Economic Discourse," *Economics and Philosophy*, vol. 1(April 1985), pp. 16–19.

24.　Antonio Gramsci, *Selections from the Prison Notebooks of Antonio Gramsci*, ed. and trans. Quintin Hoare and Geoffrey Nowell Smith (International Publishers [1929-1935], 1971).

25.　Murry J. Edelman, *The Symbolic Uses of Politics* (University of Illinois Press, 1964).

26.　Peter Bachrach and Morton S. Baratz, "Decisions and Nondecisions: An Analytic Framework," *American Political Science Review*, vol. 57 (September 1963), pp. 632–44.

27.　Aldon D. Morris, "Political Consciousness and Collective Action," in Aldon D. Morris and Carol McClurg Mueller, eds., *Frontiers in Social Movement Theory* (Yale University Press, 1992), pp. 351–73; and James C. Scott, *Domination and the Arts of Resistance: Hidden Transcripts* (Yale University Press, 1990).

28.　Robert H. Frank, *Passions within Reason: The Strategic Role of Emotions* (W.W. Norton, 1988). The desire not to be "suckered" plays a major role in addition to material reward in explaining behavior in prisoners' dilemmas and other problems of social cooperation.

29.　Kurt Lewin, "Group Decision and Social Change," in Theodore M. Newcomb and Eugene L. Hartley, eds., *Readings in Social Psychology* (Henry Holt, 1947), pp. 330–44.

30.　Lester Coch and John R. P. French, "Overcoming Resistance to Change," *Human Relations*, vol. 1, no. 4 (1948), pp. 512–32.

31.　Sidney Verba, *Small Groups and Political Behavior: A Study of Leadership* (Princeton University Press, 1961). Verba called this manipulation "pseudo-participation" (p. 224).

32.　Alexis de Tocqueville, *Democracy in America* (Vintage [1835–40], 1945).

33.　John Stuart Mill, *Considerations on Representative Government* (Forum Books [1861], 1958).

34.　Roger G. Barker and Paul V. Gump, *Big School, Small School: High School Size and Student Behavior* (Stanford University Press, 1964); and Bibb Latané and John M. Darley, *The Unresponsive Bystander: Why Doesn't He Help?* (Prentice-Hall, 1970), p. 117.

35.　On the importance of emotion as well as reason in deliberation, see Charles E. Lindblom, *Inquiry and Change: The Troubled Attempt to Under-*

stand and Shape Society (Yale University Press, 1990), p. 32, and passim on "probing volitions;" Benjamin R. Barber, *Strong Democracy: Participatory Politics for a New Age* (University of California Press, 1984), p. 174; and my "A Delibrative Theory of Interest Representation," in Mark P. Petracca, ed., *The Politics of Interests: Interest Groups Transformed* (Westview Press, 1992), pp. 32–57.

36.   Barber, *Strong Democracy*; and Jon Elster, "The Market and the Forum: Three Varieties of Political Theory," in Jon Elster and Aanund Hylland, eds., *Foundations of Social Choice Theory: Studies in Rationality and Social Change* (Cambridge University Press, 1986), pp. 112–13.

37.   Jürgen Habermas, in *Communication and the Evolution of Society*, trans. Thomas McCarthy (Beacon Press [1974], 1979), would call this an "ideal speech situation."

38.   Norman R. F. Maier and Allen R. Solem, "The Contribution of a Group Leader to the Quality of Group Thinking: The Effective Use of Minority Opinions," *Human Relations*, vol. 25 (1972), pp. 277–88, using in their experiments questions that had objectively correct answers. The same point, that a good deliberative process must actively solicit opposition, applies to deliberations far larger than the small group. See my *Why We Lost the ERA* (University of Chicago Press, 1986) and Harold Wilensky, *Organizational Intelligence: Knowledge and Policy in Government and Industry* (Basic Books, 1967).

39.   Roger Fisher and William Ury, *Getting to Yes: Negotiating to Agreement without Giving In* (Penguin [1981], 1983). On equal power, however, Joann Horaï and James T. Tedeschi, "Effects of Credibility and Magnitude of Punishment on Compliance to Threats," *Journal of Personality and Social Psychology*, vol. 12 (June 1969), pp. 164–69, found that in some contexts, when equally distributed power is high, the possibility of achieving consensual agreement was reduced.

40.   Fisher and Ury, *Getting to Yes*, pp. 86, 89, xii.

41.   Thomas C. Schelling, *The Strategy of Conflict* (Harvard University Press [1960], 1963).

42.   Fisher and Ury, *Getting to Yes*, pp. 52, xii, 86ff.

43.   Steven Kelman, "Adversary and Cooperationist Institutions for Conflict Resolution in Public Policymaking," *Journal of Policy Analysis and Management*, vol. 11 (Spring 1992), pp. 178–206, quotation on p. 180.

44.   Kelman, "Adversary," p. 185. Groups are most likely to produce these goods when they are ongoing and when talking with one another can produce joint gains. See, for example, Muzafer Sherif and Carolyn W. Sherif, *Groups in Harmony and Tension: An Integration of Studies on Intergroup Relations* (Harper, 1953). Face-to-face contact can also exacerbate tensions between individuals: athletes do better at meets in which they face their competitors in person than when they race against the clock, and removing ourselves from the presence of those who have angered us helps us regain our temper. See my *Beyond Adversary Democracy* (University of Chicago

Press, 1983), pp. 270–77, for the positive and negative effects of face-to-face contact in a town meeting and alternative workplace.

45. See Jennifer L. Hochschild, *The New American Dilemma: Liberal Democracy and School Desegregation* (Yale University Press, 1984).

46. John W. Kingdon, "Politicians, Self-Interest, and Ideas," in George E. Marcus and Russell L. Hanson, eds., *Reconsidering the Democratic Public* (Pennsylvania State University Press, 1993), and John W. Kingdon, "Agendas, Ideas, and Policy Change," in Lawrence C. Dodd and Calvin Jillson, eds., *The Dynamics of American Politics: Approaches and Interpretations* (Westview, 1993). See also my "Self-Interest and Political Transformation," in Marcus and Hanson, *Reconsidering the Democratic Public*, pp. 73–89.

47. Hugh Heclo, "Issue Networks and the Executive Establishment," in Anthony King, ed., *The New American Political System* (Washington: American Enterprise Institute for Public Policy Research, 1978), pp. 87–124, pp. 102, 104. Heclo argues that the concepts of "power," "control," and "dominance" do not accurately describe "the loosely jointed play of influence that is emerging in political administration" (p. 102).

48. Errol Meidinger, "Regulatory Culture: A Theoretical Outline," *Law and Policy*, vol. 9 (October 1987), pp. 355–86. To borrow the terminology of Joseph P. Kalt and Mark A. Zupan, in "Capture and Ideology in the Economic Theory of Politics," *American Economic Review*, vol. 74 (June 1984), pp. 279–300, we may say that some staff and officers of private interest groups engage in "ideological shirking," that is, the pursuit of their conception of the public interest against the specific interests of their members.

49. Joshua Cohen and Joel Rogers, "Secondary Associations and Democratic Governance," *Politics and Society*, vol. 20 (December 1992), pp. 393–472.

50. Peter M. Haas, "Do Regimes Matter? Epistemic Communities and Mediterranean Pollution Control," *International Organization*, vol. 43 (Summer 1989), pp. 377–403.

51. On cross-situational consistency, see in general Walter Mischel, *Personality and Assessment* (Wiley, 1968), and on altruism, Jencks, "Varieties of Altruism," and Gustavo Carlo and others, "The Altruistic Personality: In What Contexts Is It Apparent?" *Journal of Personality and Social Psychology*, vol. 61 (September 1991), pp. 450–58.

52. Latane and Darley, *The Unresponsive Bystander*; and Barker and Gump, *Big School, Small School*.

53. Levi, *Of Rule and Revenue*.

54. This may be because the more educated are also relatively well-off or can expect greater material security, so that they are more convinced the world is just.

55. Samuel P. and Pearl M. Oliner, *The Altruistic Personality: Rescuers of Jews in Nazi Europe* (Free Press, 1988).

56. See earlier attempts to measure James Q. Wilson and Edward C. Banfield's "public-regardingness" ("Public-Regardingness As a Value Premise in Voting Behavior," *American Political Science Review*, vol. 58 [Decem-

ber 1964], pp. 876–87, and "Political Ethos Revisited," *American Political Science Review*, vol. 65 [December 1971], pp. 1048–62), for example, Brett W. Hawkins and James E. Prather, "Measuring Components of the Ethos Theory: A First Step," *Journal of Politics*, vol. 33 (August 1971), pp. 642–58, and Peter A. Lupsha, "Social Position and Public-Regardingness: A New Test of an Old Hypothesis," *Western Political Quarterly*, vol. 28 (December 1975), pp. 618–34.

57.   In 1974, for instance, Harvey A. Hornstein placed on New York City sidewalks hundreds of "lost" wallets, containing small amounts of cash along with identification cards revealing the owner's name and address, and found that more than half the wallets were returned with the cash intact (*Cruelty and Kindness: A New Look at Aggression and Altruism* [Prentice-Hall, 1976]).

58.   Raymond E. Wolfinger and Steven J. Rosenstone, *Who Votes?* (Yale University Press, 1980), pp. 7–8.

59.   But see note 12 for the research of Stephen Knack, an economist.

60.   Richard B. Freeman and James L. Medoff, *What Do Unions Do?* (Basic Books, 1984).

61.   This study, by Raymond A. Bauer, Ithiel de Sola Pool, and Lewis Anthony Dexter, *American Business and Public Policy: The Politics of Foreign Trade* (Aldine-Atherton, Inc. [1964] 1972), stressed preference transformation. For European neocorporatist theory, see Claus Offe and Helmut Wiesenthal, "Two Logics of Collective Action: Theoretical Notes on Social Class and Organizational Form," in Maurice Zeitlin, ed., *Political Power and Social Theory*, vol. 1 (JAI Press, 1980), pp. 67–115, and Wolfgang Streeck and Philippe C. Schmitter, eds., "Preface," in their *Private Interest Government: Beyond Market and State* (Sage Publications, 1985).

62.   Reid Hastie, Steven D. Penrod, and Nancy Pennington, *Inside the Jury* (Harvard University Press, 1983), Phoebe Ellsworth, "Are Twelve Heads Better Than One?" *Law and Contemporary Problems*, vol. 52 (Autumn 1989), pp. 205–21; and Shari Seidman Diamond and Jonathan D. Casper, "Blindfolding the Jury to Verdict Consequences: Damages, Experts, and the Civil Jury," *Law and Society Review*, vol. 26, no. 3 (1992), pp. 513–63.

63.   James S. Coleman, *Foundations of Social Theory* (Belknap Press of Harvard University Press, 1990), p. 159.

64.   Robert D. Putnam, *Making Democracy Work: Civic Traditions in Modern Italy* (Princeton University Press, 1993).

65.   Putnam, "Democracy, Development, and the Civic Community: Evidence from an Italian Experiment," in Keohane, McGinnis, and Ostrom, *Proceedings of a Conference on Linking Local and Global Commons*, p. 141.

66.   Coleman, *Foundations*; and Elinor Ostrom, *Governing the Commons: The Evolution of Organizations for Collective Action* (Cambridge University Press, 1990) and *Crafting Institutions for Self-Governing Irrigation Systems* (Institute for Contemporary Studies Press, 1992).

Gang Behavior, Law Enforcement, and Community Values

George Akerlof and Janet L. Yellen

Between 1960 and 1990 crime rates in the United States increased dramatically: murder rates rose from 5.0 to 9.4 per 100,000; aggravated assaults increased from 85 to 424 per 100,000; and auto theft was up from 182 to 658 per 100,000.[1] The response to this upsurge has been increased law enforcement activity, with the incarceration rate more than doubling.[2] Has this policy been the correct response? Are there policy alternatives that have not been adequately pursued? The "bricks-and-sticks" approach to crime ignores the possibility that changing community attitudes toward crime and law enforcement play a role in the current crime wave and that the proper response must involve a conscious attempt to alter those values. This essay focuses on the role of community values in controlling crime. Community cooper-

We thank Jack Wang for valuable research assistance, Gary Burtless, Roger Conner, William Dickens, John DiIulio, B. Curtis Eaton, Elhanan Helpman, Benjamin Hermalin, Lawrence Katz, Lester Lave, Jonathan Leonard, David Levine, David Lilien, Richard Lipsey, David Romer, Paul Romer, Nathan Rosenberg, Ed Safarian, Andrei Shleifer, Oliver Williamson, Michael Wolfson, and Donald Vereen for comments. We are indebted to the National Science Foundation for research support under grant SES 92-10826. The first author also thanks the Canadian Institute for Advanced Research for generous financial support.

ation with local police is essential to law enforcement. Community members decide to cooperate either with the police—since the criminals have violated their values—or with the criminals, if the legal authorities represent an untrusted, alien culture, and the criminals are capable of nasty reprisals. Two conclusions follow from our analysis of the role of community values in deterring crime. First, we stress that manipulation of social values is as important in the control of crime as harsh punishments and high public expenditures for police. Second, we argue that these traditional approaches to crime control may prove counterproductive in the long run if they undermine community values.

The bricks-and-sticks approach to crime and punishment stems naturally from the economic theory of crime developed by Gary Becker. Becker's seminal article[3] provides a framework for answering basic questions: how many resources should be devoted to law enforcement? What should be the form and severity of punishments? How much crime will occur? To answer these questions, Becker developed what later became known as a principal-agent model to characterize criminal activity. The principal-agent approach has proved a productive way of understanding outcomes in a number of relationships in which one person or group (the principal) sets incentives to which another person or group (the agent) responds. Some examples are manager as principal/worker as agent; shareholder as principal/CEO as agent; voter as principal/congressman as agent; there are many others. In crime, the agent is the criminal, whose offenses are an optimal response to the incentives set by the government—the principal. The government determines the penalties imposed on offenders who are apprehended, and the intensity of the law enforcement effort determines the probability of apprehension.

In crime and punishment, as in all other situations involving principals and agents, the outcome depends on who knows what about whom. Becker's analysis implicitly assumes that police detect criminal activity with a probability dependent on law enforcement effort or "monitoring expenditures" for short. However, in reality, police do not operate in a vacuum; in solving crimes they rely greatly on tips from civilian observers. In fact, the major deterrent to crime is not an active police presence but rather the presence of knowledgeable civilians, prepared to report crimes and cooperate in police investigations. As Jane Jacobs has emphasized, crowded city streets are safe city streets, because busy streets are full of observers.[4] This chapter focuses on the fact that crime occurs in a social setting where the incentive of community members to cooperate with the police depends on the behavior of the criminals, and criminals in turn act so that community members will not reveal what they know. Thus, the principal-agent relationship between government and criminal is complicated by the presence of a third party—the community. We build a model that we use to analyze the implications of these inter-actions for the level of crime and policies to control it.

Becker assumes that criminals take the odds of detection as de-termined by factors outside their control, such as the monitoring effort of law enforcement officials. In contrast, we assume that crim-inals know that the chance of being detected depends both on law enforcement monitoring and on the behavior of the community— and that they can influence the community. This logic has little impact on isolated criminals, who know that their individual behav-ior has little effect on the community one way or another. But for youth gangs (or organized crime) the interaction is more important. These groups control territory and the openly committed crime within their neighborhoods. They thus have an incentive to control their activity in order to dissuade community members from coop-erating with the police. Our focus, therefore, is on gangs, whose members are responsible for a substantial share of inner-city crime, and who manipulate their community's willingness to report crime to their own advantage.

We describe a scenario, increasingly common in American inner cities, in which crime is limited primarily by the (rational) reluc-tance of gang members to alienate their communities: the police lack control in the sense that community members are unwilling to cooperate. Nevertheless, monitoring and penalties have an indirect effect on crime. Our model points to the necessity for strong com-munity norms against crime. Indeed, we show that in the absence of sufficiently strong norms, there is the frightening possibility that crime will increase indefinitely. This result will occur if community tolerance for local crime rises and community cooperation with the police erodes as the level of crime in society at large rises. Our entire approach thus emphasizes the role of community norms and the legitimacy of the judicial system.

The discretionary role of outside observers in offering or with-holding cooperation from the "principal" has been described in similar contexts. Gerald Mars gives numerous examples of "fiddles" with a large number of observers.[5] For example, Newfoundland dockers cause "accidents," which spill out the contents of containers. The workers appropriate the goods, while the supervisors, who share in the loot, look on. More generally, Jean Tirole shows how coalitions among agents and informed observers, supported by side payments, may arise in an organization to manipulate the information received by the principal.[6] We develop a model with a similar coalition between gangs and the community to conceal information from the police. The community conceals information to avoid retaliation and because they are more sympathetic to the gangs than to the police. The gang "bribes" the community by limiting the scope of violence and protecting the community from outside gangs. The willingness of local residents to reveal information to the police, we shall argue, depends partly on the behavior of the local gang but importantly also on the legitimacy of the police in the community.[7]

We begin by describing the behavioral building blocks of the model: the motives of gangs, members of the community, and the government. We then formalize this discussion and describe the possible outcomes in the short run, in which norms and values are fixed. Finally, we discuss long-run outcomes in which norms and values are shaped by past history and the determination of a gang's size and territory. An appendix presents the mathematical details of the model.

The Protagonists: Gangs, Community, Government

The level of criminal activity in the inner city is determined by the interactions among three groups: gangs, community members, and police. The behavior of each of these groups will be described in turn.

Gangs

Territorial control is the defining aspect of gang organization. Indeed in the Midwest gangs (or groups of gangs) commonly refer to themselves as "nations." Thus the Vice Lord Nation controls a whole area of Chicago. R. Lincoln Keiser gives a precise description of what it means to control territory: Vice Lord territory is that part of Chicago where Vice Lords but not members of other clubs are relatively free from attack.[8]

Fighting is central to gang life because of its role in maintaining territorial control. Its importance is evident, for example, in initiation rights. In Los Angeles barrios, gangs commonly require initiates to fight a group of gang members for a long count of 30. Moderately serious injuries—a broken nose or a dislocated jaw—are common. The analogy between gangs and countries is more than superficial: like countries, gangs have leaders, and governments with both civilian and military wings. The civil authority typically includes a president, treasurer, and secretary; the military authority is typically headed by a so-called warlord.

Gangs typically control the trade in drugs, protection, and numbers in their territory. Gangs are aware of activities that occur in their domain and use their fighting power to ensure that no open activities occur without their tacit consent. Outside gangs cannot freely enter (except for occasional raids). Gangs use this power to extract as much money as possible through the conduct of crime.

Our model of gang behavior is analogous to economic historian Douglass North's theory of feudal governments as rent-seeking monopolists.[9] North and Mancur Olson view feudal lords as monopolists who maximize their income by choosing the "tax rate" that maximizes their revenues. Such high tax rates considerably distort economic activity. Gangs will also try to maximize their revenues, but their control will be even more economically destructive: while a feudal lord must at least be concerned about his ability to extract revenues over the long run, because of high turnover in leadership and a lack of legitimacy, gangs will choose behavior reflecting little concern for adverse long-run effects on inner-city business.

The most important constraint on the criminal activities of gangs comes from the police power of the larger society outside its territory and the attitudes of local residents toward cooperation with the police. Local residents are quite aware of the economic dealings of the gangs in their neighborhood, since such activities as drug dealing require some degree of openness; buyers and sellers must be aware of the locations and times at which trades can take place. If the residents of poor neighborhoods cooperate with the police, then the police can exact penalties on the gangs. This constraint dictates the gang's strategy: they can pursue their activities only up to the point at which the neighborhood threatens to cooperate with the police rather than with the gang.

Martín Sánchez Jankowski provides evidence that fear of community retaliation constrains gang operations. His evidence comes from many sources: statements by members of the community (who fail to reveal to the authorities what they know about the gangs), by the police, by community workers, and also gang members themselves. The statement of Duck, a Los Angeles teenager is illustrative, showing the restraints placed by one Hispanic gang on its dealings with the community:

> When I was younger I was selling pills to young kids at school. You know, kids in grade school. Well, the parents found out about it and complained to some of the leaders [gang leaders]. Hey, at the time, I was young and thought I could do anything I wanted, I also thought that the gang would let you do what you wanted, so a couple of days later I peddled some more pills to these kids. Then at the next meeting they [the gang] really beat me up, I mean they really took me apart. I couldn't do anything for two weeks. I even had blood in my piss from getting kicked in the kidneys . . . but I got the message, and I stopped . . . I didn't like getting it at the time, but now I understand that if you [the gang] ain't got the community with you it's just a matter of time before you got to close up shop. It's crazy, but I just voted the other day to punish some homey for screwing up with the community.[10]

Other factors may also constrain the rent-seeking behavior of gangs: in the barrios of Los Angeles, gang behavior is possibly tempered by the large family sizes of the barrios, so that gang members are likely to be related by blood or marriage, if not by friendship, to large numbers of the other barrio residents.

Some criminologists have concluded that gangs are not important in crimes such as drug dealing because drug dealing is not recorded in police records as gang-related activity.[11] Nevertheless there is certainly heavy involvement in drug dealing by gang members. Jerry Sarnecki found that the thirty-five most delinquent juveniles in a Swedish community were linked by gang membership.[12] A significant fraction of other offenders in this community (30 percent) had been accomplices of the same thirty-five juveniles. Thus while many offenses are committed by individuals or small groups in underclass neighborhoods, the gang is a very important node in the networks of many people who undertake crimes.

Our model of gangs emphasizes their pursuit of economic gain and rationality. This view coincides with that of Sánchez Jankowski. However, other observers (for example, James Vigil, John Hagedorn, and Léon Bing) emphasize the importance of noneconomic motives for gang membership and the irrationality of aspects of gang behavior.[13] According to all accounts, gang members spend considerable time hanging out together, which involves verbal sparring, recreational sports, and social activities. Crime is less than a full-time activity. Moreover, not all gang violence is undertaken as a rational defense of territory for economic gain. Raids into foreign territory are sometimes undertaken simply for fun. Such observations, however, do not contradict the premises of our model. An unusual taste for fun does not imply a lack of economic motivation. There is as much reason that a person whose thrill comes from a driveby shootout will take the opportunity to earn a buck as someone whose pleasure comes from Beethoven's Ninth Symphony.

Recent ethnographies furthermore reveal an increase in the economic motivation for gang membership. This change has been associated with an increase in the age of gang members, and greater violence.[14] Jerome Skolnick's interviews of California inmates in 1988 and 1989 showed the rising importance of the gang as a business. In the words of one informant: "[Being a gang member] is just an easier way to get in [to drug dealing]. It's like if you going to get a job and you have a high school diploma. If you don't have one you ain't goin' to get the job."[15]

Lest there be any doubt about the role of gangs in drug dealing, and in community relations, an exception proves the rule. Terry Williams's careful five-year study of a teenage drug ring in the Fort Washington area of New York does not once mention the role of gangs.[16] Does this remarkable omission imply that drug dealing is just done by independent agents? The answer to this question is

supplied by Richard Neely.[17] The Fort Washington area reportedly
is controlled by big-time drug traders, who are the gang leaders in
this neighborhood. Not only do the big-time dealers control the sale
of drugs (as can be seen in Williams's account) but they also use
their armed power and inside knowledge to curb other crimes, as we
have argued above. According to Neely, "The ordinary law-abiding
residents . . . tolerated (the drug dealers) faute de mieux, because
(they) protected the neighborhood."

The Community

Gangs live and work within communities whose members are
well aware of their activities. Nonworking welfare mothers stay at
home and observe what occurs on their streets. Through a network
of contacts, their children are also aware of gang activity. Alex
Kotlowitz's vivid account of three years in the life of a typical family
(the Rivers family) in a crime-ridden Chicago public housing project
(the Henry Horner homes) illustrates how much people know and
how the information is acquired.[18] It also illustrates the motivations
for and against revealing this information to the police.

It is easy to compile a long list of unreported incidents in the
Rivers's apartment complex that, in a middle-class area, invariably
would have been reported to the police: for example, there were
frequent gang shoot-ups in which bullets entered apartments; a hole
had been dug through one wall as part of an escape route that would
be secret to the police but to no one in the complex; vacant apartments were used as a gang clubhouse; and street dealing was visible
to all residents.

Two opposing motives vie with each other in determining the
cooperation of the significant fraction of community residents with
middle-class aspirations.[19] On the one hand, and most predomi-
nantly, residents fear retaliation if they are detected revealing information to the police. On the other hand, there is considerable
hatred of the gangs and their drug dealing, even on the part of some
addicts. In the most gang-dominated neighborhoods fear typically
predominates. Again, the Rivers family is illustrative: a friend of
LaJoe Rivers (the mother) was observed tearing up the sheet of
paper on which she had outlined a recent gang shoot-up for fear of
potential retaliation; residents of the Henry Horner homes did not

use the 911 emergency number for fear that police would show up at their doorstep.

It might be thought that the fear of retaliation is so dominant that residents would never cooperate. This view is incorrect, however, because in some instances tipsters have a high probability of anonymity—partly because so many people are aware of local criminal acts. And, as Sánchez Jankowski and other ethnographers demonstrate, gang members who are apprehended have a high probability of going to jail. Thus, the benefits of tipping off the police may more than compensate the costs of possible retaliation. The fate of the local gang leader in the Henry Horner homes gives a good illustration. The local gang was the Conservative Vice Lords (one wing of the Vice Lord nation) and the well-known leader was Henry Lee. While the residents of Henry Horner homes were in great fear of him, and of the retaliation of his gang on an informer, the police did use an anonymous tip that he was in possession of unlicensed weapons. They raided his apartment with a warrant, found not only the weapons but a considerable stash of drugs, and he received a jail sentence of thirty years.

While the primary motives for and against cooperation with the police by members of the community are hatred of the gangs and fear of retaliation, other secondary motives are also important. First, there is some sympathy for the gangs because of their positive contributions to the community. Since the gangs live in the neighborhood they have an opportunity to show their human side. Thus they curb the selling of drugs to young children; they prevent undesirable outsiders from coming into the neighborhood; and on occasion they use their armed power or their money to support neighborhood functions. For example, in Chicago the gang leaders throw an annual bash in one of the parks. The Players' Picnic features free food and entertainment including games and a jazz band for dancing. The police direct the crowds and traffic with a curfew at ten o'clock, the normal curfew hour for events in Chicago's public parks.

The attitude of community residents toward the police is an important additional influence on their willingness to cooperate. More frequently than not, community residents view the police as another outside, potentially hostile gang: their procedures are often unfair and punishments do not always fit the crimes. The substantial number of false accusations and arrests by the police reinforce this attitude. Again, the experience of the Rivers family is illustrative. Over the course of three years, one son was sent to prison for a crime he did not commit (although he had committed probably hundreds like it). Another son was roughed up by the police on one occasion and convicted in juvenile court for running from the scene of a crime (theft of a radio) where he had been an innocent passerby. A friend of the family's with no involvement in crime was shot dead while running away from detectives who were looking for a suspect who, unfortuitously, had the same first name. Although part of the problem is simply police not doing their job well, one must also recognize the difficulty of their job. In underclass neighborhoods, as protection, youth with middle-class aspirations camouflage those values, so they are not prey to the gangs. Police find it difficult to distinguish those who are gang members from those who are affecting gang dress and behavior as protective camouflage.[20] Because of their own violence and error, the police are viewed far more ambiguously in the ghetto than in middle- and upper-class communities.

In the following pages the members of the community who are potential informers will be modeled as "representative agents," all with identical preferences. This use of a representative agent is a common device among economists when they wish to look at an entire group—like consumers or firms—without emphasizing individual characteristics. This tactic involves two simplifications of reality. First, because all representative agents are alike, the diversity in the community is understated. According to Elijah Anderson a central theme of black life in America is the interplay between the large fraction of the community with middle-class values that emphasize the work ethic and those with "street values" that emphasize the returns to hustling. Second, the assumption of well-formed preferences misses the factors involved in the formation of values. Anderson and William Julius Wilson have emphasized the role of community leaders in instilling the work ethic in youth, by their example of hard work and with their fund of homilies for the ready listeners from their own families and from others.[21] In former times these leaders would not only lecture the children of the community; they would also discipline them (including children who were not their own). Both Anderson and Wilson lament the flight of the black middle class from the inner city. Now, they say, the black middle class who remain preach their message warily, because they are prepared for the disdain of their young listeners who see the meager returns from low-wage jobs as offering little hope of achieving middle-class status and are attracted by the fast (but fleeting) bucks of the drug-dealing gangs. This demographic shift affects the willingness of community members to cooperate with the police. Furthermore, youth are less resistant to joining gangs; and having joined, they have less inhibition against crime and feel less shame from incarceration.

Government

The third protagonist in our drama is the government, which determines the procedures whereby offenders are apprehended, indicted, sentenced, punished, and paroled. The government also sets the budgets for the police and other law enforcement agencies and determines the penalties for various offenses.

We shall view the government as pursuing two goals: keeping crime low and holding spending down. It needs to strike a balance between them. A more general (perhaps more realistic) account would describe the government's actions in more detail. It would allow for the possibility of payoffs between the gangs and government agents who in theory are their monitors.

A Model of Gang Behavior

In the following pages we verbally describe a formal model that systematically characterizes the factors affecting the behavior of each of the three main protagonists in the drama of inner-city crime—communities, gangs, and government. The purpose is to explore how the interactions among these groups determine the level of crime and to pinpoint the parameters critical to the outcome. A technical appendix provides a mathematical presentation of the model and its solution.

The Community

Figure 7-1 shows the four factors that we assume affect the willingness of community members to reveal information to the police:

Figure 7-1. Factors Influencing Community Cooperation in Law Enforcement

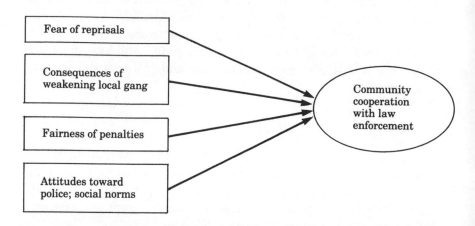

fear of retaliation, the likely consequences of a weakening of the local gang, perceptions about the fairness of penalties, and attitudes toward the police.

The community's fear of gang reprisals is the first factor limiting its willingness to cooperate in law enforcement. This fear of retaliation lowers cooperation more, the greater the severity of retaliation and the higher the probability that it occurs. We initially assume that there is a fixed probability of retaliation and later discuss the more realistic possibility that the probability of retaliation is proportional to the benefits derived from crime.

The concern of community members with the impact of revelation on the level of crime in the neighborhood is a second factor affecting the community's willingness to cooperate. The expected gain to members of the community from cooperation with the police depends on how the level of crime, with the community under the control of the current gang, compares with the level of crime in other, similar neighborhoods. Community members might reason that, if their local gang is eliminated or seriously weakened, the neighborhood will fall prey to outside gangs. The community will be disinclined to cooperate if the local gang is perceived as less destructive than gangs in other neighborhoods and more inclined to cooperate if local crime exceeds that in other communities. If increasing crime outside the neighborhood raises the tolerance of the community for local crime, the potential exists for an upward spiral of crime over the longer term.

The community's perception of the fairness of the criminal justice system is a third influence on the community's willingness to cooperate with police. Community members are assumed to be less willing to cooperate the higher the gap, positive or negative, between the penalties leveled against offenders and those considered fair by the community. Thus, if penalties are either too low or too high, observers of crimes are less likely to reveal information to the police.

Finally, the community's attitudes toward the police and, more generally, the social norms of the community concerning cooperation with the criminal justice system affect cooperation. In middle-class communities, where attitudes toward police tend to be positive, strong norms for the reporting of crime exist and revelation may even be considered therapeutic. In poor neighborhoods, however, the police play an ambiguous role, preserving some modicum of order but also imprisoning members of the community, sometimes unfairly.

Figure 7-1 omits the level of monitoring by law enforcement, which affects the community's willingness to cooperate ambiguously. On the one hand, higher monitoring raises the community's willingness to report, because with higher police expenditure there is a greater chance that information that is revealed will lead to a conviction. On the other hand, higher monitoring may discourage reporting if penalties are considered unfair, because information that is revealed may lead to the imposition of an unfair penalty. We discuss below the consequences of this potential dependence of reporting on the level of monitoring.

Faced with these factors, the representative community member must decide whether to cooperate or not. Under simplifying assumptions (specifically, a linear utility function), as the level of crime increases there is a critical level of crime where the representative community member switches from noncooperation to cooperation. We call this critical point the cooperation/noncooperation boundary. If community cooperation is needed to police crime, equilibrium typically occurs on this boundary.[22] The gang has an incentive to commit crime right up to the point where people will cooperate with the police; but beyond that point, the community will cooperate and crime will not pay.[23]

Figure 7-2.   Determinants of the Number of Crimes Committed by Gangs

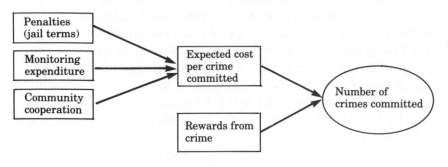

Gangs

Figure 7-2 shows that gangs determine the number of crimes committed by comparing the benefits and costs of criminal activity.

The attractiveness of outside economic opportunities is a key determinant of the costs and benefits of criminal activity. These opportunities differ systematically between rich and poor neighborhoods. The differential reward to crime is greater in poor neighborhoods, whose residents earn low rewards from legitimate economic activities. Similarly, the opportunity cost of incarceration is lower in poor than in rich neighborhoods. Anderson and Wilson have also emphasized the lack of norms against incarceration and in favor of the work ethic in underclass neighborhoods, because of the departure of middle-class leaders.[24]

Figure 7-2 also shows the factors determining expected penalties. We assume that the expected penalty, per crime, depends on three factors: the jail term (punishment) exacted; the expenditures on monitoring; and the cooperation of the community.

Gangs choose the level of crime subject to the behavior of the community.[25] For sufficiently high values of monitoring and punishments, gangs optimize by pushing the community to its limits of tolerance—on the cooperation/noncooperation boundary. Any higher level of crime would trigger the community's cooperation, resulting in expected penalties so great that crime would have a negative return. Any lower level of crime is suboptimal. Without the cooperation of the community, no penalties can be exacted on the gang, and additional crimes create benefits for the gang without imposing

Figure 7-3.   The Relationship between the Gang's Payoff from Crime and the Level of Crime

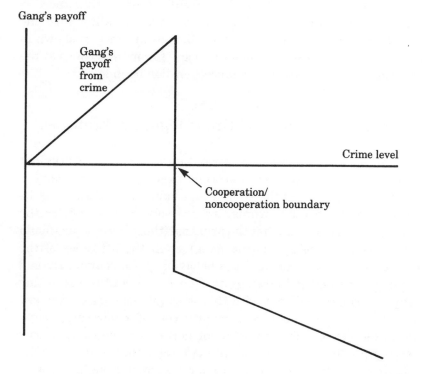

Gang's payoff

Gang's payoff from crime

Crime level

Cooperation/ noncooperation boundary

costs.[26] Figure 7-3 illustrates how the level of crime is determined by the gang.

The broken line in figure 7-3 shows how the gang's total payoff from crime varies with the level of crime, under the simplifying assumptions made in the appendix to this chapter. For sufficiently low levels of crime the community will not cooperate with the police, so crime goes unpunished. Under these conditions crime pays and the total reward to crime is proportional to the amount committed. As crime rises, however, the community's willingness to cooperate increases. Eventually, under our assumptions, there comes a point where the community switches from being uncooperative to being cooperative with the police. This is just at the cooperation/noncooperation boundary mentioned above. At this point, there is a discrete drop in the gang's payoff since at this point the police can exact criminal penalties. In the scenario depicted in figure 7-3, the gang's net benefits become negative at this critical point. And for increases in crime beyond this critical point, figure 7-3 shows the gang's net benefit declining even further. This result assumes that there is sufficient monitoring that, with community cooperation with the police, crime does not pay. Faced with the payoff function shown in figure 7-3, criminal gangs rationally choose to commit crimes at the level that is on the cooperation/noncooperation boundary.[27]

Community Norms and Crime Fighting Strategies

Our model can be used to ask what strategies the government should optimally pursue to control crime given that law enforcement is costly and, at least in the short run, community values must be taken as given. In other words, we can solve our model for the optimal incentive scheme that the principal (the government) should create to control the agent (the gang) given the attitudes of the community (the observer) and the behavior of the community and the gangs. The optimal strategy to fight crime, and the resulting amount of crime consistent with this strategy, depends on five key parameters: the social cost of crime, the cost of monitoring, neighborhood income, the fair punishment norm, and the community's reporting propensity. The community's reporting propensity depends, in turn, on community norms concerning cooperation with law enforcement efforts, the severity and probability of retaliation against informants, and the level of crime outside the neighborhood. The first three parameters represent factors that have been emphasized in previous economic models of crime and punishment. The last two parameters represent the innovation of this paper.

Table 7-1 summarizes the implications of our model. This table shows how changes in each of the five key parameters affect crime, punishment, and the law enforcement effort, when the government is pursuing the socially optimal strategy. The first column of table 7-1 shows the qualitative response of crime to its key determinants, with socially optimal punishments and monitoring. As would be expected, crime is higher the lower its social cost and the higher the cost of law enforcement. Neighborhood income also matters: poor neighborhoods will experience more crime than rich ones because the reward to gang activity will be higher in areas where outside

Table 7-1. Factors Affecting the Level of Crime and Optimal Law Enforcement Strategy

Factors affecting outcome	*Outcomes and optimal policies*		
	Level of crime	*Level of monitoring*	*Level of punishment*
Cost of monitoring	≥ 0	≤ 0	≥ 0
Social cost of crime	≤ 0	≥ 0	≤ 0
Neighborhood income	≤ 0	< 0	≤ 0
Community reporting propensity	≤ 0	≤ 0	≥ 0
Fair punishment norm	≤ 0	≤ 0	≥ 0

opportunities are poorer, and it simply does not pay to fully offset this higher incentive for crime with higher monitoring expenditure, although, as table 7-1 shows, monitoring levels would be higher in these poorer neighborhoods. This column also shows the sensitivity of crime to community attitudes: greater willingness of the community to report crimes and higher community norms concerning fair punishments contribute to a reduction in crime. Indeed, with sufficiently high norms for cooperation, a crime-free outcome may be attained.

The second column of table 7-1 shows that community attitudes also influence the cost of crime control. Other things equal, less money needs to be spent on law enforcement, and tougher penalties are possible, the higher are community reporting propensities and norms concerning fair punishments.

The third column of table 7-1 shows the qualitative impact of traditional economic factors and community norms on optimal punishments. In our model punishments are assumed, for simplicity, to be costless for the government to impose. Nevertheless, the optimal crime-fighting strategy does not call for punishments at infinitely high levels. The logic for this result is simply that such high penalties would be considered unfair: in response, the community would withhold its cooperation from the police and crime would rise, rather than fall. In many situations, the optimal punishment under our assumptions is whatever penalty the community considers fair. In some cases the government may find it optimal to set penalties a bit in excess of the levels deemed fair by the community in order to economize on costly monitoring expenditures. But any such violation of community standards is costly in that it lowers community cooperation with the police, enabling the gangs to engage in more crime without triggering community cooperation with the police.[28] The presumption in criminal cases that guilt must be established beyond a reasonable doubt is typically rationalized as a way of protecting the rights of innocent citizens against the state. Extending the logic of our model with respect to punishments, it is apparent that such a stringent criterion for conviction may actually serve to lower crime. Court decisions that are considered unfair could easily undermine the perceived legitimacy of the judicial system, thereby compromising the willingness of the public to cooperate with the police. In effect, fair rules that protect the rights of the innocent, like fair punishments, may increase the willingness of the community to cooperate in the law enforcement effort.

Our concern with the willingness of observers to reveal information applies to more than cops and robbers in the U.S. inner city; the role of informants in altering the structure of principal-agent interactions is crucial in other contexts. For example, sociologists beginning with Max Weber have described purpose, hierarchy, rules, authority, career paths, and decisionmaking in bureaucracies. Weber argued that the bureaucratic form of organization was widely adopted because it used information efficiently.[29] While economic models of information afford insight into such characteristics as the hierarchical structure of bureaucracies, there is no obvious informational interpretation of why, in bureaucracies,[30] decisionmaking procedures should have the "rule of law as [an] ideal."[31] In our model the rule of law is an ideal because well-known and fairly applied procedures maximize the willingness of members of the community of potential observers to reveal their information. Thus something approximating the rule of law is informationally efficient.

Our model takes societal norms as given, but policies to alter such attitudes provide a potentially potent strategy for controlling crime. Previous economic models have viewed punishments and monitoring as the important tools for fighting crime. This model points out that there are additional tools for fighting crime: policies that affect community willingness to report crimes, community norms for fairness of punishment, and community tolerance for crime will also influence crime. Expenditures directed at altering these other variables that enter our model may prove more cost-effective than direct expenditures on monitoring or longer jail sentences. These conclusions will come as no surprise to sociologists nor, perhaps, to the authorities who deal with crime on a day-to-day basis, but they may be very important for public policymakers, who need to understand why bricks and sticks may be self-defeating.

Long-Run Consequences of Changing Norms

In a recent interview, Los Angeles County Sheriff Sherman Block expressed fears about the long run: "If we don't make a dramatic change in our value system, in our cultural approach, in our return to a concept of individual accountability, then I really fear for the future. Because what I see happening, and what scares me more than anything, is not merely the level of violence, but the level of *tolerance* for violence that is developing."[32] Sheriff Block sees an ever-increasing norm for violence leading to ever-higher levels of crime. Our model illustrates the logic of this concern.

In modeling the short-run determination of crime in a single community, we took as given average crime in nearby communities, which conditions the expectations of community members about how the destruction of the local gang would influence crime in the neighborhood. In our model, community members assume that if the local gang is destroyed the neighborhood will not become crime free; rather, other gangs, similar to those in nearby neighborhoods, would dominate the local neighborhood, and crime would approach levels elsewhere. Thus, the community's tolerance for the local gang, in our model, depends on whether its behavior is better or worse than average. Over the longer run, however, the level of crime considered normal will change, rather than remaining fixed, and the level of crime in one community influences the expectation of crime in its neighbors. High crime outside the neighborhood raises the local com-

munity's tolerance of gang violence; high crime in the local neighborhood induces greater criminal activity in neighboring territories.

When one neighborhood's tolerance for crime depends on the
actual levels of crime in other neighborhoods, there is clear potential
for escalating levels of crime over the longer term. Indeed, under
the simple assumptions of our model, a vicious upward spiral of
crime is a distinct possibility. Suppose that the individual neighborhood we have modeled is surrounded by many identical communities. Further, assume that actual crime in each community at a
given time depends on the "expected level of crime" in neighboring
communities because higher outside levels of crime diminish community willingness to cooperate in the law enforcement effort. Finally, assume that the expected level of crime gradually changes
based on actual experience. Our model generates the extreme
outcome that, over time, the level of crime will spiral upward indefinitely in the absence of sufficiently strong reporting norms. With
sufficiently weak reporting norms, Sheriff Block's fears are
realized.[33]

This simple model could be modified in four realistic directions.
First, the set of factors assumed to influence community reporting
behavior could be expanded to include the possibility that a higher
probability of apprehension of offenders will raise the willingness of
the community to supply information. This provides a new rationale
for law enforcement expenditures: since the chance of catching criminals rises with the level of monitoring, higher monitoring expenditures raise community cooperation besides directly raising the cost
of criminal activity to gang members.

Another alteration of the model takes into account the possibility
that the gangs' incentives for retaliation depend on the profits they
are making from their criminal activities. If the probability of retaliation in our model is proportional to these profits the model is apt
to generate two possible outcomes—what economists call dual equilibria.[34] With a sufficiently large initial level of crime, the odds of
retaliation are very high, and the community will be unwilling to
report. As discussed earlier, crime then spirals upward, without
bound in our model. In contrast, if crime is initially sufficiently low,
the rewards from retaliation are small and the probability of retaliation is low, so that the community is more willing to cooperate
with the police. There is then the chance that the system converges

to a crime-free, long-run equilibrium. Thus, as Anderson and Wilson have emphasized, the norms of the community toward crime (and the work ethic) are extremely important in determining how much crime will occur in the long run.

A third alteration of the model may also lead to dual equilibria. Suppose that the willingness of members of the community to report crime depends on the probability of apprehension, which depends in turn on the willingness of other community members to report. If potential informants believe the police will be ineffective, and derive little pleasure from cooperation for its own sake, no one will inform; as a consequence, the police *are* ineffective and crime is infinite. Alternatively, if potential informants believe that the police will be effective and therefore are willing to inform, the police *are* effective and, with sufficiently high reporting norms, neighborhoods are crime free.

An example dramatically illustrates the existence of such dual equilibria. In a study of the Mafia in Sicily, Anton Blok found that the three major protagonists were the landless or almost landless peasants (the community of observers), the absentee landowners, who lived in Palermo (the principals), and their overseers, who were Mafia members (the agents).[35] The landowners faced the problem that if they did not appoint strong and violent men as their overseers, other strong and violent men would raid their holdings and rustle their cattle. Thus landlords had an incentive to appoint members of the Mafia as overseers. In turn these Mafia members had agreements, sometimes as the result of formal meetings, regarding which lands were in the hands of which members and were therefore not to be raided. If an overseer began to get into trouble with the law, the landowners would protect their own overseers because the landowners needed the support of their overseers against outsiders. The peasants, who were aware of the crimes committed by the overseers, maintained silence, except in rare instances of unusual personal harm, when their desire for retribution was overwhelming. Cooperation with the authorities would have been ineffective—because of the landowners' influence on the court on behalf of their overseers—and also dangerous—because the overseers would take reprisals.

The existence of dual equilibria is demonstrated by the complete loss of control of the Mafia in 1924 after a vigorous prosecutor used an "anti-conspiracy" law and rounded up the local Mafia in large groups.

A new equilibrium was established in which the landowners were happy without their Mafia overseers because the overseers had been taking more than their share of rent for protection as well as overseeing services. The peasantry were also happy with this outcome because they had suffered from the Mafia's impoverishing demands. In the absence of the Mafia the peasants were not afraid of informing about the odd crime that occurred. The system, however, reverted immediately to the pre-1924 equilibrium after the Allied invasion in 1943. Again the landlords were afraid of raids from the outside and felt that violent overseers constituted better protection than distant and ineffective courts.

A fourth modification of the model results in the possibility of dual equilibria for yet another reason. Community willingness to cooperate depends on the fairness of police procedures; and the fairness of police procedures, in turn, depends on the cooperation of the community with the police, because, with cooperation, it is easier to distinguish between the guilty and the innocent. There is thus the possibility that inner-city neighborhoods may be caught in a crime-ridden equilibrium in which the innocent are punished along with the guilty and, because this occurs, the community resents and frustrates the police.

Control over Territory

Our model of the determination of crime in inner-city neighborhoods takes as given the boundaries of each gang's territory. We have not thus far addressed the question of what determines the size of gangs and their territorial boundaries. This question is important, since much of the violent crime involving gangs is concerned with fighting over territorial boundaries. Insofar as these fights are for economic reasons, because of the gains from control of territory, a model of the economic behavior of gangs should explain territorial domain.

Gangs have the opportunity to control more territory by enlarging the size of their membership and fighting for marginal territory at their boundaries. If economic considerations alone determine gang activity, gangs would choose their size and boundaries by weighing the rewards from monopolizing crime in a larger territory against the cost of acquiring that territory and dividing the monopoly rents among a larger membership. The marginal cost of acquiring new turf may rise with the size of the territory. Larger memberships are more difficult to coordinate, and territory more distant from the gang's clubhouse is more difficult (requires more men) to control.

An increase in the reward to crime owing, say, to an increase in the demand for drugs or a reduction in their cost, raises the reward to territorial expansion and thus leads to more strife among gangs. Taking the sizes of other gangs as given, each gang has an incentive to increase the size of its own membership to fight for marginal territory. This yields one economic explanation why the discovery of crack has resulted in a considerable increase in gang violence and death.[36]

Increased revenues from the sale of drugs may also produce escalating violence through another channel: with higher incomes, gang members are able to buy fancier guns and cars (which are used as tanks), thus enlarging and increasing the violence of their "games" against their enemies. Although we have argued that gang members weigh costs and benefits rationally in their pursuit of crime, considerable evidence shows that some fighting occurs simply for the thrill of it. This attitude is reflected in Bing's report of a "Gang Class" at Camp Kilpatrick, a Los Angeles youth correction camp.[37] The counselor asked the boys to name good reasons to kill someone. Thirty-seven reasons were named. The first of these, reflecting the capture-the-flag-with-guns nature of gang wars, was "For the f . . . of it." Greg Davis (street name Batman and one of the last surviving founders of the Crips), commenting on the fragility of the recent truce between the Bloods and Crips in Los Angeles, noted, "A lot of us been doing this for years and don't want it to stop. We're killing each other off and a lot of us don't really care. A lot of these brothers thrill on this violence."[38]

Conclusion

This paper has developed a model of crime and punishment in which the willingness of community members—who are observers of much crime—to report what they know, is central to the success of law enforcement. The dependence of crime and punishment on the behavior of anonymous observers highlights the importance of community norms in the determination of crime and suggests that nontraditional strategies for crime prevention—measures other than increasing expenditures on police or imposing tougher jail sentences on the convicted—may have high payoffs. We have in mind social programs aimed at strengthening such value-building community institutions as churches and parent support groups, promotion of community grass roots efforts to organize citizen patrols and neighborhood cleanups, and also a return to a strategy of community policing with the objective of improving rapport between police and local community members.[39] Moreover, the model points to the possibility that the traditional tools for crime control—more police cars cruising the neighborhood and longer jail sentences— wrongly applied, will be counterproductive because they undermine community norms for cooperation with the police.

In *Pride and Prejudice*, Mr. Bennett observed: "For what do we live but to make sport for our neighbors and to laugh at them in our turn?"[40] This chapter shows that this interest in the neighbors must be harnessed for the control of crime.

Appendix

This appendix describes the mathematical model discussed informally in the text and derives its implications for the determination of crime in the short run and over the longer run. The subscripts/superscripts c, s, and m denote respectively the community, the offenders (s for sellers of drugs), and the government (m for monitors). The same letters denote the actions of the corresponding agents.

The Community

We assume that the representative community member derives "utility from cooperation" of the form:

(1) $$U^c = \{-a_c p\overline{R} + B_c(s-\overline{s}) - C_c\,|f-\overline{f}\,| + d_c\}c$$

where

U^c is the utility of a representative community member resulting from cooperation

$\overline{R}$ is the cost of retaliation by the gang

p is the probability of retaliation

s is the gang's current level of crime

$\overline{s}$ is the norm for the amount of crime expected in the absence
of the current gang

f is the level of penalty (fine)

$\overline{f}$ is the fair level of the penalty

c is the degree of cooperation.

a_c, B_c, and C_c are all positive constants; d_c is a constant, which may
be positive or negative, dependent on the norms of the community;
c, the level of cooperation, is between 0 and 1.

The first term in the utility function captures the community's
fear of gang retaliation: we assume that the level of retaliation is
$\overline{R}$, and that there is a fixed probability p of retaliation. The second
term of the utility function reflects the concern of community members with the impact of revelation on the level of crime in the neighborhood. We assume that this depends on how the actual level of
crime, s, compares with $\overline{s}$, the level of crime in other, similar neighborhoods. The third term of the utility function reflects the community's sense of fairness: community members are assumed to lose
utility from revelation insofar as the actual penalty, f, deviates from
what would be considered fair, $\overline{f}$. (In this appendix we will follow
Becker in calling the penalties fines.) Finally there is a constant
term, d_c, which may be positive or negative, reflecting other factors
influencing the utility of revealing information to the police, such as
attitudes toward the police and the norms of the community.

The representative community member chooses the level of cooperation, c ($0 \leq c \leq 1$), to maximize utility. If the community reveals
all of its information to the police, $c = 1$; if it reveals none, $c = 0$.
The community takes the fine f, the amount of crime s, the probability of retaliation, p, the norm for the crime, $\overline{s}$, and the norm for
fines, $\overline{f}$, as given. Members of the community choose c in a purely
reactive way. Accordingly they choose

(2) $$c = 1 \text{ if } A_c + B_c s - C_c \,|\, f - \overline{f}\,| > 0$$

(3) $$c = 0 \text{ if } A_c + B_c s - C_c \,|\, f - \overline{f}\,| \leq 0$$

where $A_c = d_c - a_c p\overline{R} - B_c \overline{s}$. For convenience we let $c = 0$ on the boundary at which $A_c + B_c s - C_c | f - \overline{f} | = 0$.

The assumption of a linear utility function, although restrictive, results in a tractable model that clearly emphasizes the role of the community's revelation of information. There is a unique level of crime $[s = (C_c | f - \overline{f} | - A_c)/B_c]$ at which the community switches from noncooperation to full cooperation with the police. We refer to this switching point as the cooperation/noncooperation boundary. Equilibrium typically occurs on this boundary.

Gangs

Gangs are assumed to maximize a utility function (chosen to be linear, for simplicity), which depends negatively on the magnitude of the expected penalties and positively on the number of crimes committed. The utility function of the gang is

$$(4) \qquad U^s = -A_s(\theta)r + B_s(\theta)s$$

where r denotes the expected penalties and s the number of crimes committed. $A_s(\theta)$ and $B_s(\theta)$ are constants that depend on a shift parameter θ, reflecting, in part, the outside opportunities of potential offenders. We assume that the expected penalties exacted for criminal behavior depend on four factors: the number of crimes committed, s; the fine exacted, f; the expenditures on monitoring, m; and the cooperation of the community, c. In particular we assume

$$(5) \qquad r = s \cdot f \cdot m \cdot c.$$

Gangs choose the level of crime, s, $(0 \le s \le \infty)$ to maximize utility subject to the behavior of the community.[41] If $-A_s(\theta)fm + B_s(\theta)$ is nonpositive (so that crime does not pay if the community cooperates), the utility of an offender, U^s, is maximized by choosing s on the cooperation/noncooperation boundary (or at zero, if that boundary occurs at a negative value of s). This case is illustrated in figure 7-3 of the text. In this case

$$(6) \quad s = \max \left[(-A_c + C_c | f - \overline{f} |)/B_c, \, 0 \right]$$

$$\text{if } [-A_s(\theta)fm + B_s(\theta)] \le 0.$$

In contrast, if $-A_s(\theta)fm + B_s(\theta)$ is positive (so that crime pays, *even if* community members cooperate with the police), the utility of offenders increases proportionately with s beyond the cooperation/noncooperation boundary. Utility is thus unbounded and the maximum value of U^s is obtained at $s = +\infty$. In this case

$$(7) \qquad s = \infty \qquad \text{if } [-A_s(\theta)fm + B_s(\theta)] > 0.$$

The Government

We assume, for simplicity, that the government's utility depends negatively on the number of crimes committed and also on the budget allocated to monitoring crimes. Specifically,

$$(8) \qquad U^m = -A_m s - B_m m$$

where s is the number of crimes committed and m is the expenditure on monitoring. We assume that the government chooses f and m optimally, subject to the behavior of offenders, which has been summarized by (6) and (7).

Short-Run Equilibrium

In the short run, the community's norms, $\bar{s}$, which determine its expectations about the level of crime if the crimes are reported and criminals are incarcerated, are given. (In the long-run equilibrium we assume that $\bar{s}$ is determined endogenously.)

The government's problem is to maximize its utility, U^m given the behavior of the community and the gangs. To prevent crime from being infinite even with community cooperation, fines and monitoring must be high enough to satisfy the following constraint, derived from (6) and (7):

$$(9) \qquad fm \geq B_s(\theta)/A_s(\theta).$$

We term (9) the *crime control constraint*. If it is not satisfied, crime pays even when the community fully cooperates with the police and the government's utility is $-\infty$.

The problem of maximizing U^m, as given by (8), subject to (6) and (9) turns out to be equivalent to the following simpler, constrained maximization problem: choose optimal values of f and m (denoted f^* and m^*) to maximize

(10a) $U^m = -A_m(-A_c + C_c(f-\bar{f}))/B_c) - B_m m$

subject to

(10b) $fm = B_s(\theta)/A_s(\theta)$ Crime control constraint
(10c) $f \geq \bar{f}$ Fair fines constraint
(10d) $s = (-A_c + C_c(f-\bar{f}))/$
        $B_c \geq 0$ Nonnegative crime constraint

The government's optimization problem can be rewritten in this simple form because the crime control constraint, under our assumptions, is always satisfied with equality; because the optimal level of fines is always high enough to make the level of crime on the cooperation/noncooperation boundary $(-A_c + C_c(f-\bar{f}))/B_c$, nonnegative; and, furthermore, because the level of fines is at least as high as $\bar{f}$.

According to (10b), the crime control constraint (9) is satisfied with equality. The rationale is straightforward: monitoring is costly and, from (6), the level of monitoring has no direct effect on the equilibrium level of crime.[42] According to (10c), fines are always set at least at the fair level. The logic is simple: if $f < \bar{f}$, an increase in f either decreases or has no effect on crime (according to [6]) but lowers the level of costly monitoring needed to satisfy the crime control constraint. Thus, the optimal f cannot occur in this region. If f is sufficiently low that (10d) is not satisfied, an increase in f will cause no increase in crime, since crime is zero according to (6). Again, however, such an increase permits a reduction in the level of monitoring needed to satisfy the crime control constraint. Thus, with the optimum value of f, $(-A_c + C_c(f-\bar{f}))/B_c \geq 0$. Finally, since f is not less than $\bar{f}$ at an optimum, both the utility function (10a) and the level of crime (10d) can be written without absolute value signs.

Depending on parameter values, the solution of the government's optimization problem falls into one of three distinct regimes, corresponding to which constraints are binding: only the crime control constraint or, in addition, either the fair fines constraint or the nonnegative crime constraint. Figure 7-4 illustrates the correspondence between parameter values and regimes.

Figure 7-4. Parameter Values and Crime Regimes

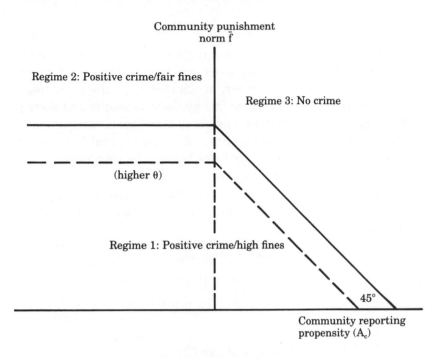

Note: This figure shows the relationship between parameter values and regimes. In the positive crime/high fines regime, $f^* > \bar{f}$ and $s^* > 0$. In the positive crime/fair fines regime $f^* = \bar{f}$ and $s^* > 0$. In the no crime regime $f^* = \bar{f} + A_c/C_c$ and $s^* = 0$. The community punishment norm is $\bar{f}$. The community reporting propensity is $A_c = d_c - a_c p\bar{R} - B_c\bar{s}$. The intercept of the boundary between regime 1 and regime 3 on the x-axis is $(B_s (\theta)B_m B_c C_c/A_s(\theta))^{1/2}$. The slope of this boundary is 45°. An increase in θ causes a decrease in this intercept, and a decline in the size of regime 1, and an increase in the size of regimes 2 and 3 as pictured by the dashed line labeled (higher θ) in the figure.

Regime 1: Positive Crime/High Fines

In the positive crime/high fines regime, only the crime control constraint, (10b), is binding. Utility is maximized by setting fines above the level considered fair by the community. Although the imposition of fines in excess of $\bar{f}$ raises crime, higher fines enable the government to economize on monitoring costs in satisfying the crime control constraint. The equilibrium levels of crime, fines, and monitoring, all positive, denoted s^*, f^*, and m^*, are

(11a) $\quad s^* = -(A_c + C_c\bar{f})/B_c + \{(B_m B_s(\theta)C_c)/(A_m A_s(\theta)B_c)\}^{1/2}$

(11b) $\quad\quad f^* = [(B_m B_s(\theta)B_c)/(A_m A_s(\theta)C_c)]^{1/2} > \bar{f}$

(11c) $m^* = [(A_m B_s(\theta) C_c)/(B_m A_s(\theta) B_c)]^{1/2}.$

Regime 2: Positive Crime/Fair Fines

In the positive crime/fair fines regime, both the crime control constraint, (10b), and the fair fines constraint, (10c), are binding. Utility is maximized at a corner, at which $f = \bar{f}$: the government sets fines at the level considered fair by the community and there is positive crime. Although the government could save money on monitoring expenditures by raising fines, it is not optimal to do so. An increase in fines above the fair level lowers the community's willingness to cooperate and raises the equilibrium level of crime. The loss in utility from higher crime outweighs the gain in utility from reduced expenditure on monitoring. In this case, the equilibrium values of s^*, f^*, and m^* are:

(12a) $s^* = -A_c/B_c$

(12b) $f^* = \bar{f}$

(12c) $m^* = B_s(\theta)/(A_s(\theta)\bar{f}).$

Regime 3: No Crime

In the no crime regime, both the crime control constraint, (10b), and the nonnegative crime constraint, (10d), are binding. The government is able to achieve a crime-free equilibrium. The community's norm for cooperation is sufficiently high that no crimes are committed when the fine is set at the fair level ($f = \bar{f}$). This provides an opportunity for the government to economize on monitoring expenses without raising crime. The government raises fines and lowers monitoring expenditures until it reaches the highest fine consistent with $s = 0$: $f^* = \bar{f} + (A_c/C_c)$. Fines are not raised above this level because the loss in utility from higher crime owing to increasingly unfair fines outweighs the gain in utility owing to lower monitoring expenditures along the crime control constraint. In this case

(13a) $s^* = 0$

(13b) $f^* = \bar{f} + (A_c/C_c)$

(13c) $m^* - B_s(\theta)/[A_s(\theta)(\bar{f} + (A_c/C_c))].$

Figure 7-4 illustrates the relationship between parameter values and regimes. The vertical axis plots the community's punishment norm, $\overline{f}$; the horizontal axis plots the parameter A_c, which measures the community's reporting propensity. This is a composite, the sum of three factors: d_c, the community cooperation norm; $a_c p\overline{R}$, the community's concern about retaliation; and $B_c\overline{s}$, the community norm for crime, reflecting crime in similar communities. A high value of A_c indicates high community willingness to report. As figure 7-4 shows, low values of A_c and low punishment norms, $\overline{f}$, lead to equilibria in regime 1, with positive crime and fines in excess of those considered fair. With low reporting norms (low A_c) and high punishment norms ($\overline{f}$), equilibrium occurs in regime 2, with positive crime and fair fines. With a high community reporting propensity and high punishment norms, equilibrium lies in the "no crime regime"—regime 3.

The location of the boundaries between regimes, as well as the equilibrium levels of crime, fines, and monitoring within regimes, depends on parameter values in intuitive ways. Consider the model's prediction concerning differences in crime between rich and poor neighborhoods. In richer neighborhoods where outside economic opportunities are better, or in neighborhoods where there is a stronger anticrime ethos, θ is higher, and the ratio $B_s(\theta)/A_s(\theta)$ is lower. A higher value of A_s reflects higher disutility of incarceration or other criminal penalties; a lower value of B_s reflects lower economic gains from crime in comparison with alternative activities and also, perhaps, greater guilt. A higher value of θ results in less crime and lower optimal monitoring and fines, assuming an initial equilibrium in the positive crime/high fines regime. Because a rise in θ shifts the boundary in figure 7-4 down, there is also the possibility that a neighborhood may switch from either the positive crime/high fines regime (1) or from the fair fines regime (3) into the no crime regime (3).

In spite of its simplicity, the model illustrates the importance of community values toward cooperation and reporting in determining equilibrium levels of crime, fines, and needed police expenditures. For example, in the crime-ridden regimes (1 and 2), an increased community propensity to cooperate, reflected in a higher value of A_c, results in lower equilibrium levels of crime. Within the crime-free regime (3), increased willingness to cooperate instead permits the government to raise fines and lower costly monitoring, thus raising the government's utility. As is apparent from figure 7-4, an increase in A_c increases the chances that the equilibrium lies in the crime-free regime 3. The model also shows how the community's attitude toward fair punishments for offenders, as reflected in $\bar{f}$, matters to the control of crime. An increase in community tolerance for penalizing offenders raises the level of fines that are optimally imposed by the government, in turn, either lowering equilibrium crime (in regime 1) or else reducing monitoring expenditures.

Long-Run Equilibrium and Extensions of the Model

In our model, the level of crime in a given community depends on the average amount of crime outside the community, which we have taken as given in the short run. Over the longer run, however, the level of crime considered normal is endogenous, rather than exogenously determined.

To analyze the longer-term behavior of crime in a given neighborhood we assume that actual crime in each community, in period t, s_t, depends on the expected level of crime in neighboring communities $\bar{s}_t$. $\bar{s}_t$ affects s_t by altering the value of A_c, which, in turn, determines crime in 11a and 12a, in regimes 1 and 2 respectively. Assuming adaptive expectations about $\bar{s}$, expected crime rises whenever actual crime exceeds expected crime; specifically, assume that $\bar{s}$ rises by a fraction γ of the gap between actual and expected crime in the previous period. The long-run behavior of crime, starting from an initial equilibrium with positive crime (in regimes 1 or 2), is then determined by the following equation:

$$(14) \quad \Delta s = s_t - s_{t-1} = -\gamma(d_c - a_c p\bar{R})/B_c$$
$$+ \gamma(C_c/B_c)\max[\{(B_m B_s B_c/A_m A_s C_c)^{1/2} - \bar{f}\}, 0].$$

The righthand side of (14) is a constant that depends on parameter values. Starting from an equilibrium with positive crime, crime will be constantly rising or constantly falling. The parameter d_c, reflecting the community's reporting norm, plays a particularly important role: reporting norms must be sufficiently high to attain a long-run outcome without crime. Otherwise, the long run is characterized by ever-rising levels of crime.

We noted in the text the possibility that dual equilibria may occur if the gangs' incentives for retaliation depend on the profits they are making from their criminal activities. In our model, those profits are $B_s(\theta)s$. Now suppose that p, the probability of retaliation, is proportional to these profits $(B_s(\theta)s)$. Dual equilibria occur if $d_c > C_c\max[\{(B_m B_s B_c / A_m A_s C_c)^{1/2} - \bar{f}\}, 0]$. With a sufficiently large initial value of s, the odds of retaliation are very high and the community will be unwilling to report. As discussed earlier, crime then increases without bound. In contrast, if s is initially sufficiently low, the rewards from retaliation are small and the probability of retaliation is low, so that the community is more willing to cooperate with the police (A_c is higher) and the system may converge to a crime-free long-run equilibrium.

Notes

1.   See Department of Commerce, *Statistical Abstract of the United States, 1968* (Washington, 1968), table 206, and *Statistical Abstract of the United States, 1990* (Washington, 1990), table 287.

2.   See Department of Commerce, *Statistical Abstract of the United States, 1965* (Washington, 1965), tables 217, 219, and *Statistical Abstract of the United States, 1992* (Washington, 1992), tables 328, 329.

3.   See Gary S. Becker, "Crime and Punishment: An Economic Approach, *Journal of Political Economy*, vol. 76 (March–April 1968), pp. 169–217.

4.   See Jane Jacobs, *The Death and Life of Great American Cities* (Random House, 1961).

5.   See Gerald Mars, *Cheats at Work: An Anthropology of Workplace Crime* (Allen and Unwin, 1982).

6.   See Jean Tirole, "Hierarchies and Bureaucracies: On the Role of Collusion in Organizations," *Journal of Law, Economics and Organization*, vol. 2 (Fall 1986), pp. 181–214. In Tirole's model, agents bribe their supervisors to conceal information from the principal. Side payments are possible because the identity of the observers is known to the agents. In contrast, in the case of social crime, observers are frequently numerous, and their identities are often unknown to the offender. Subcontracts involving private payoffs are therefore impossible; the "bribes" offered by the gangs to the observers are typically social goods; and whether or not the information is revealed depends on the "values" of the observers. While our model is for-

mally similar to Tirole's, the conclusions we draw are quite different: measures taken to enhance legitimacy are a potential policy tool of the principal in manipulating the behavior of the observers, and therefore, in turn, of the agents. Furthermore, the policies of the principal, which might be optimal, taking values and therefore legitimacy as fixed, are likely not to be optimal when these policies affect the observers' perceptions of legitimacy. One example concerns the policies of the Los Angeles police department. With values fixed, it would appear that tough law enforcement would be the best deterrent to crime. However, the negative symbolism of the Rodney King episode was, in fact, the spur to the Los Angeles riots. In principal-agent theory generally, for example in the Shapiro-Stiglitz model, workers are punished for malfeasance. See Carl Shapiro and Joseph E. Stiglitz, "Involuntary Unemployment as a Worker Discipline Device," *American Economic Review*, vol. 74 (June 1984), pp. 433–44. In fact, however, if the punishments are considered illegitimate, so that they reduce observers' willingness to report to managers, they will be counterproductive.

7.   See Martín Sánchez Jankowski, *Islands in the Street: Gangs and American Urban Society* (University of California Press, 1991).

8.   See R. Lincoln Keiser, *The Vice Lords: Warriors of the Streets* (Holt, Rinehart and Winston, 1969), p. 22.

9.   See Douglass C. North, *Structure and Change in Economic History* (Norton, 1981); and Mancur Olson, "Autocracy, Democracy, and Prosperity," in Richard J. Zeckhauser, ed., *Strategy and Choice* (MIT Press, 1991), pp. 131–57. Within their territories we view gangs as local monopolists, who act like rent-seeking feudal governments maximizing revenues.

10.   See Sánchez Jankowski, *Islands in the Street*, p. 208.

11.   Albert Reiss found that most crimes are committed either by single offenders or small groups of co-offenders. See Albert J. Reiss, Jr., "Why Are Communities Important in Understanding Crime," in Albert J. Reiss, Jr., and Michael Tonry, eds., *Communities and Crime: Crime and Justice: A Review of Research*, vol. 8 (University of Chicago Press, 1986), pp. 1–33; see also Albert J. Reiss, Jr., "Co-offending and Criminal Careers," in Michael Tonry and Norval Morris, ed., *Crime and Justice: A Review of Research*, vol. 10 (University of Chicago Press, 1988), pp. 117–70.

12.   See Reiss, Jr., "Co-offending and Criminal Careers," p. 128.

13.   See James Diego Vigil, *Barrio Gangs: Street Life and Identity in Southern California* (University of Texas Press, 1988); John Hagedorn with Perry Macon, *People and Folks: Gangs, Crime and the Underclass in a Rustbelt City* (Lake View Press, 1988); and Léon Bing, *Do or Die* (Harper Collins, 1991).

14.   See Ronald C. Huff, ed., *Gangs in America* (Sage Publications, 1990).

15.   See Jerome H. Skolnick, *Gang Organization and Migration* (State of California, Department of Justice, 1990), p. 5.

16.   See Terry Williams, *The Cocaine Kids: The Inside Story of a Teenage Drug Ring* (Addison-Wesley Publishing, 1989).

17.   See Richard Neely, *Take Back Your Neighborhood: A Case for Modern Day "Vigilantism"* (Donald I. Fine, 1990), p. 155, note 10.

18.   See Alex Kotlowitz, *There Are No Children Here* (Doubleday, 1991).

19.   See Elijah Anderson, *Street Wise: Race, Class, and Change* (University of Chicago Press, 1990).

20.   See Anderson, *Street Wise*.

21.   See Anderson, *Street Wise*; and William Julius Wilson, *The Truly Disadvantaged: The Inner City, the Underclass and Public Policy* (University of Chicago Press, 1987).

22.   We are assuming that any individual community member has only a small chance of observing any particular criminal act. Thus, while most criminal activities occurring within the community are observed by somebody, very few are observed by large numbers of individuals. Under this assumption, the average level of cooperation in the community affects the probability of catching criminals, even if there are a few cooperative mavericks who are prepared to report *any* wrongdoing. The raid on Henry Lee, mentioned earlier, is a case in point. Although Lee was captured on the basis of information supplied by a single individual, the fact that Lee was generally hated by all members of the community raised the odds that the police would receive this critical tip.

23.   Similarly, in the model of unemployment by Shapiro and Stiglitz, equilibrium occurs on the "nonshirking boundary." See Shapiro and Stiglitz, "Involuntary Unemployment."

24.   See Anderson, *Street Wise*; and Wilson, *The Truly Disadvantaged*.

25.   Our model (see, in particular equation (5) in the appendix) makes, for simplicity, the extreme assumption that, in the absence of community cooperation, there is no chance of apprehending criminals.

26.   Alternative outcomes are also possible. If the values of monitoring and fines are too low, crime pays even if the community cooperates, and the optimal level of crime for the gang is infinite. However, the government would never set fines and monitoring sufficiently low to permit this perverse outcome to occur.

27.   For sufficiently low levels of fines and monitoring, the gang's payoff may have a different shape. Beyond the cooperation/noncooperation point, the payoff function will increase with the level of crime if crime pays even when the community cooperates with the police. In this case, the optimal choice of criminal activity by the gang will be infinite. As noted, the government would not optimally set fines and monitoring sufficiently low to permit such an outcome.

28.   The possibility that increasing penalties may result in increased crime was discovered when the Puritans tried to suppress Quakerism, which was considered to be a crime in Massachusetts in the mid-seventeenth century. Despite a prior record of snitching on their neighbors for the most trivial infractions of the law, the residents of Salem allowed Quaker meetings to be held in their midst for more than twenty years without any reports to authorities. The penalty of death for offenders was

208 George Akerlof and Janet L. Yellen

considered too severe. See Kai Erikson, *Wayward Puritans: A Study in the Sociology of Deviance* (John Wiley, 1966). A. Mitchell Polinsky and Steven Shavell and James Andreoni have given other reasons for less than maximal penalties to deter offenses. Polinsky and Shavell suggest that optimal fines may not be maximal because of risk aversion and the existence of private gains from activities that exceed their social cost. See A. Mitchell Polinsky and Steven Shavell, "The Optimal Tradeoff between the Probability and Magnitude of Fines," *American Economic Review*, vol. 69 (December 1979), pp. 880–91. According to Andreoni, fines may be less than maximal because juries' standard of reasonable doubt rises with the level of fines. With higher fines, they are less likely to convict. See James Andreoni, "Reasonable Doubt and the Optimal Magnitude of Fines: Should the Penalty Fit the Crime?" *Rand Journal of Economics*, vol. 22 (Autumn 1991), pp. 385–95.

29. See Max Weber, *Economy and Society* (University of California Press, 1978).

30. See, for example, Raaj K. Sah and Joseph E. Stiglitz, "The Architecture of Economic Systems: Hierarchies and Polyarchies," *American Economic Review*, vol. 76 (September 1986), pp. 716–27.

31. Leonard Broom and Philip Selznick, *Sociology: A Text with Adapted Readings*, 6th ed. (Harper and Row, 1977), p. 208.

32. Bing, *Do or Die*, p. 275. Emphasis in original.

33. With sufficiently strong reporting norms, crime is gradually eliminated over time in our model. Our formulation of the government's optimization problem is myopic, failing to take account of the changes in levels of crime considered normal that occur because of present levels of crime. We feel that, unfortunately, governments behave in this way. As it turns out, in this simple model, there are circumstances in which the government is unable to prevent crime from drifting toward infinity through appropriate choice of fines and monitoring. The extreme simplifying assumptions of our model also generate the dramatic result that, with insufficient reporting norms, crime rises indefinitely rather than ultimately leveling off.

34. The possibility of multiple equilibria in models of crime has been discussed by Jens Chr. Andvig and Karl Ove Moene, "How Corruption May Corrupt," *Journal of Economic Behavior and Organization*, vol. 13 (January 1990), pp. 63–76.

35. See Anton Blok, *The Mafia of a Sicilian Village, 1860-1960: A Study of Violent Peasant Entrepreneurs*, 2d ed. (Polity Press, 1988).

36. This approach represents a natural extension of Steven Salop's model of the geographic distribution of firms on a circle. In that model customers who are distributed evenly along a circle prefer to frequent nearby stores; firms must lower their prices to attract customers who live farther away. In choosing their "territorial boundaries" Salop's firms thus weigh the costs owing to the price reduction needed to attract new business against the benefits of greater sales. In Salop's model, an increase in market demand, or a decrease in marginal cost, shifts up each competitor's reaction function: for given prices charged by rivals, each firm finds it optimal to

raise its own price. See Steven Salop, "Monopolistic Competition with Outside Goods," *Bell Journal of Economics*, vol. 10 (Spring 1979), pp. 141–56.

37. See Bing, *Do or Die*, p. 121.

38. *New York Times*, July 18, 1992, p. A8.

39. For a discussion of the role of community activism in combating drug dealing see Roger Conner and Patrick Burns, *The Winnable War: A Community Guide to Eradicating Street Drug Markets* (Washington: American Alliance for Rights and Responsibilities, 1991).

40. Jane Austen, *Pride and Prejudice*, (Macmillan, 1894), chap. 37.

41. Equation (5) makes, for simplicity, the extreme assumption that, in the absence of community cooperation, there is no chance of apprehending criminals.

42. In a more general framework, this constraint is not always binding. For example, if the community's willingness to cooperate varies positively with the probability of a conviction that, in turn, depends on the level of monitoring, it may be optimal to do more monitoring than is needed to satisfy the crime control constraint, since such expenditures reduce crime.

Index

Aaron, Henry J., 1
AFDC. *See* Aid to Families with Dependent Children
Affirmative action, 31–32
Affluence effect: concerns over loss of, 5, 19; defined, 17–18; evolution of, 18–19, 25–26; and expressive values, 36, 40; and family values, 35–36; greater tolerance associated with, 29; in industrial democracies, 16, 24; and marriage, 33–34; and meaning of success, 38–40; and overindividualism, 84, 91; role in changing values, 5–6, 16–17; tension generated by, 21; and traditional values, 36; validity, 27
African Americans: AFDC participation, 58; Afrocentrism multicultural demands, 117, 129, 139; changing role of community leaders, 182–83; conflict over desegregation versus cultural pluralism for, 125; scholastic achievement, 127
Aid to Families with Dependent Children (AFDC), participation in, 57, 58
Akerlof, George, 10, 12, 15, 173
Altruism: love and duty to motivate, 147; role in behavior with some self-interest, 148–49; to solve collective

action problems, 147–48, 164–65. *See also* Public spirit
Anderson, Elijah, 182, 193
Asian immigrants, and educational curriculum, 127–28
Ayers, Ian, 151

Behavior: coinciding self-interest with altruistic, 148–49; community and police crime-control, 180–83, 188–91; cultural factors and, 63–64; gang, 176–80, 186–88; habitual, 55; incentives influencing, 56; long- versus short-run self-interested, 9; moral, 56
Bell, Daniel, 92
Bilingualism, 126; effects, 142; Puerto Ricans and, 128
Bing, Léon, 179, 195
Blok, Anton, 193
Bonds, efforts to balance cultural choices and, 20, 21
Bourne, Randolph, on cultural pluralism in public education, 123, 124
Braithwaite, John, 151
Bronfenbrenner, Urie, 99
Brown, Roger, 118
Buchanan, James, 153
Bureau of the Census, 33

211

- fateball versus soccer
- music
- jeans
- how america used to be and what
  now (value, economy, family,
  people.